TWO-FOR-ONE teaching

· · · · ·

Connecting Instruction to Student Values

lauren **porosoff** · jonathan **weinstein**

Solution Tree | Press

a division of
Solution Tree

555 North Morton Street
Bloomington, IN 47404
800.733.6786 (toll free) / 812.336.7700
FAX: 812.336.7790

email: info@SolutionTree.com
SolutionTree.com

Visit **go.SolutionTree.com/instruction** to download the free reproducibles in this book.

Printed in the United States of America

Library of Congress Cataloging-in-Publication Data

Names: Porosoff, Lauren, 1975- author. | Weinstein, Jonathan (Jonathan H.),
    author.
Title: Two-for-one teaching : connecting instruction to student values /
    Lauren Porosoff and Jonathan Weinstein.
Description: Bloomington, IN : Solution Tree Press, [2019] | Includes
    bibliographical references and index.
Identifiers: LCCN 2019004081 | ISBN 9781949539332 (perfect bound)
Subjects: LCSH: Motivation in education. | Individualized instruction. |
    Classroom environment.
Classification: LCC LB1065 .P586 2019 | DDC 370.15/4--dc23
LC record available at https://lccn.loc.gov/2019004081

Solution Tree
Jeffrey C. Jones, CEO
Edmund M. Ackerman, President

Solution Tree Press
President: Douglas M. Rife
Associate Publisher: Sarah Payne-Mills
Art Director: Rian Anderson
Managing Production Editor: Kendra Slayton
Senior Production Editor: Tonya Maddox Cupp
Content Development Specialist: Amy Rubenstein
Copy Editor: Jessi Finn
Proofreader: Kate St. Ives
Text and Cover Designer: Abigail Bowen
Editorial Assistant: Sarah Ludwig

For my parents, Leslie and Harold Porosoff, who gave me every opportunity to learn, love learning, and foster a love of learning in others.

—Lauren

In loving memory of my mother, Eve Jean Weinstein, who taught me that the essence of learning is connection; and for my father, Louis Weinstein, who was afraid I would leave him out, as if I could.

—Jonathan

Acknowledgments

● ● ● ● ●

Whenever I'm asked to give new teachers advice, I say to find three mentors: one who supports you, one who pushes you, and one who inspires you. I was lucky enough to find one mentor who did all three. Thank you, Melanie Greenup. We haven't worked together in many years, but I will include your name in every book I write.

Thanks also to my teachers who made me feel seen and cared for and even loved. Janis Birt made me feel like math mattered and I mattered. John Aune made me feel like writing was more than a cute hobby and that maybe one day I'd write a whole book. (This is my fourth, Mr. Aune!) Joe Algrant and Barbara Silber showed me the wisdom of recognizing our vulnerabilities and trusting a partner who is strong in all the ways we're weak. Judy Dorros taught me that I don't need a lot of friends; I just need one who's true. Hadassah Bar-El taught me that the best teachers do smile before November.

And thanks to my rock-star students at every school where I've taught. You're why I started doing this work. You're why I still do.

—Lauren

I would like to thank my academic family, many of whom once haunted the hallways of the George Peabody Building at the University of Mississippi, for their contributions as my teachers, friends, clinical supervisors, therapists, students, and sometimes all of the above. I am also grateful to the Association for Contextual Behavioral Science, especially the friends and colleagues from this organization who took an early interest in our work. Last, I would like to acknowledge my inspirational mentors at the University of Mississippi Center for Contextual Psychology, Kelly Wilson and Kate Kellum, who taught me, as Albert Camus said, "The struggle itself toward the heights is enough to fill a man's heart."

—Jonathan

We want to thank our colleagues and friends who read our drafts and gave us the feedback that helped us improve them: Jon Alschuler, Stephanie Behrens, Olga Berkout, Yash Bhambhani, Mike Bordieri, Chad Drake, Joanna Dudek, Brad Fraver, Sharan Gill, Laurie Hornik, Kate Kellum, John Kurtz, Ciara McEnteggart, and Mollie Sandberg.

We also want to thank Barbara Swanson and Marcy Mann at the New York State Association of Independent Schools, Emily McGrath at the Northwest Association of Independent Schools, Alecia Berman-Dry at the Association of Independent Maryland and DC Schools, Rachel Folan at the New Jersey Association of Independent Schools, and the creative, committed educators who attended our workshops through these organizations.

Thanks to Matt and Jenn Villatte for their incredible work translating relational frame theory to make it more comprehensible and usable. *Mastering the Clinical Conversation* is the gift that keeps on giving.

Huge thanks to our perceptive, generous, wise editor Tonya Cupp. Giving a manuscript to an editor is kind of like putting a resistant child on a school bus—a relief for sure, yet also a knot-in-our-stomachs act of trust. But much like parents sending a child into the classroom of a talented teacher, we knew that when we sent our manuscript to Tonya, it would come back so much better than it was before. We hope this is a book that will empower teachers to empower their students. Tonya is an editor who empowers her writers to empower their readers.

Finally, we thank our families, especially our parents, to whom we've dedicated this book, and our children, Allison Porosoff and Jason Weinstein, who constantly remind us of what we value.

—Lauren and Jonathan

Solution Tree Press would like to thank the following reviewers:

David Bosso
Social Studies Teacher
Berlin High School
Berlin, Connecticut

Paul Cancellieri
Science Teacher
Rolesville Middle School
Rolesville, North Carolina

Cheryl Hermach
Language Arts Teacher
Lafayette High School
Wildwood, Missouri

Ryan Reed
Social Studies Teacher
China Middle School
China, Maine

Patricia Scriffiny
Math Teacher
Montrose High School
Montrose, Colorado

Bradley Shepstead
Eighth-Grade Teacher
Rolesville Middle School
Rolesville, North Carolina

Ashley Williams
Fifth-Grade Teacher
Sandhills Farm Life Elementary
  School
Carthage, North Carolina

Visit **go.SolutionTree.com/instruction** to download the free reproducibles in this book.

Table of Contents

● ● ● ● ●

Reproducible pages are in italics.

About the Authors xiii

INTRODUCTION
Valuing Students' Values. 1

    A Definition of Values 3

    Reasons to Do Values Work in School 5

        Connecting Schoolwork to Values Makes the Work More Intrinsically Satisfying 7

        Honoring Students' Values Can Help Create a More Inclusive Community 7

        Focusing on Values as Qualities of Action Creates Opportunities for Connection 8

        Being Able to Choose a Values-Guided Life Empowers Students 8

    Settings Where Students Can Explore and Enact Their Values 9

    Academic Tasks as Contexts for Values Work 9

    How This Book Is Organized 11

Part I: Foundations. **13**

CHAPTER 1
Creating a Culture of Willingness 15

    Design Relevant Learning Tasks 17

    Deliver Lessons to Help Students Stay Psychologically Present 19

        Portioning 20

        Pacing 20

        Summarizing 21

    Give Empowering Feedback on Student Work 21

        Make Observations 22

        Share Your Personal Experience of the Work 23

        Say Back the Student's Values 23

        Suggest Actions for Next Time 23

    Manage Your Power 26

        Participate in the Work 27

        Use Your Silence and Your Voice to Equalize Power 27

        Model Discomfort in the Service of Your Own Values 28

Respond to Student Avoidance 28

    When Students Do Something Else 28

    When Students Complain 29

    When Students Stay Silent 31

    When Students Seek Approval for Every Decision 31

Onward 34

CHAPTER 2
Using the Science of Empowerment 35

Evoking Free Choice 36

Using Language to Empower Students 37

    Deictic Framing: Taking New Perspectives on a Situation 38

    Analogical Framing: Describing a Situation in Terms of Something Else 40

    Hierarchical Framing: Seeing an Action as Part of a Meaningful Life 41

Taking Advantage of Patterns of Activity to Help Students Establish Their Values. . . 45

Helping Students Discover Meaning and Vitality at School 46

Empowering Yourself to Lead Values Work. 48

Onward 49

Part II: Protocols 51

CHAPTER 3
Protocols to Prepare for Learning 53

Values-Activating Questions 54

    Getting Ready 54

    Leading the Protocol 55

    Boosting the Impact 56

    Using the Protocol Next Time 57

Unit Partner Meet 57

    Getting Ready. 59

    Leading the Protocol 60

    Boosting the Impact 61

    Using the Protocol Next Time 62

Represent and Respond 62

    Getting Ready. 63

    Leading the Protocol. 63

    Boosting the Impact 64

    Using the Protocol Next Time 66

Intention Icons 66

    Getting Ready. 67

    Leading the Protocol. 67

    Boosting the Impact 71

    Using the Protocol Next Time 72

Intervision 72

    Getting Ready 73

    Leading the Protocol 73

    Boosting the Impact 76

    Using the Protocol Next Time 77

Onward 77

CHAPTER 4
Protocols to Explore New Material 79

Focused Annotation 80

    Getting Ready 81

    Leading the Protocol 81

    Boosting the Impact 82

    Using the Protocol Next Time 83

Discovery Writing 84

    Getting Ready 87

    Leading the Protocol 88

    Boosting the Impact 89

    Using the Protocol Next Time 90

Collaborative Conversations 90

    Getting Ready 90

    Leading the Protocol 91

    Boosting the Impact 93

    Using the Protocol Next Time 94

Track and Acknowledge 94

    Getting Ready 95

    Leading the Protocol 95

    Boosting the Impact 98

    Using the Protocol Next Time 99

Values in the Field 99

    Getting Ready 100

    Leading the Protocol 100

    Boosting the Impact 103

    Using the Protocol Next Time 103

Onward 103

CHAPTER 5
Protocols to Review the Material 105

Emotions and Values Audit 106

    Getting Ready 107

    Leading the Protocol 109

    Boosting the Impact 110

    Using the Protocol Next Time 110

Review Tournament. 111

    Getting Ready. 112

    Leading the Protocol. 114

    Boosting the Impact 115

    Using the Protocol Next Time 116

So I Will 116

    Getting Ready. 117

    Leading the Protocol. 117

    Boosting the Impact 120

    Using the Protocol Next Time 122

Booksploration 122

    Getting Ready. 123

    Leading the Protocol. 123

    Boosting the Impact 126

    Using the Protocol Next Time 126

Naming Awards 126

    Getting Ready. 127

    Leading the Protocol. 128

    Boosting the Impact 130

    Using the Protocol Next Time 131

Onward 131

CHAPTER 6
Protocols to Create Work Product. 133

Prototype Analysis 135

    Getting Ready. 136

    Leading the Protocol. 137

    Boosting the Impact 138

    Using the Protocol Next Time 138

Top-Pick Topic 138

    Getting Ready. 139

    Leading the Protocol. 140

    Boosting the Impact 140

    Using the Protocol Next Time 141

Sandbox Mode 141

    Getting Ready. 142

    Leading the Protocol. 143

    Boosting the Impact 145

    Using the Protocol Next Time 146

Exemplar Study 146

    Getting Ready. 147

    Leading the Protocol. 148

Boosting the Impact 150

Using the Protocol Next Time 151

Group Commitments. 151

Getting Ready. 152

Leading the Protocol. 154

Boosting the Impact 156

Using the Protocol Next Time 157

Onward 157

CHAPTER 7
Protocols to Refine Work Product. 159

Rubric Response 160

Getting Ready. 162

Leading the Protocol. 162

Boosting the Impact 164

Using the Protocol Next Time 165

Strategy Selection. 165

Getting Ready. 166

Leading the Protocol. 167

Boosting the Impact 168

Using the Protocol Next Time 169

Nonjudgmental Peer Review 169

Getting Ready. 171

Leading the Protocol. 172

Boosting the Impact 174

Using the Protocol Next Time 175

Considerate Editing. 176

Getting Ready. 176

Leading the Protocol. 178

Boosting the Impact 179

Using the Protocol Next Time 180

Testing for Doneness. 181

Getting Ready. 182

Leading the Protocol. 182

Boosting the Impact 183

Using the Protocol Next Time 183

Onward 183

CHAPTER 8
Protocols to Reflect on Learning 185

Concentric Self-Portraits 186

Getting Ready. 187

Leading the Protocol. 188

Boosting the Impact 189
Using the Protocol Next Time 189
Sentence Expanding 190
Getting Ready 192
Leading the Protocol 192
Boosting the Impact 194
Using the Protocol Next Time 194
Support-Push-Inspire 195
Getting Ready 195
Leading the Protocol 196
Boosting the Impact 197
Using the Protocol Next Time 198
Upcycling 198
Getting Ready 199
Leading the Protocol 200
Boosting the Impact 201
Using the Protocol Next Time 202
Values-Based Portfolios 202
Getting Ready 202
Leading the Protocol 204
Boosting the Impact 206
Using the Protocol Next Time 206
Onward 207

CONCLUSION
Creating Learning Moments That Matter **209**

APPENDIX
Reproducibles **213**
Unit Task Organizer *214*
Intention Icons *215*
Noticing Emotions Chart *216*
Review Tournament Bracket *217*
Peer Review Direction Cards *218*
Considerate Editing Chart *220*
Concentric Self-Portrait *221*
Sentence Strips *222*

References & Resources 223

Index 229

About the Authors

• • • • •

Lauren Porosoff has been an educator since 2000, most recently teaching middle school English at the Ethical Culture Fieldston School in the Bronx, New York. At Fieldston, she also served as a grade-level team leader and a diversity coordinator, and she led curriculum mapping and professional development initiatives. Before working at Fieldston, Lauren taught middle school history at the Maret School in Washington, DC; and second-, fifth-, and sixth-grade general studies at the Charles E. Smith Jewish Day School in Rockville, Maryland.

Helping students make their work meaningful has been a constant in Lauren's teaching practice, and that interest led her to learn about methods of values-guided behavior change in Acceptance and Commitment Therapy, Compassion-Focused Therapy, Relational Frame Theory, Motivational Interviewing, and other applications of Contextual Behavioral Science. Informed by research and practices from these fields, Lauren developed applications for the classroom, such as the processes for curriculum design she describes in her book *Curriculum at Your Core: Meaningful Teaching in the Age of Standards*, and the strategies for centering student values in *EMPOWER Your Students: Tools to Inspire a Meaningful School Experience*, a book she coauthored with Jonathan Weinstein.

Lauren has written for *AMLE Magazine*, *Independent School*, *Phi Delta Kappan*, the *PBS NewsHour* blog, *Rethinking Schools*, and *Teaching Tolerance* about how students and teachers can clarify and commit to their values at school. She's presented on these topics at regional and national conferences of various professional organizations, including the Association for Contextual Behavioral Science, Learning and the Brain, the National Council of Teachers of English, the Progressive Education Network, and various state and regional associations of independent schools.

Lauren received a bachelor's degree in English from Wesleyan University and a law degree from George Washington University.

To learn more about Lauren's work, visit EMPOWER Forwards (https://empowerforwards.com) and follow her on Twitter at @LaurenPorosoff.

Jonathan Weinstein, PhD, is a clinical psychologist with the U.S. Department of Veterans Affairs. He serves as the suicide prevention coordinator at the Veterans Affairs Hudson Valley Health Care System and holds an appointment as assistant professor of psychiatry and behavioral sciences at New York Medical College. Prior to serving in suicide prevention, Jonathan served as the post-traumatic stress disorder and substance use disorders coordinator at the James J. Peters Veterans Affairs Medical Center in the Bronx, New York. Before working for Veterans Affairs, Jonathan served in a variety of mental health and education roles in New York, Baltimore, and Mississippi stretching back to 2000.

Given his own experiences as a special needs student, Jonathan has had an enduring interest in the science of empowerment. As an early contributor to the development of Relational Frame Theory and Acceptance and Commitment Therapy at the University of Mississippi Center for Contextual Psychology, Jonathan studied behavior analysis and its applications for behavior therapy, social categorization, and education. More recently, Jonathan and his coauthor adapted elements of Contextual Behavioral Science for teachers to empower their students. He has also applied this work to empower veterans who are at high risk for suicide. In addition to co-authoring *EMPOWER Your Students*, Jonathan's publications appear in *Behavior and Social Issues*, *The Psychological Record*, and *Salud y Drogas*. He has presented on these and related topics at national and international conferences including those of the Association for Contextual Behavioral Science, the Association for Behavior Analysis International, the Association for Behavioral and Cognitive Therapies, Learning and the Brain, and the Progressive Education Network.

Jonathan received a bachelor's degree in history from Vassar College, a master's degree in public administration from New York University, and a doctoral degree in clinical psychology from the University of Mississippi.

To learn more about Jonathan's work, visit EMPOWER Forwards (https://empowerforwards.com) and follow him on Twitter at @jhweinstein.

To book Lauren Porosoff or Jonathan Weinstein for professional development, contact pd@SolutionTree.com.

Introduction

• • • • •

VALUING STUDENTS' VALUES

Let's begin, if you're willing, with you.

Jot down the first memory that comes to mind when you think of each grade you were in, from kindergarten to grade 12. If you can only remember your teacher's name or where you sat, then write that down. All classrooms count—gyms, fields, art studios, auditoriums—but for this activity, don't use memories of special events, trips, lunch, recess, hallways, or anything else that you wouldn't consider a regularly scheduled class. Don't overthink this, and don't cheat.

Figure I.1 features the lists we came up with.

Lauren's List	Jonathan's List
K: Total blank. I don't even remember my teachers' names.	**K:** Punching J. P. in the face for stealing my chair, thereby excluding myself from the group
1: I remember wandering the hallways when my class learned letters because I already could read.	**1:** Struggling to draw the number 2
	2: Sitting at desks that faced each other
2: Mrs. Strauss told us to be on our best behavior because when people visited our school, what did they see as they walked down the main hallway? Our room—room 2A.	**3:** Mrs. Smith telling me to give up writing in cursive because it was too hard for her to read
3: Mrs. Dorros asked us what this year's play should be about. We were studying fables, and I suggested combining them all into one big fable. That's what we did.	**4:** Ms. LaSpina telling me to go read ahead in my U.S. history textbook because I was ahead of the class
4: Mrs. Kaplan settled a fight between me and my best friend by giving us M&M's.	**5:** Moving up from the middle-level mathematics class to the high-level one, but then having to struggle to keep up

Figure I.1: Lauren's and Jonathan's school memories.

continued ⇨

5: Every time we did something right, Mrs. Freedman gave us points. Did the homework? Ten points. Aced a spelling test? Twenty points. Lined up quietly? Five points. We'd write our points on note cards taped to the corners of our desks. Every week, whoever got the most points got to be top banana.

6: My teacher was Mrs. Anziska. I remember that I liked her, but I don't remember why.

7: We all had to get daily subscriptions to *The New York Times*. We brought in our copies every day and felt very grown-up.

8: We did a project in science where cars dripped water at a fixed rate and we could measure the distance between the drops to calculate the cars' speeds.

9: My English teacher said that all literature was about only two themes: sex and death.

10: I drew a lamp in art. My teacher said I exaggerated my shading.

11: My friend Sara and I took chemistry together. We made fun of words like *stoichiometry* and *spectrophotometer*, but we both secretly loved the class.

12: My calculus teacher would explain how to do a problem, and then I'd turn to the girl who sat next to me and explain it to her.

6: Mr. Stravopolis sitting me in the back corner of the room based on my last name and then fostering competition among us to see who could complete a set number of mathematics problems first

7: Also sitting in the back corner of the classroom in science and learning about edible plants

8: Using a microscope to look at a dead fly in science class

9: Being forced to participate in a one-act scene with another student who was the only other student in class not to find a partner

10: Working in a small group in English class and being told to read books that were more challenging than the rest of the class's

11: Being ridiculed by my mathematics teacher for asking how one might use trigonometry in the real world

12: Watching films by John Kenneth Galbraith in economics, but feeling very little connection between what we learned in the films and their relevance to class

This exercise has limitations. We asked you to write down whatever came to mind first. If you thought more, you might come up with other learning experiences that felt more important in the moment or that matter more now. We also recognize that a lot of meaningful learning happens in spaces we didn't allow you to use for this activity, like the hallway or the bus. We didn't ask about what you learned at home, or in out-of-school activities such as a dance class or religious program. And we didn't ask about the years since high school.

Acknowledging these limits, what do you notice when you look over your list? What themes or connections emerge? What did academic learning look like for you?

In our lists, each memory connects to an emotion. Sometimes that emotion feels nice—excitement in trying something new, pride in a budding talent, joy in connecting with someone. And sometimes that emotion feels not so nice—embarrassment when we struggled to match someone else's expectations, frustration when our needs went unmet, anxiety when school moved too quickly and boredom when it moved too slowly. The emotional content of our classroom memories only sometimes relates to the actual learning or work. Other times, our memories reveal feelings about ourselves, our relationships with peers and teachers, or our world. What emotions would you associate with each memory on your list?

Any emotion signals that something important is at stake. If you felt excited when your history teacher invited you to read ahead, what might have been important to you in that moment? Or if you felt frustrated that you didn't get to be top banana despite your best efforts, what does that tell you about your values at the time? If you still remember these moments, what might be important to you now? Whether these moments were part of the academic curriculum or unplanned incidents and interactions, what can they teach you about who you were then, what matters to you now, and what you want to stand for in the future?

When your students look back on your class, what do you want them to remember? What do you want them to have learned about themselves, what matters to them, and what they will stand for? What if, in addition to ensuring that "students graduating from high school are prepared to take credit bearing [*sic*] introductory courses in two- or four-year college programs or enter the workforce" (National Governors Association Center for Best Practices [NGA] & Council of Chief State School Officers [CCSSO], n.d.), we could also make school a place where students discover and do what matters to them? That's what we mean by *two-for-one teaching*: it's using academic instruction as a context for students to explore and enact their values.

This book shows you how to turn academic units into opportunities for students to notice what matters to them, choose to do what matters, and accept the struggle inherent in that choice—which we call *values work*. This isn't an added thing; it's a different way to do *the* thing, academic instruction, and have students bring their values to their academic learning.

But before we discuss why, where, and how to do values work in school, we'll first define what we mean by *values*.

A Definition of Values

Our definition of values comes from Contextual Behavioral Science (CBS), which seeks to "alleviate human suffering and advance human flourishing by developing basic scientific accounts of complex behaviors" (Villatte, Villatte, & Hayes, 2016, p. 4). Psychologists who practice CBS distinguish between pain, which is an inevitable part of life, and the suffering that results when efforts to control, minimize, or avoid that pain are unsuccessful (Hayes, Strosahl, & Wilson, 2012). These psychologists help people become aware of their values and choose to do what matters—not what's easiest or most fun, not what makes them look cool or sound smart, and not what relieves them from unpleasant feelings like anxiousness, embarrassment, or frustration—so they can live more fulfilling lives (Hayes et al., 2012). Contextual behavioral scientists define *values* as "freely chosen, verbally constructed consequences of ongoing, dynamic, evolving patterns of activity, which establish predominant reinforcers for that activity that are intrinsic in engagement in the valued behavioral pattern itself" (Wilson & DuFrene, 2009, p. 64). Let's break down this definition.

- **"Freely chosen":** In this book, anytime we mention *values*, we don't mean a set of values that a teacher or school espouses. We mean values students choose for themselves. The teacher's and community's values will certainly influence students, but so will their families, friends, communities, cultural and religious backgrounds, and activities. Moreover, when schools adopt a set of core values or a values program, the students don't get a meaningful choice in whether they endorse those values. We're not arguing that schools shouldn't stand for and teach certain values; we're distinguishing between instilling certain values in students and inviting them to discover their own.

- **"Verbally constructed":** Values aren't physical, tangible things like a tree or a house; they're abstractions like courage, creativity, and excellence. We label these abstractions with words—we verbally construct them—and talk about them as if they were things, but they're not. You can't draw courage, hold creativity, or point to excellence. You *can* draw a courageous leader, hold a creative painting, or point to an excellent meatball. Leaders, paintings, and meatballs are concrete, but courage, creativity, and excellence are abstract. You cannot observe or measure them until you translate them into something concrete—like schoolwork.

- **"Consequences of ongoing, dynamic, evolving patterns of activity":** Your values come from how you interact with the people, things, and events around you, as well as the thoughts, feelings, sensations, and memories inside you. Over time, you develop a set of approaches—a pattern of activity—that you call your *values*. Students might find new ways to act on their values throughout their lives, but they don't need to wait until they're older or ask permission to start building a meaningful pattern of activity. They can start living by their values right now.

- **"Which establish predominant reinforcers for that activity":** Values aren't the same as goals or preferences. Goals help us focus our actions but only feel good when we get the outcome we want: the paper is written, the laundry is folded, the laps are run. If we don't complete our goals, we might forgive ourselves, but we don't feel satisfied. With a goal, the thing we're working for—what behavior scientists call the *reinforcer*—is the outcome, not the action itself. With a preference, the reinforcer *is* the action itself: we eat our favorite ice cream, watch our favorite show, or go on a dream vacation because it's fun. The problem with preferences is that they often aren't accessible—the ice cream shop runs out of pistachio, the television network cancels *My So-Called Life*, the trip to Australia costs too much money. But a value, like curiosity or kindness, is always satisfying and always available. You can be curious and kind even if you fail to finish your paper, fold your laundry, and get your favorite ice cream—or any ice cream at all. And if curiosity and kindness matter to you, living your life curiously and kindly becomes a source of meaning and satisfaction in and of itself.

- **"That are intrinsic in engagement in the valued behavioral pattern itself":** Although people talk about values as if they were things, they're more like approaches—*how* you choose to work, play, relate to others, take care of yourself, and otherwise live your life. For a student, values answer questions like, "How will I approach my learning?" "How will I choose to do my work?" "How will I treat my peers and teachers?" and "How will I treat myself?" When you approach the world in a values-consistent way, that approach becomes its own reward.

Because values are always available, they're available in class. Academic units can become occasions for students to notice and choose how they want to live and to accept the struggle inherent in that choice—that is, to do *values work*.

Reasons to Do Values Work in School

Even if you don't give students opportunities to discuss their values, a school already has values in it. Creating a school program means identifying the most important areas of knowledge that students need to learn, and what gets deemed most important depends on values. Boards and departments of education, professional and parent associations, textbook and testing corporations, researchers and advocates, individual teachers and administrators—almost everyone makes pronouncements about what schools should do. These are values statements. Every unit you teach, every activity your students do, every book and poster and piece of furniture in your classroom already reflects someone's values. Students should have a place at school where they can discover their own values, too.

Clarifying and committing to values at school, and learning to accept the struggle inherent in living a values-consistent life, might have mental health benefits for students. Psychologists who practice Acceptance and Commitment Therapy (ACT; Hayes et al., 2012) teach their patients how to accept painful thoughts and feelings as a normal part of committing to values-consistent action, and thus living a fulfilling life. Meta-analyses demonstrate that ACT is an effective, empirically supported treatment for depression and anxiety (Hacker, Stone, & MacBeth, 2016) and chronic pain (Veehof, Oskam, Schreurs, & Bohlmeijer, 2011). Developing values awareness, committing to values, and developing the willingness to struggle in the service of values are integral to ACT—and to the work in this book.

Also, a growing body of evidence suggests that teaching students to notice how they treat themselves and their social environments—in social-emotional learning programs that sometimes include discussions of personal values—improves academic performance (Durlak, Weissberg, Dymnicki, Taylor, & Schellinger, 2011; Taylor, Oberle, Durlak, & Weissberg, 2017). But achievement is not our agenda here. Doing values work to boost achievement risks corrupting the work; it becomes a means to an end, rather than an end in itself. Worse, doing values work to boost achievement can create the mistaken belief that lower-achieving students have social-emotional deficits that schools need to fix. If we want to boost academic achievement, let's focus on addressing systemic inequities, not fixing students.

Besides, we don't see academic achievement as school's ultimate purpose. Yes, our students need to acquire certain skills and understandings so they can go into the world ready for the next step in their journey, whether that's more education or career. And then what? We believe that the purpose of school—the reason underlying all the time and effort we put into educating students—is so they can live productive, satisfying, world-bettering lives, not just after they finish school, but right now. The point of discovering and developing their values isn't to help students achieve academically; rather, the point of their achieving academic skills and knowledge is to help them more effectively build meaningful lives.

What happens when students see school's purpose as simply to reach the next achievement? In 2010, Coxsackie-Athens High School valedictorian Erica Goldson made a graduation speech that went viral. In her speech, the video of which has gotten over a million views on YouTube, she says that even though she worked hard and got the best grades in her class, she feels like her school experience was all about compliance:

> I did what I was told to the extreme. While others sat in class and doodled to later become great artists, I sat in class to take notes and become a great test-taker. While others would come to class without their homework done because they were reading about an interest of theirs, I never missed an assignment. While others were creating music and writing lyrics, I decided to do extra credit, even though I never needed it. (Goldson, 2010)

The comic artist Gavin Aung Than (2013; https://bit.ly/2G9xyte) adapted a piece of Goldson's (2010) speech, portraying her as a robot following instructions, moving on a conveyor belt from school to university to work.

How frustrated Goldson's teachers must have felt when they heard her speech. At least some of them—and we'd guess most of them—must have tried their best to create meaningful learning experiences that she and her classmates would find appealing and fulfilling, rather than experiences that made her feel like a robot who just did as they said. At the same time, some of Goldson's teachers must have understood and even sympathized with her feelings. In school, we orient students toward achievement—we score tests, fill out rubrics, level classes, and bestow honors distinctions. Even if we gamify achievement, awarding badges or tokens or a fantasy status like *science sorcerer* when students finish tasks or master skills, we still aim for them to get to the highest level and beat the game. And to do that, they need to follow instructions. They can't win if they don't play.

Meanwhile, we've rigged the game. Some students live in districts where each student receives a computer on day one, and others live in districts where the teacher needs to start a fundraising campaign to get books. Students have drastically different experiences depending on the color of their skin, the language their parents speak, their immigration status, their gender expression, any physical or mental disabilities, and a variety of other social categories. If school is a game, then some students start with all the cheat codes, while others start at level one on a device with a smashed screen.

Knowing all of this—that they're playing a game and that the game is rigged—it makes perfect sense that students would look to beat, cheat, or abandon the game. What if we could teach our students to see school as more than just a game? What if students learned to approach school as an opportunity to live a meaningful life, instead of just a series of instructions to follow and levels to reach? That's what values work is about.

Doing values work in school benefits students in four ways.

1. Connecting schoolwork to values makes the work more intrinsically satisfying.
2. Honoring students' values can help create a more inclusive community.
3. Focusing on values as qualities of action creates opportunities for connection.
4. Having the ability to choose a values-guided life empowers students.

Connecting Schoolwork to Values Makes the Work More Intrinsically Satisfying

Most students want to do well and get the highest grades possible. Academic performance brings other things students want, such as recognition from the school, compliments from adults, approval from the teacher and family members, and perhaps access to special privileges and material things (as in, "You can have a new phone if you get straight *As*"). All of these are forms of extrinsic motivation. The students work for rewards they'll get *after* achieving some result. The behaviors associated with learning—reading, listening to a classmate, taking notes, writing an essay, solving a problem, making a video, studying for a test, meeting with a teacher—are just means to getting the rewards. If they don't get the rewards they want (they study but don't get a good grade, for example), or if they discover they can get the rewards without doing the work (they get a good grade without studying, for example), they might stop bothering. But even when they get the rewards they want, they don't necessarily find the work itself satisfying.

However, if students learn how their academic behaviors serve their values, they'll find satisfaction in the behaviors themselves, regardless of the extrinsic rewards (Villatte et al., 2016). Rather than trying to motivate our students with reminders of good things that can happen if they do their work (or bad things that can happen if they don't), we can help them notice how their actions serve their values.

Honoring Students' Values Can Help Create a More Inclusive Community

Cultural biases define our notions of good behavior. For example, do we expect higher levels of self-awareness and social awareness from girls than boys? Do we honor the ways students with disabilities manage themselves and navigate social groups? When we imagine someone who makes responsible decisions, what kinds of decisions does that person make, what life and career path does that person end up having, and what color skin does that person have? When we look at the kinds of jobs a responsible decision maker might aspire to, what do the racial demographics in those positions look like? We might say we don't have these biases, but what do our special needs referrals and discipline records say? What stories do our grades tell? Which students' names do we hear, and in what contexts? Whose names are missing from our discussions?

When students learn to notice their values and choose behaviors based on those values, they get to define for themselves what constitutes good behavior. This is not to say we can't have community rules and norms, or that dominant cultural biases don't influence students just as they influence us. But if students define what's important to them and decide how they want to approach their world, then their voices—and the process of honoring their voices—become part of our culture, too. When students have a voice at school, school becomes *their* community. Make no mistake, though: classroom teachers eliciting student voices is not a substitute for education leaders taking all students' voices seriously and creating equitable and just school systems.

Focusing on Values as Qualities of Action Creates Opportunities for Connection

If two people search for what they have in common, they might find things they both like (favorite foods, shows, or sports), places they both go (a particular restaurant, park, or city), activities they both do (knitting, racing, or gaming), or topics they both discuss (politics, science, or fashion). Our access to things, places, activities, and even topics of interest often relates to our socioeconomic class, geographic origin, cultural background, and other aspects of our identities. If we only connect with people who share our interests, it makes us more likely to stay inside our social categories, spending time with people who identify in the same ways we do.

But what if we saw our values not as *what* we want from life (the things, places, activities, and topics that matter to us), but rather as *how* we want to live? Words that describe how we live—the qualities of our actions—are adverbs like *compassionately*, *appreciatively*, and *generously*. Unlike the things, places, activities, and topics that we get out of life, which are often mediated by our social groups, the qualities of our actions transcend the actions themselves. That is, there are many different ways to live, for example, compassionately, appreciatively, or generously. One student might live generously by reading to her brother who's on the autism spectrum, while another might live generously by making sure his friends all have rides home after a party, and still another might live generously by cleaning up a park. If students think and talk about the qualities of action they want to bring to school—*how* they want to approach their learning, work, and relationships—they have a chance to notice and appreciate their diversity while also developing a sense of connection across their differences.

Being Able to Choose a Values-Guided Life Empowers Students

School is mandatory for students, but they get to choose how to approach their learning, their work, each other, and themselves. Students can choose to become curious about their own values. They can choose to make their values (and not someone else's agenda) the reason for doing their schoolwork, and they can choose to create their own opportunities to enact their values at school. They can choose to open up to each other about their genuine values, instead of avoiding the vulnerability that comes with sharing what matters most. They can choose to serve their values even when it's hard. They can choose to treat each other and themselves according to their values, rather than doing what feels good in the moment. We think the empowerment that comes from choosing what they want their lives to mean is enough of a reason for students to do values work at school.

Settings Where Students Can Explore and Enact Their Values

Many schools create dedicated settings for students to talk about their values: advisory programs, health and wellness classes, outdoor education trips, and community-building assemblies. Students who need extra support might see a counselor, psychologist, social worker, special educator, nurse, occupational therapist, physical therapist, or speech pathologist. Any of these providers might do values work with a student.

Targeted programming and more intensive interventions make space for skills that students might not otherwise learn. However, if we only talk about values in advisory, health, or other nonacademic venues, we send students the message that learning how to live a meaningful life isn't part of the *real* work at school—the academics—and doesn't need to be taken as seriously. We also send the message that the academic domain doesn't involve students' values. If we shave time off our academic classes to make room for advisory or health programs, or if we cancel academic classes for special assemblies and trips, or if we regularly pull students out of academic classes to talk about their feelings in someone's office, then we send the message that academics aren't that important, either. To honor students' academic learning and their values, we can incorporate opportunities for students to discover and do what's meaningful to them into their academic classes. When we embed values work in academic tasks, we create the time and space to do both meaningfully, and we send the message that we needn't sacrifice one for the other.

Academic Tasks as Contexts for Values Work

Even if doing values work in academic classes seems like a good idea in theory, academic teachers already have so much to accomplish in any given unit. Imagine, for example, that Jean teaches a seventh-grade science unit on cells. Her students need to be able to name the organelles, describe their functions, and explain their relationships to each other and to the cell as a whole. To ensure her students reach those outcomes, Jean could have them read an article about cells, watch a video about cells, and hear from a local biologist. Groups of students could draw and label cell diagrams, make three-dimensional models, animate different organelles, or choreograph movement sequences to represent cellular processes. Students could take samples of their own cheek cells and view them under a microscope. Student pairs could create analogies to express how the different organelles function ("If a cell is like a school, the nucleus is like the office") and then present their analogies on posters to their class. That's a lot—and it's only one unit! Where would values work fit in?

An academic unit consists of a thoughtfully sequenced set of learning tasks that culminates in a learning outcome. Usually, we assign a variety of tasks, chosen from an even wider variety of potential tasks, to help our students achieve the learning outcome. If we're willing to be flexible about *which* learning tasks our students use to reach an academic outcome, we might create opportunities for other kinds of learning *beyond* that academic outcome. For example, let's say Jean is trying to decide which learning tasks to give her seventh graders so they learn about organelles. She has many tasks to choose from. But if she also wants her students to discover the values they want to bring to their interactions with each other, then she might give her students a group task, such as having them work together to create movement sequences that represent cellular processes. If Jean wants her students to discover the values they want to bring to their time and materials management, she might have them build cell models over the course of several days. We, too, can choose learning tasks that achieve the desired academic outcomes and also help students discover the values they want to bring to their learning, their work, themselves, each other, and their world. That's the two-for-one part of two-for-one teaching.

However, just because a learning task creates a context in which students *can* explore and enact their values doesn't mean they *will*. For example, let's say Jean assigns a project for groups of students to build cell models, but she doesn't proactively help her students consider how they want to treat each other in their groups. A group's members *might* learn how to listen to each other, notice and appreciate each other's strengths, fairly divide their work, give and receive honest feedback, and consider each other's perspectives. But just as possibly, the group's members might learn how to take over, shirk responsibility, become more rigid in their roles as leaders and followers, go along with a bad idea in order to avoid confrontation, and waste time.

Jean might find herself pulling students aside to mediate conflict, or giving some students higher or lower grades than their personal contributions merit, because other group members' contributions strengthened or weakened the work. Or she might carefully group her students in an attempt to prevent problems from arising in the first place. Or she might carefully delineate each group member's rules, roles, and responsibilities so the groups have as little collective decision making and mutual accountability as possible. In time, she might become so frustrated that she stops assigning group projects and instead has her students build their cell models individually.

Given choice, people sometimes choose whatever makes them feel happiest or most powerful in the moment, or whatever requires the least investment of time and effort (Hayes, Strosahl, & Wilson, 1999; Waltz & Follette, 2009). While working on their cell models, Jean's students might choose to goof off because it's fun, assume control because they want to get an *A*, make snide comments about one group member because it gets the others to laugh, or volunteer to bring the supplies because it's easier than writing the description—even if these behaviors don't match their values. Offering an opportunity for values-consistent behavior doesn't guarantee that students will notice that opportunity or take advantage of it, any more than offering a salad on a fast food menu will ensure that people notice it next to the picture of a juicy burger, much less choose the salad.

But just as we can learn to look for healthier food options and choose them because we care about our bodies, students can learn to act in accordance with their values when we teach them how (Hayes et al., 1999; Waltz & Follette, 2009). Imagine that on the first day of the cells unit, Jean describes what the class will learn and do, and she has students consider ways they can make their work personally meaningful (as in Values-Activating Questions, page 54). As students discuss cellular processes in pairs, Jean gives them a conversation structure that helps them listen and respond to each other in values-consistent ways (as in Collaborative Conversations, page 90). Once she's assigned groups for the cell model project, Jean has her students identify how they want to bring their values to the relationships they have with their group members and to the task itself (as in Group Commitments, page 151). The protocols in this book will show you how to guide your students toward understanding and living by their values. That's the teaching part of two-for-one teaching.

This book's organization will guide you through the process of using academic tasks as contexts for values work.

How This Book Is Organized

This book has two parts. Part I, "Foundations"—which contains chapters 1 and 2—describes how to create a classroom environment that supports values work, and part II, "Protocols"—which contains chapters 3 through 8—offers instructional strategies that can help students achieve academic outcomes while also discovering and developing their own values. We call them *protocols*, not *activities*, to make clear that you can use these multiple times, in a variety of contexts—unlike an activity that might happen only once, in a particular way, as part of one particular unit, or that's disconnected from any larger learning experience. Placing gummy bears into various fluids is an *activity*: a science class would do it once, as part of a cells unit, to observe how osmosis works. If students shared their observations, inferences, and ideas about the gummy bear experiment using Track and Acknowledge (page 94), that's a protocol: a learning routine they could repeat while discussing the genetics of height during the DNA unit, and examples of mutualism during the ecology unit, and the story of Henrietta Lacks later during the cells unit.

Throughout the book, we've included middle and high school examples to show what values work looks like, and we wrote the protocols and handouts using language that middle and high school students—at least the ones we've worked with—would understand (perhaps learning the occasional new vocabulary word). We hope that if you're a middle or high school teacher, you'll find the protocols accessible and appropriate for your students. If you do not teach those grades, we hope you'll adapt, adjust, remix, and reimagine them to create versions that work for your class. And if you happen to be an intrepid elementary school teacher or college professor who was willing to pick up this book, we think you'll find a lot here that you can use with your students, too.

Chapter 1 is about how you can set your students up to do the challenging but ultimately rewarding work of connecting their assignments and interactions to their values. This involves designing relevant learning tasks, delivering lessons to help students stay psychologically present, offering feedback on student work that empowers them to act on their values, making space for all students to open up, and responding to student avoidance.

Chapter 2 describes some of the psychology behind how to help students expand their awareness of what's possible in the present, take action in accordance with their personal values, and develop the willingness to struggle in the service of living a meaningful life.

Chapters 3–8 contain the protocols. These chapters follow the chronology of a unit from beginning to end. Chapter 3 considers how to begin a unit so students can connect upcoming learning to their values. Chapters 4 and 5 focus on helping students clarify and commit to their values as they explore new academic material and then review it. Chapters 6 and 7 look at how students can create and refine work products in accordance with their values. Chapter 8 addresses how students can reflect on their learning experiences and set values-consistent goals for future assignments and interactions.

The book has a total of thirty protocols that show how teachers can use academic tasks as contexts for values work. We'd like to provide some guidance on how to select protocols that will work best for you, but we can't do that without knowing you. Whether a given protocol will work has less to do with the academic subject, grade level, population, class size, and schedule, and more to do with the individual teacher, specific students, relationships within the group, and school culture. You're the expert on those elements, not us. The best we can do is show you how the protocols work and invite you to adapt them so they work for you.

After each protocol's title, you'll see a brief summary and a Suggested Time graphic (like the one shown here) indicating the fraction of an hour-long class period we'd allocate for the protocol. We didn't estimate how many minutes the protocols will take because that depends on your class size, your schedule, your students' characteristics, how you deliver and adapt the protocol, and how much time you choose to devote to it. As you'll see, some protocols are brief lesson openers, while others are strategies to integrate into lessons, and still others are full lessons. While we expect that some will match your teaching style better than others, all will work with any academic subject.

After introducing the protocol, we offer a getting-ready checklist, steps for effectively leading the protocol, ways of boosting the impact (or how to follow up, make modifications, and handle challenges), and suggestions for reusing the same protocol next time, during future units. You can, of course, try incorporating new protocols over the course of the year, both for the sake of novelty and because different protocols will work better for different students. But we hope you'll find protocols you can use routinely. Like landmarks on a trail, these learning routines will help your students know where they are and where they're going. And just as they learn academic skills through routine practice, students can practice exploring and enacting their values and learn to choose more meaningful and empowered lives.

PART I

Foundations

Chapter 1 helps you create a classroom culture in which students willingly do values work. We offer suggestions for how to design relevant learning tasks, encourage students to stay present in the moment, offer feedback on student work that empowers them to act on their values, make space for openness, and respond to avoidance.

Chapter 2 describes tools from psychological science that help students notice what's possible for themselves, take action in accordance with their personal values, and willingly struggle in the service of a meaningful life.

Chapter 1

• • • • •

CREATING A CULTURE OF WILLINGNESS

Try this quick exercise: Draw a horizontal and a vertical axis, as shown in figure 1.1. Label the vertical axis *Fun* and *Painful* and the horizontal axis *Pointless* and *Meaningful*. In which of the resulting four quadrants would you place doing laundry? Getting a flu shot? Eating a kale salad? Listening to Prince's *Purple Rain* album? Driving a motorcycle? Hiking? Drawing? Dancing? Going to school an hour early to give a student extra help?

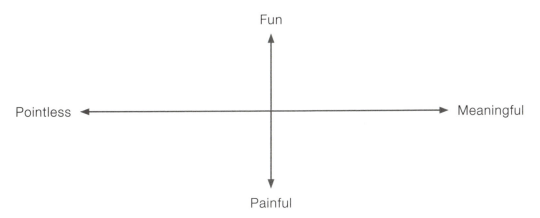

Figure 1.1: Fun and meaningful graph.

If your graph doesn't have something in each quadrant, see if you can think of activities that you'd consider both fun and meaningful, fun but pointless, painful yet meaningful, and both painful and pointless.

Psychologist Steven Hayes (2005) describes the difference between *wanting* to do something and being *willing* to do it. When we want to do something, we seek it out, look forward to it, enjoy it while it's happening, and miss it when it's over. The activities in your graph's upper quadrants are ones that you want to do—at least sometimes. You might find the ones on the Meaningful side more satisfying, and you might feel a little guilty after doing the ones on the Pointless side, but all are activities you, to some degree, *want* to do.

Willingness is different. Look at the activities you put in the bottom-right quadrant, the ones you consider meaningful yet painful. Maybe they're physically painful, or maybe they're psychologically painful—boring, tedious, embarrassing, scary, perhaps a little disgusting, or otherwise unpleasant. What makes that unpleasantness worthwhile? Maybe the activity helps you avoid an even more unpleasant outcome—laundry is a little tedious, but you'd rather do it than wear dirty clothes. Or maybe the activity serves your values. If you say you're willing to go to school an hour early to give a student extra help, that doesn't mean you want to. You'd probably rather sleep later, eat a relaxing breakfast, or work out before school. But even though you find getting to school early a bit burdensome, you might be willing to do it because you value ensuring that all students have the skills to do their best work, even if that means meeting with this particular student before school. The student, too, might not want to come in early but might be willing to because the student values learning thoroughly and acting responsibly.

Living by our values often brings deep satisfaction and vitality over time, but the day-to-day effort of committing to our values can be hard (Hayes et al., 2012). For students to do values work—that is, to discover and do what they find genuinely important—they'll need to be willing to rise to the inherent challenges of that work.

Values work challenges students in at least four ways. First, it challenges them just because it differs from what they expect to encounter in an academic class. Usually, when students show up for English class, they expect to analyze a motif in a novel, identify examples of personification, write an essay, or learn how to use a semicolon. They probably don't expect that they'll also talk about their emotions, relationships, struggles, or futures. Integrating values work means thinking more flexibly about what an academic class can be.

Second, values work involves more than noticing and talking about what matters. It's about choosing to *do* what matters. But many students have an academic comfort zone. They go back to the same topics or modalities for every assignment, like the student who always writes about otters or who always makes a poster. They use the same study strategies regardless of whether those work or make sense. They sit with the same friends, regardless of the impact on their learning. They raise their hands to answer every question in every class, or they never contribute to discussions, regardless of whether they have something important to add. Students might find the topics, processes, and relationships that matter most to them harder than what they're used to.

Third, values work might carry an emotional load, because anything a person cares about becomes a potential source of vulnerability (Wilson & DuFrene, 2009). If a student cares about a friend, she faces the possibility of feeling hurt if her friend leaves her. If she cares about playing football, she risks the pain of losing games, getting injured, and being cut from the team. In asking our students to connect their schoolwork to their values, we invite *all* their emotions into the room.

Fourth and finally, students might discover that their actions don't align with their values. They care about their friends but neglect their friendships. They care about marriage equality but tease the boy who won't say whom he likes. They care about environmental stewardship but eat meat and drive SUVs.

If students think of themselves as *bad* when doing values work, they'll distance themselves from their peers, from us, and from the work itself. They may even experience a sense of shame. Psychologists Jason Luoma and Melissa Platt (2015) explain that shame "impedes social engagement, promotes interpersonal disconnection, and interferes with interpersonal problem solving" (p. 97). However, when acting with self-compassion, a "person responds to their own behavior with the same sort of caregiving repertoire that one might apply to a friend [or] loved one" (Luoma & Platt, 2015, p. 97). Doing values work with students means helping them show self-compassion if they find their behavior doesn't align with their values.

Thinking flexibly about their classes, doing harder work, opening themselves to their emotions, and showing compassion for themselves—it's a pretty tall order. Ultimately, the students themselves have to choose these behaviors, but we can create the conditions to make that choice more likely. Our ways of designing learning tasks, delivering lessons, giving feedback on student work, and managing power will impact our students' willingness to live by their values in class. Let's see how.

Design Relevant Learning Tasks

Students can bring their values to any learning task. They can read a textbook deeply, complete workbook pages thoughtfully, write five-paragraph essays creatively, and prepare for standardized tests cooperatively. Still, some learning tasks will more easily lend themselves to values work, like reading activists' memoirs, looking at their own cheek cells under a microscope, writing dramatic scenes portraying conflicts in their lives, or calculating the total area of green space within a five-mile radius of their homes. Such tasks leave more room for students to take creative risks, make decisions, share their views, and understand what matters to them—yet they also have clearly defined parameters so students understand and can meet expectations. If students open themselves up to struggle, they do so because their struggles serve something that matters. To honor the effort it will take our students to connect their work to their values, we can design tasks that have personal, practical, and cultural relevance.

An academic task has *personal relevance* to our students if the content relates to their interests, communities, histories, goals, or daily lives—or if the task is sufficiently flexible so the students can make it relate. For example, if after reading Lorraine Hansberry's (1959/1994) *A Raisin in the Sun*, students write essays about how the author drew from her own experiences, those students who are already interested in the play's issues or in Hansberry's life will find the assignment meaningful. However, if students write original dramatic scenes based on conflicts in their lives, every student can potentially find a way to write something personally relevant. To prepare for the latter assignment, students could still explore how Hansberry based her play on her experiences, but instead of writing about that, they could use her work process and product as a model for their own while incorporating stories that matter to them.

An academic task has *practical* relevance if students can see how they will use what they are learning, not just in some undetermined future, but right now in their current settings. For example, calculating the area of green space within a five-mile radius of their homes gives students mathematical skills they might need in the future and also gives them a way to talk about resources they have access to in the present. Or take the example of Marjory Stoneman Douglas High School students in Parkland, Florida, studying gun regulation in advanced placement government class (LeTourneau, 2018) and learning debate, drama, and journalism through school programs (Lithwick, 2018). In the wake of the deaths of fourteen students and three staff members from the 2018 shooting at their school, a group of students gathered together and organized a mass youth movement to end easy access to firearms (Lopez, 2018). Over eight hundred coordinated demonstrations occurred on a single day in March of 2018 (Carlsen & Patel, 2018)—with the Washington, DC rally reaching close to one million participants (Reilly, 2018)—largely due to the skills the students learned at school. Imagine if academic classes became places where all students develop the skills to rise to the challenges in their lives, however big or small.

Taking these definitions into account, we propose that an academic task has *cultural relevance* if it opens multiple paths to excellence, helps students honor and preserve their home knowledge while also extending their capabilities, elevates knowledge from traditionally marginalized groups while also exploring the variety and complexity within the group, and equips students with tools to challenge systems of power and privilege (especially those that impact the students themselves; Ladson-Billings, 1995, 2014).

If this sounds like a lot to manage, consider the alternative. Should some students find it easier to see their experiences, histories, and worldviews in the curriculum while others are excluded, erased, marginalized, or reduced to a stereotype? Should some students feel entitled to academic and social status because they only ever see people who look like them in the curriculum, to the point that they think their own way of life is *normal*, everyone else is *other*, and they're generous to let *others* into the room? Should students leave school lacking the tools to dismantle injustices that affect their lives and communities? How can students freely choose to approach their learning and their relationships in accordance with their values if their only choices replicate oppression?

In attempts to make the curriculum more culturally relevant, too many schools use what professors James A. Banks and Cherry A. McGee Banks (2010) call an *additive* approach, or attaching "content, concepts, themes, and perspectives to the curriculum without changing its basic structure, purposes, and characteristics" (p. 240). To create a context for our students to live by their values, we can try what Banks and Banks (2010) call the *transformation* approach, which "changes the basic assumptions of the curriculum" (p. 242) so that students learn multiple ways to approach the world. Transforming the curriculum means more than adding one book by a First Nation author, or spending one day during a Civil War unit discussing women's contributions, or using ethnically coded names in word problems that describe situations only wealthy people would encounter. Transformation means confronting the stereotypes and privilege embedded throughout the curriculum, and choosing materials that affirm diverse experiences within multiple groups. Addition is an event, but transformation is an ongoing process.

We can begin—and only begin—transforming our curriculum for cultural, practical, and personal relevance by asking three questions about each learning task.

1. **"Who contributes?"** We proceed from the assumption that any knowledge that meaningfully advances learning is valuable. That knowledge might come from traditionally privileged sources such as a textbook, but it might also come from the students' families and neighborhoods. To increase cultural relevance, we can engage in what Christine Sleeter (2005) calls the "process of retrieving subjugated knowledge"—that is, finding and studying the contributions of a "sociocultural group whose experiences, perspectives, and/or intellectual work relates to the big idea [of the] curriculum, but is marginalized in it" (p. 91).

2. **"Who participates?"** In doing values work, you might find that the students who make their work meaningful are the very same ones who already love learning and get good grades, and who are eager to do even more. In "Promoting the Non-Obvious Candidate," Raghu Krishnamoorthy (2014) argues that "in addition to grooming obvious high performers who are accomplished in a particular domain," we should also look at "high performers in other domains who do not automatically fit the bill." Though this advice is about how companies should hire, it applies just as well to academic classes. In designing relevant learning tasks, we might think of two or three students who typically struggle, act out, or fly under the radar. Instead of labeling such students as "at-risk, disadvantaged, and underachieving" (Ladson-Billings, 2014), try considering these particular students' strengths and imagining learning tasks that would best leverage them. By rejecting deficit thinking and noticing all kinds of excellence, we can design tasks that define success more flexibly, according to multiple sets of values.

3. **"Who benefits?"** We can also consider how academic work products could solve problems in our school or community. Imagine, for example, an eighth-grade physical science teacher who has students make solar-powered chargers for their phones. If you were to take your students on a walk through your school or neighborhood and look for problems they could solve through the work they do in your class, what might they find?

A task has personal relevance when it connects to students' lives, practical relevance when it teaches skills students can use within and beyond school, and cultural relevance if it affirms multiple experiences and creates equity. Designing tasks that have personal, practical, and cultural relevance helps students engage more fully with their work and more willingly with their values.

Deliver Lessons to Help Students Stay Psychologically Present

Meaningful learning isn't necessarily fun. Students could care about gun violence but find the work of researching it exhausting. They could write about being bullied but feel anxious when they remember the experience. They could choose to work carefully on a science project but feel isolated when their friends finish more quickly and go out without them. They could practice speaking in French class but feel embarrassed when they use the wrong word. Knowing that a learning task will challenge them more—academically, intellectually, emotionally, socially, and sometimes even physically—students often choose a less meaningful but more comfortable route.

In any of these cases, the student's focus on what happened before, what might happen next, what's currently happening elsewhere, or what's happening inside their skin keeps them from fully engaging with a meaningful task *here* (in the classroom) and *now* (at that moment). To help our students stay psychologically present, we can portion and pace our lessons such that their focus remains on the here and now. At the end of the lesson, we can summarize how they might have brought their values to their work.

Portioning

Portioning a task helps keep students from feeling overwhelmed. Getting ten problems at once might feel like too much, but getting two or three at a time feels more manageable. Portioning also helps prevent students from choosing the easiest option. Let's say that a history teacher wants his ninth graders to describe what appears in a photo, infer when and where the photo was taken, and imagine what the people in the photo were thinking. One student might rush through the describing and inferring because he thinks the imagining prompt sounds more fun. Another might spend all her time describing, because inferring and imagining seem hard and she's not sure she'll do those right. If the class gets ten minutes to respond to all three questions, these two students could spend nearly all that time responding to only the question they like but still remain on task. But if the teacher gives the questions one at a time, the students can only stay on task by responding to that one question. Portioning can prevent students from avoiding difficult but potentially meaningful work.

Revealing one step at a time also helps students bring their values to each step, instead of anticipating the next one. Let's say a geography teacher plans to have her eighth graders list all the places they go during a typical week, choose one that matters to them, and then notice how the place reflects its physical location. (Is the soccer field built for drainage or drought resistance, or both? Is their house built to let in the breeze or keep out the cold, or both?) If the teacher gives all the prompts at once, some students might choose a place because they can immediately think of ways it reflects its physical geography, and not because the place is particularly important in their life. But if the teacher gives the prompts one at a time, the students can first choose which place matters to them, and then analyze that place.

Pacing

Once you've broken your lesson into portions, how much time should you spend on each one? Imagine that same geography lesson about how places reflect physical geography. After writing about their places, students will share their responses in small groups and read an article about how Latin America's diverse terrain influences life there. How much time should the teacher allocate to each part of this lesson? If she doesn't give enough time for students to analyze their places, they could end up with nothing to share. If the teacher gives too much time for individual analysis, then students who quickly understand might get bored, and it won't give the class enough time to hear each other's analyses and find patterns. If she cuts the sharing short, students might lack the foundation to understand the article about Latin America. If she lets the sharing go on too long, they'll run out of time for the article.

Whatever amount of time you devote to each task will be too much for some students and too little for others. The best you can do is estimate how much time you'll spend on each portion, and then, while teaching, watch your students and the clock. When students whisper or put their heads down or ask to get water, they might be ready to move on, or they might need help seeing how to go deeper. Meanwhile, students who are still working might feel stressed out because they think they're too slow. Since there won't be a point when everyone is ready to move on, wait until most students seem ready, and then give the next portion—but point out how continuing to work on the current portion might serve students' values. For example, a mathematics teacher could say, "If you're still working on problem one, that means you're making sure you thoroughly understand how this formula works instead of just plugging in numbers, or that you're coming up with your own creative way to solve the problem, or that you're carefully checking to make sure you didn't make any mistakes. Those are good things to be doing. If and when you're ready for problem two, here it is."

Summarizing

At the end of each portion, you can help students observe how their actions matched their values. Maybe the geography teacher says something like, "At this point, you've all spent fifteen minutes having a discussion. Wanda's group had a deep debate about one point that she shared; it seems like you all care about depth and listening deeply, too. Nikki's group had lots of mini discussions about all the different details they noticed; it seems like your group cares about paying close attention and being thorough. And Taj's group made connections between what different people noticed; it seems like you all really care about thinking creatively and collaboratively."

Summaries like these help students notice their values so they can choose to learn, work, and relate to each other according to those values. Summarizing also reminds students of what the lesson's overall purpose was, so they can see where they are in the present moment and anticipate where they might go next.

Give Empowering Feedback on Student Work

In between collecting and returning student work, you do something with it. What do you call the thing you do? Some teachers call it *grading* or *marking*, as if our main jobs are to approve the work (or say exactly how much we disapprove of it) and to tattoo it with our ink. In grading and marking student work, we establish our dominance and legitimize grading itself.

At the same time, we see things in our students' work that they don't, and passing along our knowledge can be an act of empowerment and even love. You might not have the ability to change the system that ranks and subjugates students—at least not quickly or easily, and certainly not by yourself—but you can give feedback that acknowledges your common humanity and that lovingly empowers students to evaluate their actions and improve their skills, according to their own values.

Psychologist Russell Kolts (2016) explains that eliciting self-evaluation—as teachers do when they give their students feedback—"works a good deal better when it's presented in a warm manner" (p. 16), because people are more willing to share their vulnerabilities when they have reason to think they'll get understanding and support as opposed to judgment and shame. Compassionate self-correction involves noticing what didn't work and "turning the focus toward doing better in the future" (Kolts, 2016, p. 16). By *better*, we mean more in line with community standards of excellence as well as students' own values; if they willingly improve, it's because that improvement matters to them. Our feedback empowers students to improve willingly when we deliver it with warmth and compassion, connect students' work to their own values, and help students turn their focus toward the future.

Empowering feedback consists first of making observations and sharing our personal experience of the work, which shows students that we are not standing over them in judgment but rather beside them in fellowship. As teachers, we have a different role than they do, and we have the power to give them grades, but we're also *people* who see them as people. If the students then willingly act upon their values, it's not because we've told or convinced them to; it's because we see and appreciate who they are. Empowering feedback also includes saying back the student's values and suggesting actions for next time. Instead of pointing out every flaw in their work and every mistake they made, these types of feedback keep students focused on what matters to them, how well their actions served them for this assignment, and what they could try in the future.

Make Observations

Empowering feedback begins with observations: What do you see? So often, we go directly to judgments ("Excellent work" or "This isn't quite there yet") or assumptions about a student's actions ("You needed to proofread this more carefully") without describing what we actually see ("You sometimes left out apostrophes, like in *Wendell's* and *Jasmine's*"). When we look at student work, we notice things that they, their peers, their parents, and even our colleagues who teach the same subject and grade level don't notice.

Seeing takes time. We have to slow down and pay attention, looking at the work and looking again. Then, we have to pick out details we want to mention: "One especially powerful description was of five-year-old you doing your own makeup and hair for your ballet recital because unlike the other girls, you had only a dad who wasn't allowed into the dressing room." Or, "Your explanation of the relationship between your brother's toys and tantrums showed how well you understand the concept of proportionality—and gave me an idea of what your brother is like." Seeing can get tedious, especially when we have a hundred or more tests, projects, or papers. But when students read our descriptions, they know we paid attention to the details of their work. We see their work, and through their work, we see them (and they see us seeing them).

Share Your Personal Experience of the Work

As we describe the work itself, we can also describe how we experience it. Unlike the computer programs that score standardized tests, we're human beings. A student's work evokes our emotions (such as a mathematics teacher feeling delight on seeing a student's clever solution), thoughts (such as a Spanish teacher picturing her student making the favorite foods he listed), memories (such as a science teacher recalling a recent fishing trip when his student mentions the smell of the water she tested), and sometimes physical sensations (such as an English teacher wincing while reading an essay about a student injuring her arm). Sharing how we experience our students' work shows them that they made an impact on another person.

Say Back the Student's Values

Within our feedback on students' work, we can also say back to them what they seem to value. What topics or qualities of action seem to matter to the student? If Jordan mentions his grandparents in every Spanish composition, or if Sophia keeps connecting her ideas in history class to contemporary racial justice issues, or if Dante lines up his equations carefully and precisely, their teachers can say back what seems important to them. Because the students haven't necessarily stated what they value, we can express an inference ("It *sounds like* your grandparents are important to you"), a pattern ("*Once again*, you've pointed out how racist ideas that took hold in the past persist in the present"), or a question ("*I wonder*, do you think about doing your problem sets carefully, or do you just sort of do them that way?"). Reflecting back their values helps students notice more ways to connect their schoolwork to those values. It also might encourage them to experiment with values they weren't aware of having, and to notice new ways to live their values day to day.

Suggest Actions for Next Time

We can suggest topics, strategies, and techniques students can keep using, and new ones they can try. When we orient students toward their past actions, we do it not to judge the actions as good or bad but rather to help the students notice whether their actions serve their values. If their actions feel satisfying and meaningful, then students now have the power to keep choosing similar actions, thus building a pattern of actions that serves their values. If they don't feel satisfied, they now have the power to recommit to their values by trying something else next time.

When students hand in their work, imagine that instead of submitting it for evaluation, they're starting a conversation. Your role in that conversation is to help them discover their own values, notice the extent to which their work product reflects their values, and develop a greater repertoire of actions that match their values.

Table 1.1 (page 24) summarizes the types of empowering feedback and their functions, and it provides examples of these feedback types.

Table 1.1: Types of Empowering Feedback

Feedback Type	Functions	Examples
Observations What do you see?	• Show students you paid close attention. • Build students' awareness of their actions.	"You've created an informative guide to coyote behavior for people who live in our county. The color-coded backgrounds help readers navigate the different categories, and the side-by-side labeled photos of a fox and coyote give readers ways to tell these animals apart. The matching game is an especially engaging way to help readers review and remember what they learned."
Personal experience of the work What do you think about, feel physically or emotionally, and remember as you experience the student's work?	• Show students how their work impacted another person. • Emphasize your common humanity.	"When I read your solution to problem six, I actually laughed out loud with delight because of how you described *unwrapping* a cylinder and getting two circles and a rectangle. It reminded me of when I was little and used to peel the labels off all the soup cans, and my parents would get mad because they wouldn't know what kind of soup was in each one. Little did I know then that this was a great way to measure the surface area of a cylinder!"
Tentative statements of the student's values Who or what does this student seem to care about? What qualities of action seem most important to this student?	• Help students notice what matters to them. • Help students notice how their schoolwork can be an expression of what matters to them.	"It sounds like the 84th Street movie theater is special not because of the films or seats or snacks, but rather because your family goes there together, and because seeing it outside your bus window is part of your daily routine."
Suggestions for next time What should the student keep doing in future work? What should the student do differently next time?	• Orient students toward future opportunities to recommit to their values. • Help students choose topics, strategies, and techniques that work for them.	"During some parts of your speech, you spoke a bit too quickly for me to understand every word. I still got the overall message, and I know the fast pace was intended to convey a sense of urgency about plastic pollution. In future spoken presentations, slow yourself down so your audience can get the full impact of your words and ideas. Try looking for parts you feel strongest about, and practice delivering those parts extra slowly."

Figure 1.2 has a sample response to student work that integrates these four types of feedback. For this activity, a science teacher asked his sixth graders, including Olivia, to create board games that teach others about an endangered animal. If it's prohibitively time consuming to write a comment this long for every student, you can create a list of observations and suggestions you find yourself making for multiple students. This way, you don't have to think of how to phrase them every time they apply.

Elements	Basic	Effective	Exemplary
The game includes **accurate scientific information** about the animal's characteristics, behavior, and habitat; why this animal population is threatened; and what people can do to help.		✓	
The board, pieces, and object of your game **directly relate** to the animal, its habitat, and the issues affecting it.		✓	
The game is **thoughtfully organized** based on your purpose; it's easy to set up and play; and the rules are clear and complete.		✓	
The game and its components are **appealing** because they're neat, colorful, and free of capitalization, punctuation, and spelling errors.	✓		
The game uses at least three **properly cited sources** of information.		✓	

Comment:

Olivia, you've created a lively and informative game about proboscis monkeys. You put a lot of care into cutting the game board into the shape of Borneo and thinking of appropriate rewards (like finding unripe fruits to eat) and pitfalls (like having to cross a river full of crocodiles). I especially enjoyed the rule that every time a player overtakes the others, that player has to make a honking sound like a male proboscis expressing his position! You made this game a fun experience while also sharing serious threats to proboscis monkeys.

I appreciated the "Did you know?" cards, but since they weren't part of the game, I'm not sure a player would read the cards. The facts about habitat destruction were right on the board and therefore more noticeable. Next time you make something that will be used to educate others—whether it's a game, a poster, a slideshow, or something else—think about how your audience (in this case, the game players) will interact with the information so your message gets across.

Something else to work on next time is proofreading. While the game was clear and well-made overall, the game cards had several misspelled words, such as omnivore and floodplain. Write unfamiliar words slowly, paying special attention to spelling them correctly, so nothing ends up distracting your audience from your important ideas.

Figure 1.2: Example response to student work.

Visit **go.SolutionTree.com/instruction** *for a free reproducible version of this figure.*

Finally, consider creating a hub for all the feedback you give a student throughout the year. Imagine that at the beginning of the year, Olivia's science teacher shares an electronic document with her that gives his feedback on her first piece of work, a field journal containing quantitative and qualitative descriptions of items found at school. After the science skills unit ends, Olivia's class moves on to a new unit on eco-systems and makes the endangered animal games as part of that unit. The teacher posts his feedback on Olivia's game in the document that already has his feedback on her field journal. Over the course of the year, the teacher posts feedback on all of Olivia's work in that same document. The teacher keeps the document private, sharing it only with Olivia and making it editable only by him. Students in the class each have a similar document that only they and the teacher can access. If your school doesn't use electronic document sharing or have secure ways to share information with students, you can keep file folders for each student with your handwritten or printed comments from each assignment.

In any case, if you put all your feedback for a student in one place, students will be more likely to notice their progress from one assignment to the next. You'll be more likely to notice their progress, too. You'll be able to see what you've said to a student in the past and decide what to say next. Most of all, when students can see their feedback on multiple assignments all in one place, they can track what happens when they act on their values and make better-informed decisions about where they commit their energy.

Manage Your Power

As much as we try to build a safe community for our students, a power dynamic still exists in the class-room. We're in charge; they're not. We make the assignments; they do them. They raise their hands; we call on them. Even if we let them make the rules, arrange the room, decide what and how they learn, and evaluate their own progress, we are the ones allowing that autonomy. The power is ours to give away, and at any moment, we can take it back. That doesn't mean we would, but we could. We know it, and they know it.

That power dynamic is part of the context that shapes our students' experience. Many students comply with whatever their teachers ask, whether out of blind trust, fear, or obligation. In values work, we're ask-ing our students to share their genuine stories and struggles, and it would be unethical to use our power to coerce them into doing so. If we want to create a safe and consensual environment for values work, we need to recognize and account for our power.

At the same time, we aren't that different from our students. We have our own values and vulner-abilities, just like they do. We're always learning, just like they are. Any learning will involve making mistakes, revealing ignorance, overcoming previous misconceptions, asking questions, and not knowing what questions to ask—for us and for them. Making ourselves vulnerable in the service of our values helps us understand what our students go through as learners. Making ourselves vulnerable in front of our students—telling them about how we've struggled and grown—opens the way for them to do the same. Of course, we shouldn't tell them anything about ourselves that will make them worry or that will otherwise detract from their learning experience. But just as our power shapes our students' learning context, our vulnerability can, too. Ways to have vulnerability with your students include participating in the work, using your silence and your voice to equalize power, and modeling discomfort in the service of your own values.

Participate in the Work

Make yourself an equal participant when possible. Instead of always leading the discussion, take part in the discussion sometimes. Instead of only assigning work, also do the work yourself. Do your own bridge-building project. Write your own essay. Take your own notes on the assigned chapter. By doing classwork alongside your students, you show them that you don't ask them to do anything you wouldn't do, and that they have something to contribute to your learning, just as you contribute to theirs. Although you're still the teacher and they're still the students, you're all learning together.

You'll also better equip yourself to relate to their experiences if you've had a similar one. While you might not struggle in the same ways they do, you'll understand the start-to-finish process of doing work in your class. You'll be able to say things like, "When I first started building my bridge, I felt positive it wasn't going to support any weight" or "I don't like proofreading either, but I caught some comma mistakes when I read my draft, and I think I would have been embarrassed if I hadn't fixed them," or even "You can take your notes in a Venn diagram, but to be totally honest, I get weirdly perfectionistic about drawing the circles and it becomes a huge distraction, so I put my notes into a chart instead."

Comments like these show your students that self-doubt, reluctance, embarrassment, distraction, perfectionism, and other such emotional challenges are normal—and that it's possible to approach those challenges in an open, playful, self-compassionate way. Doing your own assignments allows you to have authentic conversations with your students about how you bring your values to your work—thus showing them how they might bring their values to their work.

Often, it won't be possible for you to participate equally. You'll ask questions you already know the answers to, or your role will be to facilitate and manage learning rather than to learn yourself. If you can't do the work alongside your students, you can do similar work with your colleagues. Many protocols in this book lend themselves to teachers' work. Just as students can use the Exemplar Study protocol (page 146) when working on an academic project, teachers can use it when working on a lesson plan. Just as students can use the Collaborative Conversations protocol (page 90) to talk about course content, teachers can use it to talk about pedagogy. Just as students can use the Intervision protocol (page 72) to observe their classmates, teachers can use it to observe their colleagues. If you belong to a teaching team, see whether the team would be interested in using some of this book's protocols in the professional work you do together.

Use Your Silence and Your Voice to Equalize Power

When you can't equally participate in class, do your best to equalize the power. In situations when speaking up would give you more power, consider saying less. For example, when students share their interpretations of historical texts or solutions to a geometry problem, the teacher's contributions will sound like the *right* ones. Students might stop sharing because, in their minds, the master has spoken. The less you say, the more room you create for your students to talk, showing them that their talk matters.

In situations when silence would give you more power, consider saying more. Professor, writer, and activist bell hooks (1994) explains:

> Professors who expect students to share confessional narratives but who are themselves unwilling to share are exercising power in a manner that could be coercive. In my classrooms, I do not expect students to take any risks that I would not take, to share in any way that I would not share. (p. 21)

What hooks says of university seems even more true for middle and high school, when students are younger and not as good at filtering themselves. Before you invite your students to become more vulnerable than they already are—such as when you ask about their personal histories, struggles, families, and values—consider sharing your own narrative and not requiring, expecting, or even asking them to share theirs. And if you do ask students to share, consider sharing first.

Model Discomfort in the Service of Your Own Values

Finally, you can point out moments when you're willing to be uncomfortable, not because you're tougher or more self-assured than your students, but because the very action that makes you uncomfortable is also important to you. Imagine a history teacher who plans to have her ninth graders analyze each other's photos as a way to get to know each other, practice making inferences, and understand the limits of interpreting primary sources. The teacher hasn't tried this activity before and doesn't feel confident. She says, "I'm not sure this activity will work, but I'm hoping it'll give us a chance to get to know each other and see how it feels to be historians." If you, the teacher, take risks, you'll show your students that your classroom is a place where they can take risks, too. If you explain how your risks serve your values, they'll learn when risk taking is worthwhile.

Respond to Student Avoidance

So far, we have explored how designing relevant learning tasks, delivering lessons to foster psychological presence, giving empowering feedback, and managing classroom power dynamics supports a culture of willingness. But even if you do all of this, you won't prevent students from avoiding the challenges associated with living by their values. Let's look at four ways students avoid fully engaging with their work—(1) doing something other than the assigned task, (2) complaining, (3) staying silent, and (4) seeking approval for every decision—and how you can help them return to their values.

When Students Do Something Else

Some students avoid their assignments by doing something else instead, whether that means drumming with a pencil, talking to a friend, making jokes, leaving their seats, texting, or staring into space. We might call these students *disruptive*, *distractible*, *impulsive*, or *out to lunch*, but they're all avoiding the assigned task. We have various ways to address such problem behaviors, like providing more fun activities, reducing demands on the student, or eliminating the possibility of escape, among others (Geiger, Carr, & LeBlanc, 2010). However, even if these strategies reduce or eliminate one particular behavior, avoidance is not a single behavior but rather a "generalized response class" (Stokes & Baer, 1977). That is, an almost unlimited number of behaviors could function as avoidance moves (Friman, Hayes, & Wilson, 1998).

Imagine that Allison wants to avoid doing her mathematics work. She doodles in her notebook. When her teacher takes away her notebook and tells her she's supposed to use her tablet, she uses the device to watch geometry videos. When she gets caught doing *that*, she argues, "But I'm learning math!" The teacher takes the tablet away, and Allison just stares at her desk. Her teacher can't prevent her from doing that because she can insist she's thinking. He assigns what he thinks will be a fun game, but one of the students in Allison's assigned group sometimes teases her, so she hangs back. A creative child like Allison can always find another way to avoid an unpleasant task. The teacher closes a door; the student opens a window.

When students do something else instead of their work, we can first ask ourselves whether our assignments are too boring or difficult, or create the potential for embarrassment or social exclusion. We can then ask questions to help students describe their own behaviors and assess for themselves whether those behaviors match their values.

- "What's happening right now?"
- "What happens if you keep doing this?"
- "How does it affect your learning?"
- "How does it affect your classmates?"
- "What if it becomes a pattern?"
- "What other choices do you have?"
- "What happens if you try that instead?"

According to psychologists Matthieu Villatte, Jennifer Villatte, and Steven Hayes (2016), asking such questions—rather than simply telling students what we think the answers are—means we "evoke rather than provide observations and descriptions," so that the student "learns the overarching process of observing and drawing conclusions based on his or her own experience" (p. 16). Instead of following someone else's rules, students learn what works for them from their own experience, giving them agency in their own lives. Moreover, when students see how their avoidance behaviors prevent them from serving their values, they have a choice: they can keep avoiding the task but avoid their values too, or they can approach the task and accept the discomfort that comes along with doing something important (Hayes et al., 2012).

When Students Complain

Some students complain about things they can't control as a way to avoid taking responsibility for things they can control. They complain about their grades instead of reflecting on what they could have done differently. They complain about their assignments instead of actually working. They complain about their classmates instead of considering how they might treat their classmates more kindly. We might perceive such students as whiny, pushy, or entitled. Depending on who the students are, how they express their complaints, and whether they bring in a parent for backup, we might give in to their demands, or we might minimize their experiences by trying to convince them that things aren't so bad—or even shaming them for complaining in the first place.

When students complain, we can first ask ourselves the hard question of whether we should do something differently. Maybe our grading practices really are unfair, or our assignments are problematic. Maybe we need to learn some new ways to teach our lessons and build community. We can also listen for the values underneath our students' complaints and say those values back to the students. If they feel upset enough to complain, something important must be at stake.

For example, if a student complains about a grade on a history test, we could say something like, "It sounds like it's important to you to know about history." If students disagree with our restatement of their values, we can apologize and ask them to tell us what does matter to them in class. Once we or they have summarized the values at stake, we can ask questions to help the students discover where they still have control.

- "What did you do to prepare?"
- "How much time did you spend?"
- "How were you thinking about the assignment?"
- "What strategies could you use next time?"

Questions like these help students reconsider their process even if they're focused on outcomes, and choose values-consistent action next time even when they're not happy this time.

Sometimes, students complain because they did put forth effort but didn't get the results they hoped for. Professor Carol S. Dweck (2015) cautions:

> Certainly, effort is key for students' achievement, but it's not the only thing. Students need to try new strategies and seek input from others when they're stuck. They need this repertoire of approaches—not just sheer effort—to learn and improve.

If students (or their parents) insist that they worked hard and therefore deserve a good grade, we can express empathy ("Oh, that sounds so frustrating"), ask questions to help them connect their efforts to their values ("What about this work was so important to you that it was worth all your effort?"), and collaborate with them to find new strategies that would more effectively serve their values next time ("Can you think of a different way to have studied?" or, if they can't think of anything, "How about if next time, you try making and taking a practice test instead of using flash cards?"). Even if they continue to complain, we can keep moving the conversation from achievement and effort to process, and from the past to the future, thus reminding students that they still have control over their actions, and that those actions can still reflect their values.

When Students Stay Silent

Some students do their assigned work but stay silent whenever they can. These students get labeled *quiet* or *reserved*; they'll answer questions when called on but rarely ask questions, volunteer to share, or offer comments. Teachers often coax these students to talk by suggesting that they make it a goal to raise their hand at least once per class period. When these students do share their thoughts, whether because they've volunteered or because they were called on, teachers often praise them, saying, "You got it" or "Excellent question." Such statements of praise might feel good in the moment, but as education professor Peter T. Johnston (2012) explains, praising a student creates an environment of judgment:

> If we say 'I'm proud of you' when they're successful, they will fill in the other end of the conversation and infer our disappointment when they are unsuccessful. We don't have to say anything. They are learning that, in this domain, we judge people. (p. 38)

If students stay silent because they fear judgment, creating an environment that judges responses (even positively) risks making them less likely to offer theirs. If they stay silent because they're thinking about the ideas, praise might just distract them from that thinking, and coaxing might get them to speak before they're ready.

When students stay silent, we can first check if we've explained the material clearly and engagingly enough for all students to understand it, connect to it, and have something meaningful to say about it. We can also wait longer before calling on students to give everyone a chance to volunteer. Then, instead of praising students who contribute, we can ask questions to show interest in their ideas, or simply thank them for their contributions. While praising asserts our power to judge something as good or bad, thanking helps the students notice they've offered something meaningful to the group, whether by sharing an idea, asking for clarification, challenging an assumption, or otherwise contributing. We can also thank students for less conspicuous contributions, such as listening, trying a new strategy, or helping a classmate. Acknowledging all kinds of contributions gives students a choice in how they participate and helps them appreciate moments when their efforts match their values.

When Students Seek Approval for Every Decision

Some avoidance behaviors don't look like avoidance at all. When students seek your approval for every tiny decision—"Is this good? How about now? Is it OK if the last two lines printed on the second page? Should I add another sentence? Do I have to add another sentence?"—they're avoiding making these decisions themselves. We might say these students are *anxious* or *perfectionistic* and respond either by giving them the approval they seek (if only to get them off our backs) or by telling them to stop asking us questions (which might only make them more anxious that they've upset us).

When students seek approval, we can look for ways we unintentionally send the message that their job is to please us. For example, are we explaining why it helps *them* to make an essay a certain length or to put a heading on the paper, or do we make these demands seem like *our* personal preferences? We can also make sure we've expressed our expectations clearly and specifically enough that our students understand them, and that we haven't left the students to guess some secret right way to complete the assignment. Beyond that, we can ask questions that give the decisions back to the students. If they ask if their work is good, we can ask, "How would you know it's good?" If they ask if a choice is OK, we can direct them back to their resources: "Where can you look to find out how long your paper should be? What if the assignment doesn't say?" If they ask if they're doing a task correctly, we can help them notice whether their approach is working: "What happens if you subtract x from both sides? Does that look right?" or "Why is it important to you to learn how calculate correctly?" Questions like these put the responsibility for making values-conscious decisions back on the student.

Figure 1.3 summarizes common classroom avoidance moves and how teachers can move students back toward their values.

Student Avoidance Moves		Teacher Responses	
Students sometimes . . .	**in order to avoid the challenge of**	**Teachers can . . .**	**to help students move toward**
Do something else, such as have a side conversation, fidget, look out the window, or ask to leave the room	Putting forth the necessary effort to complete the task	**Ask questions** that help students notice their actions, such as: • "What's happening right now?" • "How does this affect your learning? Your classmates?" • "What if this becomes a pattern?" • "What other choices do you have?" • "What happens if you do that instead?"	Monitoring their own behaviors Exploring the costs of their actions in terms of their values Holding themselves accountable to their values

Complain about their assignments, classmates, or grades	Putting forth the necessary effort to address the problem or try a new strategy	**Say back** students' values and ask what they want to do next, such as by saying: • "It sounds like you really care about . . . ." • "What can you do?" • "How will you . . . ?" • "What will you do if that doesn't work?"	Noticing what they can and can't control Noticing their values Choosing values-consistent actions
Stay silent when it comes to their thoughts, questions, or experiences	Subjecting themselves to judgments from their peers, their teacher, or themselves, including: • Being wrong • Looking stupid • Looking too smart	**Thank them** for their contributions, which may include: • Making a connection • Offering an interpretation • Asking for clarification • Asking for more information • Raising a concern • Challenging an assumption • Listening • Working hard • Trying something new • Helping someone	Understanding their own values Noticing values-consistent action in the moment
Seek approval for every decision by asking the teacher questions such as: • "Is this good?" • "Is it OK if . . . ?" • "Should I . . . ?" • "Does it have to be . . . ?" • "Do you mean . . . ?"	Subjecting themselves to judgments from their peers, their teacher, or themselves • Being wrong • Looking stupid • Getting a low grade	**Ask questions** that give the decision back to students, such as: • "How would you know if it's good?" • "What happens if . . . ?" • "Where can you look to find out . . . ?" • "What strategies have you used so far?" • "What are you going to try next?" • "Why does that matter to you?"	Making decisions in terms of their values Finding out for themselves what works

Figure 1.3: Responding to common avoidance moves.

*Visit **go.SolutionTree.com/instruction** for a free reproducible version of this figure.*

We can use communication strategies such as questions, summaries, and expressions of gratitude to help students notice the costs of their avoidance and the benefits of approaching their work instead. These aren't magic tricks; students might continue to avoid in the same old ways or new ones. If nothing else, though, our responses show our students that we are listening to them and care about them, and that when they're ready to commit to their values, we'll be there to support them.

Onward

In this chapter, we explored the relationship between values and willingness. Connecting their assignments and interactions to their values challenges students to think more flexibly about their academic classes, choose more difficult work, bring their emotions into the classroom, and face feelings of inadequacy. To create a context in which students approach these challenges, we can design meaningful learning tasks, deliver lessons in a way that helps students stay fully present, give feedback that shows students we see them, and manage power dynamics in the classroom so that all students can open up about what matters. When students inevitably avoid challenges by doing something else, complaining, staying silent, or seeking approval for every decision, we can respond in ways that help them notice that they have a choice between doing what's easy or fun and doing what's consistent with their values.

Most of the rest of this book consists of protocols that embed values work into every stage of academic learning. But before we get to the protocols, we'll explore the psychological science behind how they work.

Chapter 2

• • • • •

USING THE SCIENCE OF EMPOWERMENT

In the last chapter, you saw how to create a culture of willingness so students accept the challenges inherent in living by their values. In the coming chapters, you'll see how to embed values work into academic classes, so that everyday lessons, assignments, and interactions become contexts for students to discover and do what matters. But what *is* values work?

Before we can define *values work* in the classroom context, we'll need to acknowledge its roots in clinical psychology, and Contextual Behavioral Science (CBS) in particular. Of course a teacher has very different goals from a therapist's, but one goal we can share is to help the people we serve live more fulfilling lives. A wide range of contemporary psychotherapies deemphasize the importance of symptom reduction and focus instead on behavior change. For example, in Dialectical Behavior Therapy (DBT), the overall goal is to help patients "increase…resilience and build a life experienced as worth living" (Linehan, 2014, p. 1). In Compassion-Focused Therapy (CFT), patients with high levels of shame and self-criticism learn to develop inner warmth, safety, and soothing via compassion and self-compassion (Gilbert, 2009). Motivational Interviewing (MI) involves "arranging conversations so that people talk themselves into change, based on their own values and interests" (Miller & Rollnick, 2013, p. 4). In Acceptance and Commitment Therapy (ACT), the aim is "to create a rich, full, and meaningful life while accepting the pain that inevitably goes with it" (Harris, 2009, p. 7). These four approaches all help people *increase* their range of behaviors so they can live more meaningful lives—as opposed to seeking to *decrease* symptoms of psychological distress.

Villatte and associates (2016) describe how people can live more meaningful lives when they develop two capacities: (1) *flexible context sensitivity*, or the ability to notice various external and internal influences on their behavior and selectively attend to the ones that matter, and (2) *functional coherence*, or the ability to choose responses that most effectively serve their values.

For students, having flexible context sensitivity means noticing the internal and external factors that might influence their actions at school—their thoughts, emotions, and physical sensations, the assignment guidelines and available resources, their history with that type of assignment and the overall subject, their relationships with their teacher and classmates, any local or global conditions and events, their personal and cultural histories—and responding to the most relevant factors. Behaving with functional coherence means choosing to do what most effectively builds a life they find meaningful.

Based on CBS, *values work* in school includes any endeavor that helps students notice more features of their context and attend to the ones that matter to them, and choose to do what effectively serves their values. To more fully explain what values work entails, we'll return to the way contextual behavioral scientists define *values*: "freely chosen, verbally constructed consequences of ongoing, dynamic, evolving patterns of activity, which establish predominant reinforcers for that activity that are intrinsic in engagement in the valued behavioral pattern itself" (Wilson & DuFrene, 2009, p. 64). We already broke down this definition in the introduction (pages 3–5) so we could explain what values are. In this chapter, we'll discover, within the definition, four keys to using the science of behavior change to help students live values-guided lives: (1) evoking free choice, (2) using language to empower students, (3) taking advantage of patterns of activity to help students establish their values, and (4) helping students discover meaning and vitality at school.

Evoking Free Choice

If values are *freely chosen* (Wilson & DuFrene, 2009), then every aspect of values work must be the student's choice. You might wonder about the apparent contradiction between leading a protocol—telling students what to do, step by step—and doing values work. Shouldn't we just let students do as they please if values should be freely chosen? When students (and adults) have the freedom to do whatever they want, they sometimes choose what's easiest or most fun in the moment, as opposed to what serves their long-term values (Hayes et al., 1999; Waltz & Follette, 2009). A social or academic status goal might also motivate a student's choice. Given free rein, students sometimes choose whatever they think will maintain their image as cool or smart or funny, or they choose whatever they think provides the clearest path to an *A*.

If we want to empower our students to choose actions guided by their values—as opposed to their momentary preferences or status goals—we can create a context for them to make those choices. When our students fall into habitual behaviors, as if on autopilot, they aren't really choosing. Values work asks them to try new behaviors: to use unfamiliar learning and work strategies, think about academic content and processes in unconventional and sometimes deliberately weird ways, and relate to each other and themselves differently. In the moment, students might feel like they aren't choosing these behaviors, if only because so much of school is mandatory. But after trying a new behavior, students can make a meaningful choice—between the same old behaviors they've always done without necessarily thinking about them, and these other behaviors that might better match their values. Even if they return to their old behaviors, having exposure to something else shows them they have a choice.

Just because it's up to students to notice what matters and choose what workably serves their values, doesn't mean you can't intervene when they struggle. But instead of telling them what to notice ("She's talking to you") or how to respond ("Say something to show her you're listening"), you can ask questions to build their capacities for awareness and values-consistent action. Psychologists William Miller and Stephen Rollnick (2013) explain that people often feel ambivalent when choosing behaviors, as if they have an argument going on inside their head. One side is saying, for example, "I don't really care what my partner thinks," and the other side is saying, "Maybe I want to be the kind of person who listens." According to Miller and Rollnick (2013), taking up one side of this internal argument (such as by saying, "Listen to her!") risks the student taking up the other side ("But I don't care what she's saying!"). Such students might not argue with us; outwardly, they might make it look like they agree with us. Faced with a teacher telling him to listen to his partner, a student might make eye contact, nod, and respond in a way we'd find appropriate. But that's not values work; it's compliance. Instead of the teacher attempting to convince the student to do something and thus evoking resistance or mere compliance (which is just resistance in disguise), values work involves asking questions that help students examine for themselves how well their actions match their values, and based on those values, choose for themselves what they want to do.

Using Language to Empower Students

Since values are *verbally constructed* (Wilson & DuFrene, 2009)—not tangible things but ways of describing actions, like *generously* or *independently*—we can use language to help our students notice the choices available to them during any given class period and make choices that match their values. The language we use includes not only what we say to individual students, but also the questions, prompts, and information we give our classes—what we'd usually call a *lesson* or *assignment*. Even when we communicate with pictures (like in a map or diagram) or gestures (like when we put a finger to our lips to ask for quiet), we are still using symbolic communication, which is language.

According to Relational Frame Theory (Hayes, Barnes-Holmes, & Roche, 2001), a contemporary scientific account of how language works, we make sense of the world by relating the things, ideas, and experiences we encounter to things, ideas, and experiences we've already encountered. As a teacher, you already know this. When you introduce a new concept to students, you relate it to something they've encountered before: The Reconstruction happened *after* the Civil War. The electrons in the outermost shell of an atom are *like* lonely people looking for company. A sonnet is a *type* of poem. Subtraction is the *opposite* of addition.

When we relate things, ideas, and experiences to each other, we change what they mean to us—a process called *transformation of function* (Berens & Hayes, 2007; Hayes at al., 2001; Weinstein, Wilson,

Drake, & Kellum, 2008). Imagine you're a U.S. citizen traveling in Southeast Asia, and you encounter a big, green, spiky, stinky fruit. Knowing nothing but what your five senses tell you, you'd probably avoid this fruit. If your experience with fruits such as apples, oranges, and bananas further tells you that fruits should smell sweet and delicious, then you might think that a stinky fruit is rotten and not good to eat. But then you learn that this fruit is called *durian*, and you remember a friend telling you that durian is sweet and delicious even though it smells bad. You become curious and decide to try it. You haven't changed anything about how the durian looks or smells. You haven't changed your past experience of fruits, or of things that smell stinky. But you have reframed what this big, green, spiky, stinky thing means, using only language (your friend's description of durian as "sweet and delicious"). You've transformed the function of this fruit; you relate to it differently (Roche & Barnes, 1997). You approach it instead of avoiding it. If you like the fruit, you're rewarded by its pleasurable taste. Even if you don't like the fruit, you might still be rewarded by a sense of adventurousness and accomplishment for having tried something new.

The protocols in this book use language to help students transform the functions of their lessons, assignments, projects, and interactions. More specifically, the protocols use three types of relational framing—deictic, analogical, and hierarchical—to expand the functions of academic tasks so that they serve the student's values and thus become a source of meaning and vitality in the student's life. Even if they can't choose or change the tasks themselves, students can choose how they frame the tasks. Choosing to frame their actions in terms of their values—to make their lives meaningful in any context—is the very definition of empowerment.

Deictic and analogical framing help students develop flexible context sensitivity; that is, these two framing types help students notice more features of their academic tasks and attend to the ones that matter to them. Hierarchical framing helps students behave with functional coherence; it helps students choose actions that effectively serve their values.

Deictic Framing: Taking New Perspectives on a Situation

When we use *deictic framing*, we help students take new perspectives on their current situation. By imagining their situation as if they were another person, or as if it were occurring at another point in time or in another place, the student begins to notice values-consistent possibilities for themselves in their class at this moment. Deictic framing empowers students to develop more flexible context sensitivity; by seeing their task in a different way, they notice more of its features and can attend to the ones that matter to them.

But before we explore deictic framing, let's make sure we understand what *deictic* means. Let's say Barry is vacationing in the British Virgin Islands, and he texts a photo to his daughter Sasha, who's at school in Washington, DC. Barry says, "I'm having so much fun! Wish you were here! Now, get back to studying for your math test." Sasha texts back, "I'm so jealous right now. Things are fine here, though." Barry and Sasha each mean something different when they say *I*, *here*, and *now*. The words *I*, *here*, and *now* are all speaker-dependent. That is, they're deictic.

Psychologists sometimes refer to *I-here-now* to denote the perspective of a specific individual in a specific place at a specific moment in time. Everything we do and experience throughout our lifetimes happens to I-here-now. We might remember the past and anticipate the future, but we act *now*. We might imagine what we would be doing if we were in a different place, but we do that imagining *here*. And we might consider how other people experience the things we experience, but we consider them from the perspective of *I*.

Each aspect of I-here-now implies other perspectives. *I* implies a *they*: another person with another point of view. *Here* implies the existence of *there*: other locations where the situation could be different. *Now* implies that there must be a *then*: a past and future (Hayes, Barnes-Holmes, & Roche, 2001; McHugh & Stewart, 2012). When we imagine the perspectives of *they*, *there*, and *then*, we begin noticing more possibilities for I-here-now. Let's see how that works.

Imagine that the seventh-grade science students are using microscopes to view planarian worms. The teacher could ask questions to raise students' awareness of what they might possibly see, think about, and do during the lab.

- **I-here-now:** "What do you notice in your body right now?"
- **I-*there*-now:** "If you were writing a poem for English class, how would you describe what you see under the microscope?"
- **I-here-*then*:** "What did we learn about microscopes the last time we did a lab?"
- ***They*-here-now:** "What would Antonie van Leeuwenhoek, the 17th century Dutch microbiologist credited with advances in microscopy, think if he were watching us do this activity?"
- **I-*there-then*:** "How will learning to make careful observations benefit you in other classes?"
- ***They-there*-now:** "Do you think your peers are having as much fun in their classes as you're having in yours?"
- ***They*-here-*then*:** "How do you hope your partner will describe your contributions to this activity?"
- ***They-there-then*:** "What do you think the eighth graders learned from doing this activity last year that's helping them this year?"

Notice that these questions start with *I-here-now* and then vary one, two, or all three aspects of perspective, for a total of eight different deictic variations. Really, though, the ways we can vary our perspective are limitless, since there are so many different people, points in time, and places from which we can imagine our current situation.

Many of this book's protocols use deictic framing to help students notice features of their current context. For example, in the Values-Activating Questions protocol (page 54), students hear about an upcoming unit and then respond to three questions: (1) "What about this unit interests you, or how will you make it interesting for yourself?" (2) "What about this unit will challenge you, or how will you make it challenging for yourself?" and (3) "Imagine a future version of yourself. Why will this future self be glad you did the work in this unit?"

The first two questions ask students to notice how their upcoming work (I-here-then) connects to interests they've developed and challenges they've faced in the past, in or beyond school (I-there-then). If nothing about the work seems interesting or challenging, they imagine how they can make it interesting and challenging for themselves in the future (I-here-then). The third question asks them to imagine a future self—themselves next year, or in the next phase of school, or as adults who have jobs, partners, or families (I-there-then). Asking a question like, "Why is this unit important?" doesn't invoke that same perspective taking; it keeps them here and now. But looking at the unit as their future self helps them notice how their current work might be important there and then so they can choose to approach it differently here and now.

With the three questions, we transform the upcoming unit's function, so that instead of coming to class and *only* learning material someone else finds important (or avoiding that learning, as the case may be), students can *also* see the unit as an opportunity to do something they find interesting, challenging, or meaningful.

Analogical Framing: Describing a Situation in Terms of Something Else

Teachers can also help students approach their classroom experiences in accordance with their values by using *analogical framing*: developing an analogy or metaphor through which students notice features of their context that they might not have otherwise perceived. While deictic framing helps students notice what's possible in their situation by imagining it from a different perspective, analogical framing helps students see the situation itself as something entirely different—and thus discover new possibilities within it.

Let's take the example of failure metaphors. When describing a failure, we commonly use metaphors of total destruction, such as, "I bombed the test," "My team went down in flames," "My ex-girlfriend broke my heart," and "That paper was a train wreck." But let's imagine other metaphors that frame failure as temporary pauses: "I got stuck in traffic when I was writing that paper" and "The game was like getting caught in a rainstorm." Traffic and storms might be unpleasant, but they eventually pass. We can wait, take care of ourselves, and try again. If you got stuck in traffic while writing that paper, what can you do to find a new route for next time? When you get stuck, who is your GPS? If your team got caught in a rainstorm, what can you do so that the sun comes out next time—or so that you at least have your umbrella? Let's also imagine metaphors that frame failures as opportunities for creativity and growth: "That game was lacking in artistry, but it added new colors to my palette" and "That paper didn't land the way I wanted it to, but it did fly to some interesting places."

By directing our attention to overlooked aspects of our situation, a metaphor or analogy helps us respond to that situation differently (Foody et al., 2014; Stewart, Barnes-Holmes, Hayes, & Lipkens, 2001; Torneke, 2017; Villatte et al., 2016). A loss, breakup, or low grade often comes with feelings of disappointment, if not outright sadness and anger. We might seek to console or distract ourselves, act like we don't care so we maintain our image, or harm ourselves or others when attempting to win the next time. But if we notice our situation's impermanence, we might instead ride it out and use that time to take care of ourselves, reconnect with loved ones, discuss our feelings, and seek help. If we notice how our situation provides opportunities for values-consistent action, we might end up trying something new and growing. Thinking metaphorically "allows the efficient development of entirely new ways of thinking, while providing the guidance or a model drawn from a more known domain" (Stewart et al., 2001, p. 86). That is, when we think of our situation in terms of something familiar, such as getting stuck in traffic or painting a picture, we quickly discover a different, unexpected, yet comprehensible way to see the situation itself.

Depending on which metaphor they use, students will notice different features of the situation and respond to it differently. If, for example, Anton thinks of his history paper as a train wreck, then he'll likely feel embarrassed and anxious, and possibly avoid writing assignments in the future. But if he looks at the paper as a time when he got stuck in traffic, then he'll be more likely to pause, reflect, and seek solutions for next time. If he looks at the paper as a plane that flew to interesting places, he'll likely revisit the topic he wrote about and keep experimenting with voice and structure the next time he writes.

A few protocols in this book rely on analogies or metaphors. For example, Sandbox Mode (page 141) compares a project's generative stage to playing. Early in a project, in their rush to start the work, students sometimes don't come up with enough ideas, and they go with one that ends up not working. By the time they realize it doesn't work, they think they're too deep into their project to start over. If we called this early stage *step one*—comparing it to the first step on a staircase, ladder, or pathway—some students might move quickly past it and go with any idea in order to get to step two and eventually to the end. But when we call this early stage the *sandbox*, we compare it to a playful, low-stakes activity that exists for its own sake. Students might play in the sandbox for a little longer without worrying about what happens next. The sandbox metaphor transforms the function of early generative writing, so that instead of getting a task out of the way, students are playing with their ideas. Protocols that use analogical framing help students notice features of their context that they might not otherwise pay attention to and then act on their values.

Hierarchical Framing: Seeing an Action as Part of a Meaningful Life

So far, we have seen how deictic and analogical framing help students develop flexible context sensitivity, or the ability to notice factors that might influence their actions and respond to factors that matter most. *Hierarchical framing* helps students behave with functional coherence: they choose to do what most effectively builds a life they find meaningful, as opposed to what's easy or fun, or what brings them status. It is called *hierarchical framing* because students learn to see their actions within a hierarchy, where the top of that hierarchy is a life they'd find meaningful, and all of their behaviors serve values, which in turn serve a life of meaning. When we use hierarchical framing, we help students see their actions as contributing to something larger: a meaningful life. They not only understand why they're doing their schoolwork; they see that work as serving their values.

Sometimes in school, we tell students what to do without explaining why. We tell them things like, "Review your Spanish vocabulary for fifteen minutes every night," "When you write a research paper, cite at least three different sources," "Sit down," and "Be quiet."

Often, though, we do explain why our students should do the things we ask them to do, framing these behaviors as causes of particular outcomes, or at least as necessary conditions.

- "*If* you review your Spanish vocabulary for a few minutes each day, *then* you'll learn it better and get a better grade" (perhaps without mentioning grades aloud).

- "When you write a research paper, you must cite at least three different sources *so that* you've accounted for multiple perspectives and come to your own conclusions, which will affect your grade."

- "Sit down *so that* you can focus on the material, which will appear on the test, which will be included in your grade."

- "*If* you're not quiet, *then* your classmates won't be able to focus, and your grade will be lowered."

One problem with making such causal and conditional statements is that they're not necessarily true. For example, many students would focus better if they were to stand instead of sit. Some students would undoubtedly learn their Spanish vocabulary by reviewing it every day, but others learn it just fine from hearing it in class, and even those who would learn it better through daily practice still might not do well on the test if they're anxious, or if they misunderstand the directions.

But even when our causal and conditional statements are true, they don't necessarily empower students to make their schoolwork meaningful. When we frame an action, like studying Spanish vocabulary, as a cause of a specific outcome, the student only feels satisfaction on achieving the outcome, not from doing the action itself (Villatte et al., 2016). If a student knows she has a Spanish quiz coming up, she might study because it's a necessary precondition for getting the grade she wants. She might like her grade, but that doesn't mean she finds the act of studying vocabulary any more satisfying, and she might not study again unless and until another quiz approaches.

However, when we frame an action not as causing a desired outcome but as contributing to a meaningful life, the student can find satisfaction in performing the action itself (Villatte et al., 2016). If a student could somehow see studying Spanish vocabulary, citing multiple sources, sitting down, or maintaining quiet as parts of living in accordance with her values, then she'd derive a sense of meaning and vitality from these actions themselves. In the process, she'd also learn more about her values, which she could then use to help her frame other actions, too.

For example, let's say Kara is a tenth grader who really cares about equity—and hasn't felt so motivated in Spanish class. We can imagine her Spanish teacher's pep talk: "Kara, if you want to practice immigration law one day, you should really study Spanish. Some of your clients will come from Spanish-speaking countries." But studying Spanish might not feel particularly satisfying when Kara's goal remains so far in the future. Also, it might not be true that she'll need Spanish for that work; maybe she wants to work with refugees from Syria and would be better off studying Arabic, or maybe she wants to be a lobbyist and could get by with just English. The teacher could add something about how studying Spanish will help her get a better grade and get into the college of her choice, where she can study immigration, but again, studying doesn't guarantee her the grade or the acceptance.

But if Kara instead frames the difficult and sometimes tedious work of studying Spanish vocabulary as part of building her stamina for facing challenges (which she will need no matter how she ends up working for equity), then she might derive satisfaction just from the act of studying, regardless of the short-term and even long-term academic outcomes. If she's also struggling to stay in her seat and work quietly but frames these behaviors as part of respecting herself and her classmates so that they all have a fair chance to do their best work, then she might feel a sense of purpose when she sits and stays quiet, rather than only doing it to stay out of trouble.

It's not that the outcome doesn't matter. Most students prefer *As* to *Bs*, and even those who prefer lower grades are still seeking status (perhaps as rebels). But if we teach our students to see their actions as parts of a meaningful life—the way notes make up a song—they can choose to make their actions matter, even if they don't get the outcomes they want.

Many of this book's protocols use hierarchical framing to help students see their behaviors as serving their values and thus contributing to a meaningful life. For example, in the Focused Annotation protocol (page 80), students choose a theme that matters to them and look for it when reading a unit text. Their highlighting and margin notes don't have to relate exclusively to this theme, but connecting the text to something they care about helps them read it more purposefully. Teachers ask students to annotate because it helps them read more deeply and critically, but students might do it just to get a good grade or avoid getting in trouble. Instead of framing the task as *causing* a particular outcome (a good grade, a happy teacher), Focused Annotation frames it as *serving* the student's values. Using hierarchical framing, we've transformed the function of reading and highlighting from *only* fulfilling an assignment to *also* exploring sources of meaning in the student's life. When we use hierarchical framing, we not only motivate students to do what we want them to do (like annotate or study Spanish), but also help them understand how they want to approach their learning, their work, and each other.

Table 2.1 (pages 44–45) summarizes which kinds of framings each protocol in this book uses. We invite you to think about the different types of framings as you read, and to develop your own ways to use deictic, analogical, and hierarchical, framing. This way, you can help your students see their assignments and interactions differently and respond to these situations more flexibly, in the service of their values.

Table 2.1: Protocols by Framing Type

	Deictic Taking new perspectives on a situation	**Analogical** Describing a situation in terms of something else	**Hierarchical** Seeing an action as part of a meaningful life
Prepare for Learning			
Values-Activating Questions	•		
Unit Partner Meet	•		
Represent and Respond	•		
Intention Icons	•	•	
Intervision	•		
Explore New Material			
Focused Annotation			•
Discovery Writing		•	
Collaborative Conversations	•		
Track and Acknowledge	•		
Values in the Field			•
Review the Material			
Emotions and Values Audit	•		•
Review Tournament		•	•
So I Will	•		•
Booksploration			•
Naming Awards		•	
Create Work Product			
Prototype Analysis	•		•
Top-Pick Topic	•		•
Sandbox Mode		•	
Exemplar Study			•
Group Commitments	•		•
Refine Work Product			
Rubric Response	•		
Strategy Selection			•
Nonjudgmental Peer Review	•		
Considerate Editing	•		•
Testing for Doneness	•		

Reflect on Learning			
Concentric Self-Portraits	●		●
Sentence Expanding	●		
Support-Push-Inspire	●		●
Upcycling	●	●	●
Values-Based Portfolios			●

Taking Advantage of Patterns of Activity to Help Students Establish Their Values

Values are "consequences of ongoing, dynamic, evolving patterns of activity" (Wilson & DuFrene, 2009, p. 64). That is, values emerge over time, in the course of our daily lives. We don't spontaneously start valuing, say, gratitude, and then immediately start dancing down the street every time we see a sunrise, hear a chirping bird, or taste a new coffee drink (unless we're in a commercial for said coffee drink). We come to value gratitude if, for example, we say a prayer on waking up, pause for ten seconds to listen to the birds, thank the person who made our coffee, or write to the coffee company to express appreciation for how it pays its workers a fair wage. Such small actions probably wouldn't change our lives if we only did them that one day. But if we regularly showed gratitude—as we walk to work and once we get there, and in class with our students and in the faculty room, and at home with our families and while we exercise, this month and next month and the month after that—we would build a pattern of grateful actions.

It's easier to develop a pattern of values-consistent actions—that is, to gain what psychologists call *behavioral momentum* (Nevin & Grace, 2000)—when we can build those actions into our existing behavior patterns. For example, if you want to live more gratefully and you buy coffee every day, you could decide to smile when you thank your barista so she knows you appreciate the coffee, and you could close your eyes when you drink your first sip so you savor the experience. Every day, the act of buying coffee reminds you to behave gratefully, and over time, showing gratitude becomes as much a part of the experience as adding milk and sugar.

If we want to help students build patterns of values-consistent actions, it makes good sense to embed these actions into their existing patterns of activity. Just as a person who already buys coffee every day can embed grateful actions into that routine, our students can embed actions they value into their classroom routines throughout a given unit, and from one unit to the next.

Another way we can help students build patterns of values-consistent actions is to make each task novel enough to excite and challenge our students, yet at least somewhat similar to previous tasks. If students choose activists' memoirs to read in a history class, let's give them other opportunities to choose readings. If, in a mathematics class, they learn about radius and area by calculating the area of green space within a five-mile radius of their homes, let's give them other opportunities to solve real-world problems. If students choose to stay comfortable and avoid what really matters *this time*, a *next time* will come when they can practice their values. The new task's novelty keeps it fresh and engaging, but the familiarity reminds students that they have a new opportunity to continue their pattern of living by their values— or to start that pattern.

The following unit task organizer (figure 2.1) shows six stages of a unit: (1) preparing for learning, (2) exploring new material, (3) reviewing the material, (4) creating work product, (5) refining work product, and (6) reflecting on learning. As you plan a unit, you can use the "Unit Task Organizer" reproducible (page 214) to jot down ideas for tasks, noticing how each stage of the unit is another opportunity for students to explore and enact their values. The six remaining chapters in this book contain protocols that embed values work into these six unit stages. As you read, we hope the unit task organizer and this book's organization will help you use your course's existing academic activities as opportunities for your students to develop their own patterns of values-consistent actions.

Helping Students Discover Meaning and Vitality at School

Values "establish predominant reinforcers . . . that are intrinsic in engagement in the valued behavioral pattern itself" (Wilson & DuFrene, 2009, p. 64). Put more simply, we get a deep sense of satisfaction and vitality from doing something that genuinely matters to us.

Students do not have control over most elements of their context—the various factors that influence how they learn, work, and relate to each other at school. They don't usually have much say in what or how they're taught, how they're assessed, when or how often they're in class, who their classmates and teachers are, or which resources they have access to. Nor do they choose the cultural, political, economic, technological, and environmental factors that shape their school experiences. Neither, for that matter, do we; teachers have little control over many contextual factors that influence students' ability to learn.

But even if students can't choose much of what school *is*, they can always choose what school *means*. Values work is about empowerment—creating a context in which students find meaning and purpose in their lives. Although the protocols include lots of instructions and prompts, students do much of their work in the privacy of a notebook, graphic organizer, or partner discussion. Most protocols do not require students to share their work with the teacher—which means some students might not do the work at all, or they might take the easy or comfortable way out. For example, the Collaborative Conversations protocol (page 90) asks students to listen and respond more actively when talking to a peer about academic material. The protocol does *not* include the teacher grading students on how well they listened to each other, or assigning points to different types of responses. Instead, the students share with each other how they felt about their conversation, and they're invited to share their experiences with the class.

Although you can integrate the values work in this book into lessons and assignments that you grade, you won't grade the students on how aware they are of their context or how well their actions match their values. In values work, students are not accountable to an outside set of standards or rules. They're

Unit:
GRAPHING FUNCTIONS IN THE COORDINATE PLANE

Outcome:
Describe functions verbally and alphabetically in slope-intercept form

Create a research question

Collect and display data

Create tables, scatter plot graphs, best-fit lines, and questions in slope-intercept form

Prepare for learning
Battleship-style game on plotting point

Explore new material
Problem set on graphing data sets

Matching game to associate graphs, tables, and equations

Worksheet on writing formulas for functions and describing those functions verbally

<u>Collaborative Conversations:</u> Why are most graphs correlations, not functions? What would need to be true for the graphs to be functions? How can we use graphs to help us make decisions about our behaviors?

Review the material
<u>Problem sets:</u> Graphing data sets, determining whether tables and graphs show correlations or functions, describing functions

Create work product
<u>Group Commitments</u>

<u>Exemplar Analysis:</u> mini-posters with graphs

<u>Top-Pick Topic:</u> choosing a research question (Like, do hours of sleep relate to quiz scores? Does $ we spend on clothes relate to how we feel about ourselves? Is there a relationship between time spent with friends and how we feel?)

Make tables, scatter plot graphs, best-fit lines, and equations in slope-intercept form

Refine work product
<u>Rubric Response</u>

<u>Nonjudgmental Peer Review</u> of graphs

Groups use the comments and discussion to help them write an easy-to-understand description of their findings. They turn their graphs and descriptions into mini-posters.

Reflect on learning
Support-Push-Inspire

Figure 2.1: Example unit task organizer.

accountable to themselves. They also don't get an external reward like a good grade or an approving comment. The deep sense of satisfaction and vitality that comes from doing meaningful work, building meaningful relationships, and living a meaningful life is its own reward.

Empowering Yourself to Lead Values Work

We've now seen what values work entails: empowering students to notice various internal and external influences on their actions and selectively attend to the ones that matter to them (develop flexible context sensitivity), and choose to respond in ways that most effectively serve their values (behave with functional coherence). How successfully you lead that work will depend on *you* noticing various internal and external influences on *your* actions and selectively attending to the ones that matter *to you*, and choosing to respond in ways that most effectively serve *your* values.

Figures 2.2 and 2.3 offer two self-assessment tools you can use, one for before leading any protocol in this book, and one for after. These will help you develop your own flexible context sensitivity and functional coherence—and thus build a more meaningful experience for your students and yourself.

Directions: Before leading a protocol, respond to the following questions by rating yourself on a scale of 1 to 10.	**Hardly**			**Somewhat**				**Very**		
How **important** is it to you to do this sort of values work with your students?	1	2	3	4	5	6	7	8	9	10
How **willing** are you to try this protocol in your class?	1	2	3	4	5	6	7	8	9	10
How **confident** do you feel that this protocol will go well in your class?	1	2	3	4	5	6	7	8	9	10

If your importance rating is higher than your willingness rating, what's getting in the way? What would make you more willing to try the protocol?

If your importance rating is higher than your confidence rating, what concerns do you have? Who can help you address those concerns?

What would you add, cut, or change to make the protocol work for your students, subject, and time frame?

Figure 2.2: Self-assessment before leading a protocol.

*Visit **go.SolutionTree.com/instruction** for a free reproducible version of this figure.*

Directions: Before leading a protocol, respond to the following questions by rating yourself on a scale of 1 to 10.	Hardly			Somewhat				Very		
How satisfied are you with this protocol's **outcomes**?	1	2	3	4	5	6	7	8	9	10
How satisfied are you with the **process** of doing this protocol?	1	2	3	4	5	6	7	8	9	10
How satisfied are you with **yourself** for making an effort to embed values work into your unit?	1	2	3	4	5	6	7	8	9	10

What did you notice during the protocol? What came up in the room? In you?

After doing the protocol, what questions do you have?

If you try this protocol again, what will you do similarly and differently?

Figure 2.3: Self-assessment after leading a protocol.

Visit **go.SolutionTree.com/instruction** *for a free reproducible version of this figure.*

Onward

In this chapter, we dug more deeply into the science of values-guided behavior change. Values work in school consists of empowering students to notice influences on their actions, selectively attend to the ones that matter to them, and choose to respond in ways that match their values. To promote this work, we reframe how students see their academic tasks. Deictic framing helps students imagine their current situation from other perspectives, so they can respond here and now, according to their values. Analogical framing helps them notice features of their situation that they might not have noticed, so they can respond in the service of their values. Hierarchical framing helps them notice how their actions can be part of a meaningful life pattern, so they can choose to act in the service of their values, rather than only seeking pleasure or escaping pain. Using these framing tools, we can embed values work into academic units to help students develop patterns of values-consistent living. And then we can ask questions that help them assess the impact of choosing (or not choosing) a values-consistent approach to school.

The remaining chapters in this book offer protocols that use deictic, analogical, and hierarchical framing during each stage of a unit to help students notice their choices in class and respond in a way that serves their values.

PART II

Protocols

The protocols in chapters 3–8 follow a unit from beginning to end: preparing for learning, exploring new material, reviewing the material, creating work product, refining work product, and reflecting on learning.

Every protocol is structured the same way: a suggested time, preparation in Getting Ready, instructions in Leading the Protocol, ideas for following up and overcoming challenges in Boosting the Impact, and how to reuse the protocol during future units in Using the Protocol Next Time.

Chapter 3

• • • • •

PROTOCOLS TO PREPARE FOR LEARNING

New units don't necessarily begin with much fanfare. Maybe students get a new book to read, or maybe they turn to a new chapter in their old one. Perhaps students do an activity in which they discover what they already know about a new topic: "Who knows what a watershed is?" Perhaps the teacher just makes an announcement: "Today we start learning about World War I." Handing in a project might show students they've finished learning about some set of ideas and must therefore move on to another. Or the shift from one unit to the next can be imperceptible—students take a test on algebra, and the next day, they go to algebra class and do more algebra.

Outside the classroom, we see rituals to mark beginnings, from baptisms to bat mitzvahs to driving tests to engagement parties to first-day-of-school welcoming assemblies. Our beginning routines raise our awareness, signaling that something new is about to happen and that we therefore have a new opportunity to enact our values.

Studying something new creates a context for students to reflect on what they've learned in the past, what they want to accomplish in the future, and how they want to behave in the present. This chapter's protocols offer ways to help students bring their values to their learning from the very beginning of a unit.

- Values-Activating Questions helps students connect the new unit to their past interests, present challenges, and future goals so that their learning becomes more meaningful for them right here and now.

- In Unit Partner Meet, pairs look together at their past learning experiences so they can begin developing a meaningful learning partnership.

- In Represent and Respond, students appreciate common and diverse learning experiences within the whole class.

- Intention Icons helps students bring valued actions from other contexts into your class.

- Intervision helps students model positive behaviors for their peers while also learning positive behaviors from their peers.

Values-Activating Questions

Students identify how to make a new academic unit interesting, challenging, and meaningful for themselves.

Suggested Time:

When you design units, you define learning goals, map out lessons that will move your students toward those goals, and determine how you'll assess understanding. Unit plans help *you* organize your teaching time, so you are your own audience. In the unit description for this protocol, *students* are the audience. Much like a book-cover blurb or a movie trailer, the unit description gives just enough information to stimulate students' thinking without overwhelming them or spoiling any surprises.

An example unit description for a tenth-grade French unit on daily schedules follows. (In an actual French class, a unit description would most likely be in French!) It tells students what they'll learn (outcomes) and what they'll do to learn (tasks).

> How does where we live influence our daily schedule? During this unit, we'll explore that question. We'll look at websites from high schools in France, Quebec, Senegal, and Haiti to find similarities and differences between their school schedules and ours. We'll also have a video call with a class in Brussels so we can interview each other about life in each place. During this unit, you'll learn vocabulary associated with daily schedules, as well as reflexive verb conjugations. At the end of the unit, you'll choose a country and write a composition that compares and contrasts daily life there with daily life here. You'll present this composition to the class.

During the Values-Activating Questions protocol, students hear or read a description of the upcoming unit. Then, they respond to three questions that help them connect their upcoming work to sources of meaning in their lives: (1) "What about this unit interests you, or how will you make it interesting for yourself?" (2) "What about this unit will challenge you, or how will you make it challenging for yourself?" and (3) "Imagine a future version of yourself. Why will this future self be glad you did the work in this unit?"

Getting Ready

Do the following in preparation for the protocol.

❑ Write a short paragraph describing an upcoming unit. Include outcomes (what students will learn), tasks (what they'll do in order to learn), any important readings or resources they'll use, any work products they'll create, and how they'll be assessed.

Leading the Protocol

The following five steps will help you most effectively lead the protocol.

1. **Have students read a description of the upcoming unit.**

   You can include the description in a slideshow, post it on the wall, or hand out copies of it.

2. **Give the first writing prompt: "What about this unit interests you, or how will you make it interesting for yourself?"**

   This question helps students connect the material they're about to study to their existing areas of interest. If they don't find the subject matter particularly interesting, something about the process of studying it might invoke their curiosity. If nothing seems interesting, then this question gives students an opportunity to take responsibility for making the unit interesting for themselves.

3. **Give the second writing prompt: "What about this unit will challenge you, or how will you make it challenging for yourself?"**

   This question frames challenge as an expected and positive aspect of learning. The prompt also calls on students to contextualize challenges within the specific unit. For example, imagine a tenth grader in the French class that's about to start the daily schedules unit. He usually fears and hates public speaking, but asked to consider what in the unit will challenge him, he writes, "I think it will be hard to stand up in front of my class and read my composition out loud, especially since I have to do it in French!" Even as he expresses his (common and understandable) worries, he describes them as specific to this unit, not as general fears, and not as personal deficits. Meanwhile, students who think the material sounds easy can consider how they'll challenge themselves. Challenge becomes something students can approach and even create.

4. **Give the third writing prompt: "Imagine a future version of yourself. Why will this future self be glad you did the work in this unit?"**

   This question gets students to consider what about this unit has potentially lasting importance. If instead we directly asked them why the unit is important, they might say that everyone learns this, that this will appear on a standardized test, that they'll look stupid if they can't do this, or that they need to know this in order to get into a good college. Such responses define importance according to someone else's terms. Asking students to consider their future selves helps them notice what about the unit will have lasting importance to *them*.

   You can help students visualize a future self by giving them some examples. A tenth-grade teacher could say, "Imagine a future version of yourself—your eleventh-grade self, your twelfth-grade self, your college self, your adult self at work, yourself as a partner, or yourself as a parent."

In visualizing a specific future self, students might notice aspects of the upcoming unit that don't seem particularly interesting or challenging at the moment, but that could matter in that future. They can then choose how they want to engage with that material, even if it doesn't seem fun here and now.

5. **Invite volunteers to share their responses.**

Students might connect with each other or with you in discovering shared interests, challenges, or goals. Also, when students hear their peers share, they might identify aspects of the unit they, too, find meaningful but didn't notice on their own. For example, if Genevieve says that the upcoming Russian Revolution unit will teach her about the misuse of power and might give her new ideas as an antibullying ally, a classmate who hadn't thought about the unit that way might see that he can learn more about the misuse of power, too.

Finally, when students share, you can listen for and affirm any willingness to struggle in the service of their values. Imagine that a twelfth-grade literature class is about to begin a unit on Albert Camus's (1946) *The Stranger*. Harley says she thinks it will really challenge her because she's not sure she'll understand the vocabulary, let alone the themes of colonialism and existentialism. Her teacher says, "This book *is* hard. It's great that you're thinking about that challenge right from the start, because it'll help you slow yourself down and pay attention in a way that you might not usually do when you read." Not only Harley but all the students hear that slowing down and struggling are *positive* behaviors. Even if she and her classmates don't enjoy *The Stranger*, they can choose to approach the challenge of reading it.

Boosting the Impact

Responding to the three questions gives students multiple ways to make the unit meaningful. They might find the unit interesting or challenging right here and now. It might have lasting value over time. Even if students won't always find the work fun, they can always find it meaningful for reasons the students themselves articulate at the outset.

Some students might overstate their enthusiasm because they want to please you. Or they might try to provoke you with responses like, "Nothing about this unit interests me," or "My future self will be glad I did this unit because if I don't do my schoolwork, I won't get into college, and I'll have to rob convenience stores." Such responses alert you to which students are struggling to make the material meaningful for themselves.

Try finding time to meet with these students individually so you can learn more about their interests, backgrounds, homes, and other sources of meaning in their lives. Even if you don't immediately find ways to connect those sources of meaning to your class, one-on-one conversations will show your students that you care about them and that you want to work with them to make your class as meaningful as possible. The conversations will also get you thinking about these students, so you might come up with solutions later on. If you continue to have trouble, you can reach out to the parents or guardians and your colleagues about how you all can support these students in making their classes more meaningful.

Using the Protocol Next Time

If you use this protocol to begin each unit, some students will come to expect the three questions. When that happens, you can ask whether the last unit was as meaningful as it could have been, and have them consider how they can make the upcoming unit even more meaningful—regardless of whether the material appeals to them.

 Unit Partner Meet

Each student gets to know a classmate, who becomes the student's learning partner throughout a unit of study.

Suggested Time:

When students work with partners, they can share their responses to recently learned material, ask each other questions, see each other's ways of doing a task, exchange feedback, and fill in each other's knowledge gaps. If partners stay together throughout a unit, they can develop a working relationship, benefit from each other's thinking and work styles, understand each other as people and as students, and understand themselves as contributors to a partnership.

Unit partnerships are low stakes; pairs learn together without creating graded work together. Also, although one member can avoid participating in a conversation in a group of three or more, there *is* no conversation without input from both people in a pair. Putting students in twos prevents anyone from being left out or ganged up on. In classes with an odd number of students, you'll have to create a group of three, but you can make sure those students are in twos next time.

If students choose their own partners, they get a say in their learning experience, but they often choose based on their preferences instead of their values. For example, students who enjoy hanging out together might have trouble working together. And students sometimes choose partners based on their biases and assumptions, avoiding classmates they perceive as academically or socially weak, or as different from themselves in terms of race, ethnicity, gender, or other identifiers. You can ask students to let you know in private if there's anyone they'd like to work with, and tell them you'll consider but won't be bound by their requests.

Pairing students can show them—and you—that there are many ways to be academically strong. For example, a creative but disorganized student could work with a student who's organized but rigid. Or a student who has loud, emotional reactions could work with a quieter student who asks occasional probing questions. A student who gets lots of his ideas from reading fantasy could work with a student who gets lots of her ideas from her social life.

To make such pairings, you need to know your students. Over time, you can learn a lot from making observations in and out of class, talking to the students and their parents, hearing from your colleagues, and reading the students' work. Early in the year, before you really know your students, you can give out a questionnaire to gauge their interests, strengths, and needs. You can use the domains of life questionnaire in figure 3.1 (adapted from Wilson, Sandoz, Kitchens, & Roberts, 2010) to help you get to know your students well enough to be able to pair them for units.

When the new unit begins, you could simply pair your students and begin whatever introductory lesson you've planned. However, even if they've been together in your class for months and together in school for years, partners might not know each other as learners. The Unit Partner Meet protocol allows partners to get to know each other as learners at the unit's outset, when they're about to learn together.

The following are domains of life that some people find important. You might find some domains very important to you, some less important, and some not important at all.

Directions: In each box, write things you do in this domain of your life. Think of this as an opportunity to share what matters to you. Share only what you feel comfortable sharing.

The first four domains relate to school—at least to some extent.

Social Life	**Academic Life**
What do you do to build and maintain relationships with your friends and peers?	What do you do to study or learn, within or beyond school? Be specific about the kinds of books, materials, or places that help you learn.
Athletic Life	**Artistic Life**
What do you do to develop physical skill? This might involve formal competitive sports, or it might involve informal or noncompetitive activities, like pick-up ball, dance, yoga, or biking.	What do you do to create for the sake of creating? This includes any creative act, such as painting, music, cooking, writing, theater, building, coding, and fashion design.

The last four domains relate to areas of your life outside school. They're here both because they might be important to you and because your school life and your out-of-school life often affect each other. Please be mindful of your own privacy and your family's if you choose to respond to these questions.

Family Life	**Civic Life**
How do you spend time with different family members or your family as a whole? What do you do to take care of your family?	What do you do to participate in a community, such as your neighborhood or a group you belong to?
Spiritual Life	**Physical Life**
How (if at all) do you practice a religion, connect to a higher power (if you believe in one), or discover your larger purpose?	How do you take care of yourself (for example, through fun, relaxation, exercise, or nutrition)?

Source: Adapted from Wilson et al., 2010.

Figure 3.1: Domains of life questionnaire.

*Visit **go.SolutionTree.com/instruction** for a free reproducible version of this figure.*

During the protocol, students discuss significant moments in their lives as learners, which means they'll first need to identify these moments. To help them, you can choose questions about their significant learning moments from figure 3.1 or write your own, but use no more than three. Unit partners will get to know each other throughout the unit as they share ideas, solve problems together, and give each other feedback. This protocol just helps them introduce themselves to each other so they can do that work.

Getting Ready

Do the following in preparation for the protocol.

- ❑ Get three sticky notes or small slips of paper for each student.
- ❑ Create student partnerships based on complementary interests or strengths.
- ❑ Choose three questions to help students identify significant learning moments. You can select from the following unit partner meet questions or you can write your own.

Leading the Protocol

The following five steps will help you most effectively lead the protocol.

1. **Pair students. Give each student three sticky notes.**

   The small papers prevent students from elaborating. At this point, they are only identifying the learning moments.

2. **Ask three questions about significant moments in the students' lives as learners, and have them jot down each response on a different sticky note.**

   - What are some important learning experiences you've had in school?
   - What are some important learning experiences you've had in your out-of-school life?
   - Who have been some of your greatest teachers? What did you learn from them?
   - Which peers have taught you? What did you learn from them?
   - When did you struggle to learn something?
   - When did you have fun while learning?
   - What have you learned at home (or in a place that felt like home)?
   - When have you learned from being out of your element—in a new place, with new people, or in a new role?
   - What were some times when you learned to relate better to others?
   - What were some times when you learned to relate better to yourself?
   - When did you learn from teaching others?
   - When did others learn from teaching you?

3. **Students arrange their three learning moments in roughly chronological order. Then, they share their resulting time lines with their partners.**

   Tell your students that it's OK if they cannot remember exactly when a particular learning moment happened. Making a roughly chronological time line might help students see connections between their learning moments, and sharing the whole time line means each partner has one longer turn to speak rather than three shorter turns. The students also have a longer listening turn, which helps them hear their partner's experience rather than just waiting for their own turn to speak.

   You'll probably want to specify how much time your students get for this step, and let them know when half that time is up.

4. **Post the following questions so partners can collaboratively reflect on the learning moments they've just shared.**

   - What does meaningful learning look like for my partner?

- How does meaningful learning look different for this person than it does for me?
- Even with all the differences between us, how do our meaningful learning experiences reveal similarities?

These questions require analysis—interpreting the partner's responses, finding differences, seeking common ground—which is harder than the storytelling in the previous step. Have your students move their sticky notes so that both partners can see both time lines. That way, they have the responses they're analyzing right in front of them.

5. **Post these questions so volunteers can share with the class anything they learned just now.**

- What did you learn about your partner?
- What did you learn about yourself?
- What kinds of learning moments are you hoping to have with your partner during this unit?

Boosting the Impact

Your students might have trouble talking about their own learning experiences, listening to each other, and noticing their differences and similarities. (Taking notes usually helps.) If students struggle, notice any urges you have to save them from their discomfort by filling the silence yourself. Your discomfort with their discomfort shows that you care about them, and *not* intervening allows them to learn for themselves how to listen to each other. You can ask about their experience afterward, and if they say they were uncomfortable, you can name that discomfort as a sign that they might want to become better listeners—*and* that they can practice their listening skills when they're working with their partners throughout the unit.

As for the pairings, you'll get some wrong. You'll pair a student with his ex-boyfriend or her third-grade bully, or you'll pair two students who have every class together and need a break from each other, or you'll pair two friends who suddenly get into a fight and aren't speaking. You can switch partners in the middle of the unit if things are a complete disaster, but you can't just split up one partnership without creating ripple effects. You'll have to have those two students work alone (thus stigmatizing them and putting them at an academic disadvantage), give the two students new partners (but split up another partnership in order to do so), add the two students into existing partnerships (thus creating two trios and all the associated problems of threes), or switch everybody's partner (and break up good teams).

Instead of breaking up a pair because of conflict between them, you can work with the two students. Imagine that Caroline and Prashant constantly bicker because Caroline wants to get right to work and finish the task, and Prashant makes jokes and works more slowly. The teacher could privately meet with the two students and ask questions that help them explore what they can learn from each other. Can Caroline name something Prashant does better than she does? Can Prashant do the same about Caroline? Can they each name something they want to work on in their partnership? After the unit, can Caroline and Prashant identify why their future selves might be glad they kept working together even when they experienced conflict? Questions like these can help students become better partners to others in the future, even if they still wouldn't want to work with their past partners again.

Using the Protocol Next Time

When students stay with the same partner, they have time to develop a relationship, persist through challenges, and repair any rifts. When students work with different partners, they have a chance to build working relationships with multiple peers and benefit from more peers' perspectives. Maintaining partnerships throughout a unit, but then assigning new partners for each new unit, balances the need for deeper relationships with the need for diverse relationships.

If you use the Unit Partner Meet protocol multiple times, you can vary some but not all of the questions about significant learning moments. Let's say that for the first unit, partners discuss their responses to these questions: "When did you have fun while learning?", "When did you struggle to learn something?", and "What were some times when you learned to relate better to others?" Then, for the second unit, students get new partners and discuss their responses to "When did you have fun while learning?", "When did you struggle to learn something?", and "What were some times when you learned to relate better to yourself?" Changing some questions creates novelty, but reusing other questions allows students to see how they can make new connections from old topics. Or they might respond to the same question in a new way, which creates some flexibility in how they see themselves.

 Represent and Respond

Students create work that shows what they already know about a topic they're going to study. As a class, they notice connections and outliers among their representations, thus building a learning community and appreciating their classmates' diverse perspectives.

Suggested Time:

When students begin a unit, they need opportunities to connect what they'll learn to what they already know—from previous units in your class, other classes at school, home and community experiences, travel, books, or popular culture.

Many units, and even individual lessons, begin with students accessing prior knowledge. For example, many elementary school teachers use KWL charts (Ogle, 1986). When starting a unit on rainforests, students could chart what they already know (K) and what they want to know (W) about rainforests, and throughout the unit, they add what they have learned (L) to the chart. Middle school students might agree or disagree with a series of statements about contemporary immigration when preparing to study its history. High school students might begin a trigonometry unit with a problem set that has them review what they know about right triangles. Such activities help students connect new material to what they already know.

Often when students take stock of their knowledge, they do it only for themselves. For example, if students journal what they already know about plant adaptations, only they will see their work. In the following protocol, students represent what they already know about the topic they're studying *for each other*. Then, they explore the connections and outliers in their responses. This step helps students notice what they have in common, appreciate each other's diverse contributions to their learning, and prepare to do further learning together.

Getting Ready

Do the following in preparation for the protocol.

❑ Choose an aspect of your upcoming unit that your students will have prior knowledge, beliefs, or feelings about.

This could be the unit topic itself (the Louisiana Purchase, rainforest ecology, *Romeo and Juliet*); a related topic (New Orleans, rainforest animals, Shakespeare); or a larger theme (negotiation, interdependence, choice).

❑ Decide what kind of representation they'll make.

They might create mini posters showing images they associate with growing up, cartoon characters of periodic table elements, maps of their state, sketches of tattoos they'd imagine a book character getting, clay sculptures representing democracy, or black marker drawings showing their emotional responses to a current event. Written representations such as stories and outlines work just fine, but artistic representations allow students' classmates to interpret their work in a variety of ways. In any case, keep the prompt and materials simple, because this is meant to give students a low-stakes way to display what they already know, think, or feel.

❑ Obtain any supplies that your students need to make their representations.

Leading the Protocol

The following five steps will help you most effectively lead the protocol.

1. **Students represent their initial knowledge, beliefs, or feelings on a topic they're about to study.**

Keep the time frame short so your students know this is not a big project but rather an entry point to further learning. This is not to say that the knowledge isn't important or doesn't merit more time, and in fact, students will get more time to develop their understandings throughout the unit.

2. **Students silently view each other's work.**

After putting their own finished or in-progress work on their desks, all the students walk around the classroom to view each other's. Rather than students each presenting what they created, the work speaks for itself. No one puts on a show, justifies choices, or even gives an explanation. This first look—just a minute or two for each piece of work, and possibly even less—gives students a chance to see each piece of work on its own terms.

3. **Students notice and note patterns: anything the representations have in common.**

Patterns might be obvious; if students made mini posters of images they associate with growing up, maybe several students drew car keys. But encouraged to look deeper, some students might notice lots of images associated with independence and mobility. Listing these patterns individually in their notebooks requires students to all make their own observations. Working together to list patterns on the board means everyone benefits from the group's collective observations.

4. **Students notice and note outliers: any images or ideas that come up only once.**

Again, outliers might be obvious, such as a funny picture of a mustache to represent growing up. But outliers might be less obvious, such as a picture of a recycling bin to illustrate how growing up means taking more responsibility for the planet.

5. **Ask questions to help students interpret the patterns and learn from the outliers.**

Try some of these questions.

- "What do the patterns tell us about _____?" (Fill in the blank with the topic or theme your class is about to study, like *plant adaptations* or *racial justice*.)
- "What do the patterns tell us about our group?"
- "What's interesting about some of the outliers, and what do these outliers tell us about _____?" (Fill in the blank with the topic or theme your class is about to study.)
- "What do the outliers tell us about the individuals who thought of them, and what could we potentially learn from these classmates?"
- "What's not here? What don't we know or understand about _____?" (Fill in the blank with the topic or theme your class is about to study.)

Students could respond in writing, have discussions in pairs or small groups, or talk as a whole class. Once they've explored their individual and collective understandings of the topic, they're ready to apply these understandings to the new material they'll encounter in the unit.

Boosting the Impact

Now that students have represented their prior experiences with the content, you could simply begin teaching it. However, since the protocol brings up common and diverse experiences within the class, you could take advantage of the opportunity to help students appreciate, connect with, and learn from their peers. Try asking one or more of these questions.

- "Did anyone notice a connection between your representation and a classmate's? How did that feel?"

- "Did anyone notice that your own representation was an outlier? How did that feel?"

- "Why would you want to have classmates who have some of the same experiences or knowledge as you do?"

- "Why would you want to have classmates whose experiences and knowledge differ from yours?"

Asking students to share their understandings of a topic exposes the diversity of background knowledge in the room, giving students with greater knowledge a chance to be experts. Some of these experts will be excited to share what they know, and some surely will not. Imagine a class is about to study immigration, and Victor knows quite a lot because his family recently moved from Canada to the United States, but other students constantly assume that he's from China due to his ethnicity. Or imagine that in a science class about to study plant adaptations, Jala would love to tell stories about plants she's seen on vacations to Hawaii and Costa Rica, but she knows she'll get teased about her family's wealth. Or imagine that when a class is sharing knowledge about right triangles, Zoe pretends she doesn't know the Pythagorean theorem so her classmates won't groan that she knows everything.

The things students know and don't know reveal information about their lives, families, heritage, and socioeconomic status—or just how much time they spend watching internet videos on the subject. Displaying their knowledge can make students feel exposed, vulnerable to judgment, or afraid of being associated with a stereotype. *Stereotype threat* is a phenomenon where people who think they're at risk of being prejudged on the basis of group membership tend to underperform, distance themselves from the stereotyped group they belong to, and disengage from the activity that makes the stereotype more salient (Steele, 2010). To keep students from underperforming in class, and dissociating themselves from their groups or from their work, we need to carefully avoid invoking stereotypes.

Instead, we can make sure students genuinely want to share their knowledge with their classmates by soliciting their authentic consent. Rather than approaching specific students whose representations indicate that they know a lot about the unit topic, invite all students in the class to email you or tell you privately if they're interested in sharing their knowledge more fully. That way, students who feel excited to share still can, students who feel mixed can think about it, and students who don't want to share don't have to refuse a personal request from you. You can also offer lots of choices in how they share—such as in a class or small-group discussion, a video, or a piece of writing or art—while making *not* sharing a legitimate option, too.

If your students seem particularly invested in their representations, then you might give them a way to revisit their personal experiences with that topic in a longer-term project, *after* they have learned more about the topic during the unit. For example, if eleventh graders seem excited to share stories of their personal journeys before reading Homer's *Odyssey*, then perhaps after reading it, they could reimagine a personal journey as a fantasy story and then write about it in free verse. Or if, before a unit on plant adaptations, sixth graders are excited to bring in photos of plants growing near their homes, then at the end of that unit, they might assess how those plants are adapted to their climate. If you already have a different idea for a culminating project, you can keep thinking about ways to incorporate students' backgrounds and passions into future units.

Using the Protocol Next Time

If you use this protocol to begin multiple units, vary the way students represent their understandings each time. For example, in an English class, students could write poems about personal journeys before reading the *Odyssey*, make mini posters of images they associate with growing up before reading *American Street* (Zboi, 2017), and create time lines of books that have impacted them before reading *Fahrenheit 451* (Bradbury, 1953).

Bringing the students' knowledge into the classroom at the beginning of each unit shows them that their own experiences merit academic inquiry and that their new learning will meaningfully expand what they already know. Having them notice connections and outliers among their representations shows them that each classmate is a potential source of worthwhile information—and by extension, so are they. With that awareness comes a choice: how will they treat their classmates, themselves, and their own knowledge? These choices are at the heart of values work.

 Intention Icons

Students identify values they want to bring to their classwork and create icons that will remind them to behave in a values-consistent way.

Suggested Time:

Everything meaningful is a potential source of uncomfortable emotions. When we feel uncomfortable, we often take action to make that feeling go away. We pull out our phones when we're bored, take deep breaths when we're anxious, and vent when we're annoyed. Sometimes our efforts to make uncomfortable feelings go away work well for us. For example, if a student has a headache the day of a group presentation, he might take a pain reliever. Other times, the actions we take to escape discomfort go against our values. If a student panics during his group presentation and runs out of the room, that might make him feel less anxious, but he also violates his values of contributing to his team and approaching new learning experiences with an open mind. The Intention Icons protocol helps students recognize how they respond to uncomfortable emotions they feel in your class. Then, they identify alternative responses that better serve their values.

Getting Ready

Do the following in preparation for the protocol.

❑ Make enough copies of the "Intention Icons" reproducible (page 215) for each student. Figure 3.2 is a filled-out example.

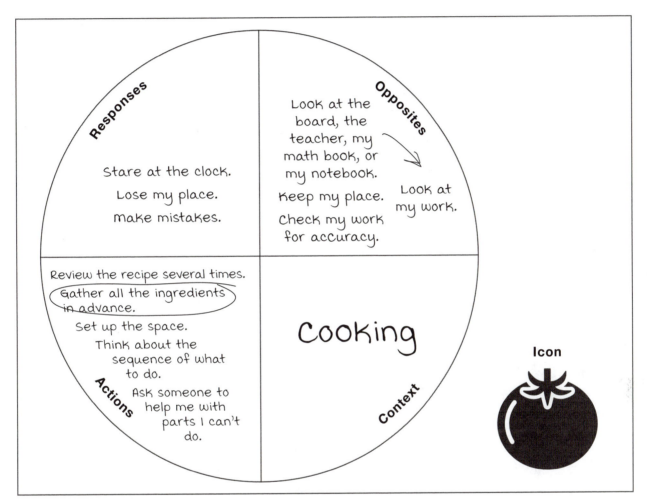

Figure 3.2: Example Intention Icons protocol graphic organizer.

Leading the Protocol

The following nine steps will help you most effectively lead the protocol.

1. **Students brainstorm uncomfortable or unpleasant emotions.**

   Suggest that there are many ways to feel uncomfortable, and ask your students to share some varieties. They might say boredom, frustration, anxiety, embarrassment, exhaustion, physical pain, sadness, annoyance, anger, and so on. Write your students' list on the board, and feel free to add to it yourself.

Your students might make side comments or jokes as they share uncomfortable emotions they've encountered. You can, of course, modify this step as you see fit or just make the list yourself. However, if your students become a bit rambunctious in listing uncomfortable emotions, this probably signifies how often they feel these emotions and how rarely they get to express them to someone with the power to provide relief.

2. **Students identify the specific uncomfortable emotions they expect they might feel during the upcoming unit.**

   Just asking this question might make your students feel uncomfortable! They're not used to teachers acknowledging that learning experiences can be tedious, frustrating, anxiety provoking, and otherwise painful. This is a good moment to tell them that while teachers are always looking to create stimulating and productive learning environments, anything meaningful—including meaningful learning—will involve some of the emotions they've just listed. You can even tell a quick story about a recent learning experience that made you feel an uncomfortable emotion.

   You can also ask your students to notice that any uncomfortable feelings they experience during this upcoming unit might be the same as what they usually feel in your class, or they might experience different feelings. A student who generally feels frustrated in Spanish class because he has trouble remembering the vocabulary might not feel frustrated during a food unit, since he's picked up a lot of Spanish food words from watching cooking shows. However, he might still think the grammar will be hard and he'll feel tired because the class is last period.

3. **Hand out copies of the "Intention Icons" reproducible (page 215), or have students draw their own. In the Responses wedge, students list things they do in your class when they feel the uncomfortable emotions they identified.**

   Imagine that Raul finds mathematics difficult and tedious due to the effort it takes him to write neatly. He might say that when he feels that way, he stares at the clock, loses his place, and makes mistakes. Or imagine Camdyn has trouble keeping track of the many names, dates, and events in history class. She might say that when she feels anxious, she spaces out, doodles, and sometimes sends text messages under her desk.

   In order to help your students be completely honest as they list their behaviors—which will often be against the rules or embarrassing—you'll need to assure them that this writing will remain totally private. You will not require them to share these lists with you or each other at any point.

4. **In the Opposites wedge, students list the opposite of each behavior they just wrote.**

   Raul—who said he stares at the clock, loses his place, and makes mistakes in mathematics—might list the following as opposite behaviors.

   - "Look at the board, the teacher, my math book, or my notebook."

   - "Keep my place."

   - "Check my work for accuracy."

These opposite behaviors should include positive *dos* as opposed to *don'ts* so that students know what to do rather than what to avoid. If students doodle, stare at the clock, or call out, that behavior serves a function, such as attracting attention or providing escape from boredom, so telling themselves *not* to do these things won't help. Also, most students don't consciously choose to behave in these ways, but they can actively choose to try a more positive behavior.

Still, students might have trouble coming up with *dos* that are the opposites of behaviors on their original lists. For example, if Camdyn doodles and texts during history class, she might very reasonably say the opposite behaviors are "Don't doodle" and "Don't text." If students can't think of a positive opposite behavior, ask what they would be doing instead of the unhelpful behavior. Camdyn's teacher could ask, "If you're not doodling, what *are* you doing in your notebook?" At that point, Camdyn might come up with a positive behavior, such as, "Writing only history notes in my notebook."

Since your students might need help thinking of opposite behaviors, you can circulate while your students make these lists and encourage them to ask you or their classmates for help if they're comfortable doing so. You can also have them write behaviors on slips of paper that they turn in anonymously, and then recruit the class's help in coming up with opposite behaviors. After you've given students a few minutes to think of opposite behaviors themselves, offer a few unhelpful student behaviors you typically see, along with their opposites, such as texting friends or communicating with people in the room, interrupting or listening to others, and having side conversations or contributing to the class discussion. In any case, be sure to repeat that the original Responses lists are private and that you'll help only if students request it.

5. **Students think of another class, activity, or situation in their lives where they do at least some of what appears on their opposite lists. They write this in the Context wedge.**

Raul, who loses his place and makes mistakes on mathematics problems, might keep his place and get all the steps correct when he cooks. Camdyn might be all over the place in history but have laser focus when writing a story.

Many students will have to rephrase the behaviors they wrote down, or interpret them more broadly, to make this comparison. Let's say Camdyn has made the following opposite list.

- "Stay focused on the history lesson."
- "Write only history notes in my notebook."
- "Keep my hands on my desk and my phone in my backpack."

There won't be another situation where Camdyn stays focused on a history lesson. She might need help coming up with more general versions of the behaviors she identified. Her teacher could ask, "Is there something else besides a notebook that you keep organized and use only for its dedicated purpose?" If she needs an example, the teacher could ask, "Do you maybe organize your dresser so that each drawer has only a certain type of clothing, or do you have your apps organized on your phone?" Questions like these can help students discover a more general action (in this case, using a particular space for a particular purpose) and a context in which they have success with it.

Some students might have items on their list for which they can't identify any successful areas of life. Maybe Camdyn doodles in all her classes and therefore never has only class notes in her notebooks. If Camdyn struggles to use her notebooks just for class notes, she might struggle to keep her dresser, nightstand, backpack, computer, and phone organized too. If she doesn't have an area of life where she successfully dedicates a space to a purpose, her teacher could have her look at the other items on her list: "What about staying focused? When are you most successful at that?" These questions might lead Camdyn to realize she can focus when she writes, so she puts *Writing* in her Context wedge.

6. **In the Actions wedge, students list things they do in the class, activity, or situation they just wrote in the Context wedge.**

Raul, the mathematics student who feels successful when cooking, makes the following list of his cooking behaviors.

- "Review the recipe several times."
- "Gather all the ingredients in advance."
- "Set up the space."
- "Think about the sequence of what to do."
- "Ask someone to help me with parts I can't do."

Camdyn, who has trouble staying focused in history class, identifies writing as an area of life where she very successfully maintains her focus (even though her writing notebooks are as doodled in as those she uses for class). Her writing behaviors might include working in a quiet place, writing down her ideas whenever she has them so she can come back to them later, working on stories that interest her, making an outline so she knows what she needs to do, and going for a walk when she gets stuck.

7. **Students identify a behavior in the Actions list, or some version of that behavior, that they can try during the upcoming unit. They circle that action.**

Raul could try reviewing mathematical algorithms several times, the same way he reviews recipes. Or, just as he sets up the kitchen before he cooks, he could try arranging all his mathematics materials in a way that will help him stay focused. Or he could write the various terms and formulas he learns throughout a unit on an index card, so that he has these mathematical *ingredients*, so to speak, on hand when the time comes to do a challenging problem. Making his ingredient card would also give him something useful to do when he gets bored in class.

Students might have trouble thinking of how to adapt their actions from the other context to your class. You can circulate and help them think of ideas, and you can also encourage them to ask each other for suggestions. This gives them a good opportunity to share their successful work behaviors and benefit from each other's advice.

8. **In the little Icon box, students create a very simple drawing to represent the action they circled.**

   The drawings might depict what the students will do in your class, or they might depict the context in which the students feel successful and serve as a metaphor for what they'll do in your class. Let's say Raul decides to make an index card with the mathematics terms and formulas he'll need, much like how he gathers his ingredients to help him stay focused and organized while cooking. His favorite thing to cook is chicken cacciatore, so he draws a little tomato to represent gathering ingredients in mathematics class. Camdyn wants to keep her history notebook dedicated to history, so she draws a sheet of paper with the letter *H* on it. Both drawings represent the students' commitments to try something new that will benefit them in their classes.

9. **Students draw their icon in the corner of every notebook page they'll use during the unit, or on other materials they'll use every day, so the icon reminds them to keep trying their chosen behavior.**

   Often we set intentions, but then we forget to do what we said we'd do, or we backslide into old behaviors. You can imagine Camdyn starting to doodle without even realizing it, because doodling has kept her stimulated in the past. Her H-paper icon reminds her that she wants to keep her notes focused on history. When she notices the icon, she resumes taking notes. When Raul opens his notebook and sees his tomato icon, he remembers to take out his mathematics ingredient card so he can use it and add to it during that day's lesson.

   At the beginning of the unit, you can estimate how many page corners on which your students should draw their icons. Every so often, remind them that they might need to draw more. Predrawing ensures that the icons are already there during each lesson, when the students need them as reminders to stay committed to their chosen behaviors.

Boosting the Impact

As a teacher, you'll have a sense of which behaviors will most likely benefit students. You might think, for example, that Camdyn should try doodling *about* history, and that Raul should use graph paper to line up his equations and make fewer mistakes.

If you have students who choose behaviors that will make their situation worse, of course you can intervene. But you might be wrong about whether a strategy will or won't work. Although the idea for Camdyn to doodle about history sounds good, she might get as distracted by doodling about the U.S. Constitution as she does when she doodles swirls and flowers. More importantly, experimenting with new strategies, even if the strategies fail, can help students become more attuned to what works for them and what doesn't. If Raul tries setting up his workspace but then still loses his place and makes mistakes, he might realize on his own that he needs to try something else, or at least become more open to his teacher's idea to use graph paper.

Instead of making suggestions, try asking your students to reflect on how well their chosen strategies benefit them in class. If a strategy isn't working, they might need to try something new (and create a new icon). Or your students might not be using the strategy they chose, in which case they can either recommit to trying it or choose a different strategy they're more likely to use. If you see students really struggling, you can always redirect them. However, every time you tell students what is and isn't working, and what to do instead, you take away an opportunity for them to notice and choose for themselves.

Finally, you can use this protocol to help you notice behavior changes you might need to make. If a lot of students are trying to stay focused, maybe your class needs more variety or challenge. If they're looking to ask more questions or review the material, maybe you need to slow down or give clearer directions. Once you've identified a behavior you want to try, you can make your own intention icon and post it somewhere in your classroom. Just as your students can set intentions to align their actions with their values, so can you.

Using the Protocol Next Time

After using their icons throughout a unit, students can decide whether they want to keep working on that same behavior during the next unit, or whether they'd like to try something new—especially if they expect the next unit to be painful in different ways. It might sound funny to continually discuss the ways your class brings up uncomfortable emotions, but that pain can help your students clarify and commit to their values.

 Intervision

Students make behavioral commitments based on the example they want to set for their peers and the examples their peers set for them.

Suggested Time:

Of the many forms of professional learning—books, articles, conferences, webinars, social media chats—a particularly powerful one is peer observation. Some fields call this *intervision*, to distinguish it from *supervision*. In supervision, someone with more institutional power observes someone with less, with the goal of evaluating how well that person has met performance standards. If we're lucky, our supervisors do more than tell us about areas where we don't measure up; they also point out our strengths, listen to our stories, pass along useful resources, and give us feedback that helps us grow. Still, even the most supportive administrator-teacher relationships have a power imbalance. It's supervision.

Intervision is different. During intervision, peers observe each other so that both can grow. If you've observed a colleague, you probably learned a lot just from being in the room. Maybe your colleague had a great strategy for regaining students' attention, transitioning between activities, explaining a concept, or using wall space. Or perhaps a colleague observed you, and your teaching improved just from having that colleague in the room. Maybe it made you a little more patient. Maybe you circulated more while your students worked instead of grading papers or checking your phone. Maybe you explained that day's content a little more clearly. If you and a colleague watch each other teach, you both learn.

The following protocol assumes that students can benefit as much from intervision as teachers can. Just as we learn instructional and management techniques from watching our colleagues, students can learn study and participation techniques from watching each other. Just as our better teaching selves often emerge when our colleagues are watching, students' better learning selves can emerge when their class-mates are watching. The Intervision protocol works well during the second half of the year, once students have established behavioral patterns in your class and started noticing each other's.

Getting Ready

Do the following in preparation for the protocol.

- ❑ Gather one sheet of paper and two sticky notes per student.
- ❑ Identify colleagues you would learn from observing, and identify what you hope your colleagues would learn from observing you.

To model for your students how they can both learn from and set an example for their classmates, you can share ways you would both learn from and set an example for your colleagues. Before leading the protocol, think of some colleagues you would learn from observing, and some actions you take (or want to take) that your colleagues would learn if they were to observe you. Even if you don't end up sharing specifics with your students, considering these questions for yourself might help you help them—not to mention that it might make you a better teacher!

Leading the Protocol

The following eight steps will help you most effectively lead the protocol.

1. **Lead a brief discussion about what people can learn from observing other people.**

   Ask questions like, "What have you learned from observing your family members? Your friends? People you don't know? People on TV or online?" This shouldn't be a long discussion; get just a few examples of different things students have learned from different people in different contexts.

2. **Give each student a sheet of paper. Have the students fold their papers in half and then open them. On the left side, they identify classmates they could learn from observing, and they write about what academic behaviors they'd learn from observing each of those classmates.**

Expect some awkwardness when you ask students to write what they can learn from observing each other. Some might never have thought about their classmates' work behaviors; they might regard each other as friends, teammates, crushes, minor annoyances, threats, or nemeses, but not models of how to learn. The very idea that other students might behave in ways that merit their attention and emulation could be brand new.

Other students might have noticed each other's learning behaviors but feel weird writing about them. You can encourage the students to acknowledge any discomfort yet continue to write. Discomfort doesn't necessarily mean something bad is happening; it often means something *different* is happening, and writing about their peers' learning behaviors probably differs from what students usually do in class.

You might also share examples of colleagues you would learn from observing and what you'd learn: "I'm also a learner, and one of the best ways I can learn to become a better teacher is by watching really good teachers. I can learn from Mr. Cardinelli how to balance the needs of individual students with the needs of the group. I can learn from observing Dr. Ramos how to incorporate humor and play into my classroom. I can learn from observing Mx. Owens how to keep students focused on respecting the thinking process over finding a right answer."

As the students continue to write, encourage them to look around the room and consider what they might learn from observing each person. "What skills do some of your classmates have that you don't? How are their work habits different from yours? How do they engage in discussions? How do they approach projects? What qualities of action—like creativity, kindness, persistence, or curiosity—could you learn from them?"

3. **Invite volunteers to share what they said they could learn without sharing whom they wrote about.**

Sharing gives students a chance to hear what kinds of behaviors their peers find valuable to learn. You could have everyone share in small groups to establish a sense of privacy and allow more students to contribute, or you could have a few volunteers share with the whole class.

The share-out also gives you a chance to affirm learning behaviors that students and teachers don't usually notice. For example, many students (and teachers) equate class participation with talking a lot. If a student says that she wants to emulate the behavior of a good listener, you could say something like, "Listening isn't always recognized as a type of class participation, but it's a big one. Some of you might think it's important to learn how to listen more deeply, and you have classmates who are really good at it."

4. **On the right side of their papers, students write about academic behaviors they'd hope their peers would learn from observing *them*.**

They can write about things they already do that they think their peers could learn from observing, and things they want to get better at, which their peers would then learn from observing them.

Again, you can share what you'd hope your colleagues would learn from observing you. If it feels challenging or strange to name your teaching strengths and goals in front of your students, you might notice and name that feeling so they see you're willing to do the same kinds of values work you're asking them to do.

If your students need more help figuring out what they want to say, you could write sentence starters on the board, like, *My classmates could learn how to _____ from watching me, My classmates could get better at _____ from observing me, and I want to set an example for how to _____.*

5. **Invite volunteers to share what they wrote.**

This gives you a great opportunity to say back to students what they value—and to amplify the voices of students who aren't perceived by their classmates or even themselves as having academic strengths their peers would benefit from emulating. This sharing allows you to call on these students (assuming they raise their hands) and affirm contributions they find meaningful.

Some students, particularly those with an internalized sense of failure or oppression, might turn this share-out into a joke. For example, a student might say his classmates could learn from him how to attract girls, or how to play video games in class without getting caught. Such statements are probably signs that these students want attention, are stuck in a particular self-image, can't think of academic behaviors that would serve as examples for their peers, or feel vulnerable sharing their academic strengths and goals. In any case, you can respond to such statements with compassionate encouragement: "It sounds like you're still thinking about how our classroom behaviors could serve as examples for our peers. Let's see if we can come up with some more ideas." Privately, you might brainstorm more with these students to help them understand their values and identify strengths they bring to the classroom.

6. **Give each student two sticky notes. On the first one, the students write, I will _____ so my classmates can learn from observing me. They fill in the blank with a specific academic behavior they want to practice.**

Even if it feels awkward, you might share what you wrote (*I will ask lots of questions so my colleagues can learn from observing me*) or what you would have written when you were a student their age (*I will write stories so my classmates can learn from observing me*). Then invite your students to share their examples. It can be a scary yet powerful experience to state a commitment out loud in front of others.

7. **On the second sticky note, students write,** *I will observe _____ so I can learn _____.* **They fill in the first blank with a specific classmate's name and the second blank with a specific academic behavior they want to get better at as a result of observing that classmate.**

   If it's helpful, you can share some examples from your life (*I will observe Dr. Ramos so I can learn how to incorporate humor and play into my classroom*) or of your former classmates (*When I was a student, I would have observed Kofi so I could have learned how to use my creativity when I did Latin assignments*).

   If you share your own statements about people you want to learn from, you might be tempted to invite students to share their statements as a way of appreciating each other, but sharing can create problems. The same few names might come up repeatedly, leading those students to feel awkward and others to feel ignored. A student might consider a peer's behavior to be positive and worth imitating, but the peer might not feel that way about their own behavior. One student's "active participation" could be another student's "talking too much." A well-meaning classmate could appreciate a behavior that other classmates have ridiculed in the past, and the share-out could resurrect that teasing: "Oh yeah, we can *definitely* learn from Zora how to ask questions." In any event, recognition isn't the point. Learning is.

8. **Students put their sticky notes somewhere among the upcoming pages of their notebooks, or within other materials they'll soon use.**

   At some point during the coming unit, they'll rediscover these sticky notes, which will remind them to learn from observing a classmate and to set a positive example for their classmates to observe.

Boosting the Impact

After a week or so, you can ask your students if anyone has tried observing a classmate yet. Without saying that classmate's name, can the students say what they learned? You can also see whether any students have tried setting an example for their classmates to observe and ask how that felt. You can also ask questions to help students explore why they haven't used the sticky notes.

- "Did anyone see a sticky note and ignore what it said? What got in the way?"
- "For those who haven't come across their sticky notes yet, how do you feel about the possibility?"
- "Have any of you observed and learned from a classmate's behavior without needing the sticky note to prompt you? What did you notice?"

Questions like these can help students become more aware of how their classmates might set behavioral examples and how they themselves might set behavioral examples for others.

Using the Protocol Next Time

This protocol works in part because of its novelty. If you repeat it more than once or twice throughout the year, you might change up how students identify peers to observe. For example, if students have unit partners (as described earlier in this chapter on page 57), you might pair them with former partners for intervision. In this case, they would know who is observing them. Each student would then have a unit partner to work with during day-to-day lessons *and* an intervision partner to work with on academic habits. In that case, since the two students were partners before, they might have enough to give each other feedback on their classroom behavior—what's working and what isn't. But even if you don't get to a point where students know who is observing them and talk about their behaviors, just noticing their roles in one another's learning can help them more actively choose how they want to approach your class.

Onward

This chapter's protocols help students prepare for academic learning; students anticipate upcoming content, tasks, and relationships, and connect these to previous experiences. In the course of preparing for learning, students also notice the values they want to bring to their upcoming learning, work, and relationships.

In the next chapter, we'll see how students can continue to discover and develop their values as they explore the new material.

• • • • •

Chapter 4

PROTOCOLS TO EXPLORE NEW MATERIAL

When students learn new material, they might read an article, chapter, poem, story, essay, or other verbal text. But they could also read a painting, photograph, video, film, talk, data set, interactive website, or diagram. We might even regard events, such as music performances and art exhibits, and locations, such as the school library or a local stream, as texts for students to decode, comprehend, and interpret.

Verbal or otherwise, most assigned texts serve one of three purposes.

1. The text contains information about a topic—for example, a diagram of the nitrogen cycle or a time line of the Vietnam War.

2. The text shows students how to do something—for example, a video on how to take a logarithm or a blog post about using a semicolon.

3. The text itself is the subject of study—for example, a literary work, a historical document, a parabola, or a park.

If we predetermine what students are supposed to get out of an assigned text, then they look to extract that knowledge as quickly and easily as they can, or read to the extent necessary for them to sound smart and get the best grade. The protocols in this chapter are more about exploration than extraction; students make observations, ask questions, experiment with ideas, use their imaginations, and listen to each other's perspectives. If after this exploration you find your students didn't pick up on some concept or detail, you can simply point it out.

In *Understanding by Design*, Grant Wiggins and Jay McTighe (2005) distinguish between *coverage*, when "the student is led through unending facts, ideas, and readings with little or no sense of the overarching ideas, issues, and learning goals that might inform study" (p. 28), and what they call *uncoverage* of "the core ideas at the heart of understanding a subject" (p. 58) through inquiry-based learning. During such learning events, we can guide students to uncover something more: their values. This chapter's protocols turn exploring new material into opportunities for students to consider how they want to approach the content they learn, the ideas and imaginings that emerge as they learn, the peers they learn with, and the resources they learn from.

- Focused Annotation helps students connect academic reading to ideas they care about.

- Discovery Writing challenges students to think about material in personal and creative ways, and to persist in the presence of doubt and discomfort.

- Collaborative Conversations helps students listen more deeply to each other and appreciate a partner's ideas and experiences.

- Track and Acknowledge also helps students listen to and appreciate one another, but within the context of a whole-class discussion.

- Values in the Field helps students notice how they want to interact with new settings where they learn.

 Focused Annotation

Students annotate a unit text based on what they value.

Suggested Time:

Teachers often have students think about new material by asking them to annotate—to record their thoughts about a text in the margins as they read. According to researchers Jolene Zywica and Kimberley Gomez (2008), annotation supports deeper learning: "because students are focusing closely on the structure and content of the text, they become more active and engaged readers" (p. 156). The pen in their hand (or, if they're reading digitally, the open panel of markup tools) reminds students that this reading experience will be interactive and participatory. They'll make knowledge and not merely receive it.

When students share their annotations in class, they start deeper conversations about the material. They'll notice different parts or interpret the same parts differently, and they'll have questions they can either answer for each other or grapple with together. Annotations also reveal your students' thinking to you. After students read, you can quickly check their annotations and discover sources of confusion and curiosity to address during the lesson.

When students read and annotate new material, teachers often give them something to focus on. History students reading a website about the former Yugoslavia might annotate causes of Yugoslavia's dissolution, different perspectives on it, or evidence of the author's bias for or against it. Mathematics students reading a textbook chapter about logarithms might annotate steps in the process that they think are confusing, or aspects of problems that remind them of problems they've seen before. Having a focus makes the act of reading more purposeful; students are learning about something specific.

In this protocol, students choose their own focus for their annotations based on their values. They get all the benefits of annotating—reading more deeply, critically, and purposefully—while also using their reading task as an opportunity to explore and express what matters to them. It works best a few days into the unit, once some of the unit's larger themes have come up.

Getting Ready

Do the following in preparation for the protocol.

❑ Make enough copies of the kinds of annotations handout (figure 4.1, or create your own version) for each student.

- **Reactions:** What I feel or think
- **Questions:** What I wonder
- **Inferences:** What I think is happening
- **Predictions:** What I think will happen
- **Summaries:** What I think has happened so far
- **Interpretations:** What I think something means or represents
- **Patterns:** Ideas, phrases, or images that come up multiple times
- **Connections:** How the reading relates to my life, material I've learned in other classes, my communities, historical or current events, natural or built phenomena, or systems of power and privilege
- **Disruptions:** How the reading conflicts with my experience or upends previously held notions

---

Figure 4.1: Kinds of annotations.

*Visit **go.SolutionTree.com/instruction** for a free reproducible version of this figure.*

Leading the Protocol

The following five steps will help you most effectively lead the protocol.

1. **Review different kinds of annotations.**

   First, ask students what kinds of annotations they've used before. They'll have a chance to recall what they've learned, and you'll get a chance to assess their prior knowledge and find out what terms they use. Then, hand out a list of annotation types with student-friendly definitions (figure 4.1, or your own version with terms you use). If your students have already been annotating, you can ask them to look back through their annotations and categorize them. Or have students share interesting annotations they've already made and see if their classmates can categorize what they did. Any of these methods helps students review the concept of annotating, but asking students to share examples of recent annotations also allows them to review the material itself.

2. **As a class, identify what makes a set of annotations exemplary.**

   Perhaps you'd consider a set of annotations exemplary if students use a variety of types; respond to what's important, as opposed to having too many or too few notes; and respond in depth, as opposed to just underlining and occasionally writing a word or two. Whether you consider annotations exemplary will also depend on the reader's purpose and the text itself.

3. **Discuss the difference between free annotating and focused annotating.**

   Free annotating means the students write whatever thoughts and feelings come to mind as they read. *Focused annotating* means the notes relate to a specific topic or concept.

4. **Ask students to list themes that have come up so far during the unit.**

   To encourage all students to participate, have them make lists individually in their notebooks, and then invite them to share themes that you record in a single list on the board. They might identify themes you brought up in previous lessons, those they've learned about in other classes or on their own, but that connect to the material in some way. Listing themes helps students review what matters in the unit as well as what matters to *them* about the unit.

5. **Students choose a theme they find particularly important and, while doing the next reading, they annotate with this theme in mind.**

   Whether that theme comes from your previous lessons or their previous experience, it matters to them. While reading, they'll experience the text selectively, looking for how the material relates to the theme they've identified as important.

   Let's say a science class is studying systems in the human body, and today's reading is about the digestive system. One student's annotations concern how the circulatory system connects to other systems in the body, because the teacher has emphasized interconnectedness and this student thinks it's important. Another student focuses his annotations on the digestive system's role in physical and mental wellness. A third student annotates for evidence of bias in the text. She notices that in the digestive system chapter, the food examples presume a Western middle-class lifestyle, compelling her to look back at the musculoskeletal system chapter to see if its exercise examples are similarly biased. Even if analyzing the book for bias isn't at the top of the teacher's agenda, this student will engage more deeply with the digestive system chapter because she's connecting it to something she genuinely cares about.

Boosting the Impact

After students do the Focused Annotation protocol, ask them to reflect on their experience of the process, using questions like these.

- "How does *focused* annotating compare to *free* annotating?"

- "What changes for you when you're annotating about a theme *you* find important, as opposed to what the teacher deems important?"

- "What did you find hard about focused annotating? Why was the hardest part worthwhile?"

- "What do you want to get better at?"

- "Which kinds of annotation did you use?"

- "Did you find that the thematic focus helped you read more deeply? Or do you think the theme you chose to focus on distracted you from thinking about some of the key points in the text?"

You always have the option of telling students what to focus on next time or reviewing key points you think they might have missed.

While students do that day's classwork, you can walk around the room and assess their annotations. Did the student annotate at all? If not, what got in the way? Students sometimes say they stopped annotating because it slows them down, and you can respond that slowing down is part of the point; at a slower speed, they notice more. What happens when they intentionally slow themselves down? How does it feel? Even if you feel disappointed that they haven't done their work, ask with a tone of curiosity rather than shame.

As for those who did annotate, how deeply are they thinking about the text? Do they use a broad range of annotation types or just one or two? Do some students underline too little, which suggests they miss key points, or too much, which suggests they have trouble identifying what's most important? You're not checking whether the students stay focused on their chosen themes; you're looking for diversity and depth in the annotations themselves.

As you check their annotations, you can briefly coach students on how effectively they annotated and what else they might try. For example, if Ella underlines huge swaths of text, you might suggest that she only underline a sentence or two on each page, just to see what that self-imposed limitation feels like. Or if Luke fills his pages with emotional reactions, you could frame that as a strength—he's really taking in the material and letting it impact him—and then gently suggest that he try asking some questions or connecting the material to events in the news.

You can ask students to share their annotations, and then ask other students to offer their own thoughts about the same passage or to say how their classmates offered them a new perspective. Sharing annotations and responding to each other's helps students notice points they might have missed, practice listening to each other, and understand the values their classmates bring to the work.

Using the Protocol Next Time

After doing Focused Annotation once or twice, you most likely won't need to review annotation types or what makes a set of annotations exemplary; you can skip to having students identify themes in the unit and choose themes to focus on when they read.

Discovery Writing

Students respond to a series of three prompts for which there are no right or best answers. The prompts intentionally promote analysis and creativity, which helps students discover and deepen their thinking about a text.

Suggested Time:

Instead of seeking the *right* or *best* interpretations of a text, we can design prompts that elicit creative thinking about the text and the issues it raises. Professor Alice Lesnick (2009) calls these kinds of prompts *odd-angled*; they approach the text in compelling and sometimes playful ways. Lesnick (2009) explains that while "study questions locate authority within [the] teacher and text," odd-angled questions "distribute authority and enable, indeed depend on, divergent thinking and dissent" (p. 75). Discovery Writing prompts invite students to bring their diverse personal experiences and imaginations to the text. We use the word *prompt* instead of *question*, because while a question compels an answer (often a particular kind of answer, if not a specific right answer), a prompt compels any kind of thinking—knowing, not knowing, wondering, guessing, making stuff up, telling stories, and otherwise engaging with the text. There is never a right answer; the only way to do Discovery Writing wrong is to avoid writing at all.

For this protocol, you'll provide three prompts: (1) one that draws attention to an odd detail and invites personal connection, play, and speculation; (2) one that asks about a structural or stylistic feature of the writing itself; and (3) one that helps students think beyond the text—how it connects to other texts, issues in students' own lives or communities, current or historical events, or concepts from other units or courses.

Consider, for example, the essay "Conformation: The Body No Longer Policed by Gender," where transgender author S. Bear Bergman (2018) writes about his experiences trying to conform to his parents' expectations of girlhood. He offhandedly mentions that during the '80s, girls' clothing always "came with shoulder pads [he] learned to snip carefully out and save (for what, who could say)" (Bergman, 2018). It's an odd detail, almost a throwaway to amuse the reader. Instead of ignoring the detail, we might ask as a first prompt, "What could he have been saving all those snipped-out shoulder pads for?"

A more traditional version of this question might be, "Why do you think the author mentions saving his shoulder pads?" This phrasing suggests students can know the author's unstated motivations, and the task becomes figuring out the best or smartest answer. Asking, "What could he have been saving the shoulder pads for?" invites students to empathize with the author and to imagine for themselves what one might do with a collection of snipped-out shoulder pads. They might get to a deeper theme this way—maybe the shoulder pads symbolized the gender expectations he'd one day reject—or they might not. Either way, students learn to wonder about odd details rather than discount them, to experiment with new perspectives, and to develop their creativity.

For the second prompt—the one that asks about a structural or stylistic feature of the writing itself—we could consider how, at various points in his essay, Bergman (2018) compares himself to animals. We could ask students to pick out specific instances when he does this and explain how these comparisons impact their understanding of his story. Such a prompt draws students' attention to the fact that the text they're reading is a composition—even (and perhaps especially) it's the sort of text they don't think of as having authorship, like a geometry worksheet or a news video. The prompt helps students notice that the text has an author, the author made choices, and these choices impact them as readers. Asking how these instances affect *their* understanding (instead of asking, for example, why the writer made this choice or what the device does in the text) shifts the students' burden from figuring out the author's intention to exploring the work's impact.

For the third prompt—the one that helps the student think beyond the text—we could consider how Bergman's (2018) essay comes from a series called *Unruly Bodies*. We could ask, "What can make bodies unruly at school?" Students might consider impacts of gender and race, abilities and disabilities, the difficulties of controlling oneself in classrooms, changes during puberty, embarrassing odors and noises—there are so many ways to reinterpret the concept of an unruly body.

Table 4.1 has examples of Discovery Writing prompts, based on texts in various disciplines and formats. We don't intend for you to use these prompts or texts. Rather, the table is here so you can get a sense of what these prompts sound like and imagine how to write your own, based on the texts you use in your class.

Table 4.1: Discovery Prompt Examples

	Odd Detail Prompt Invites personal connection, play, and speculation	**Structural or Stylistic Feature Prompt** Draws attention to authorship and readership	**Connection Prompt** Helps students situate the text within a larger conversation of ideas
"Coffee and Cancer: What Starbucks Might Have Argued," *an article about how to consider the statistical risks of drinking coffee (Spiegelhalter, 2018)*	Toward the end of his article, David Spiegelhalter distinguishes between *hazards* and *risks*. Make a list of hazards and a list of risks in your life.	Spiegelhalter links to a variety of studies and articles that further support his claims. If you could only click on one of these links, which one would you choose?	How does mathematics help us make decisions? Can mathematics get in the way of decision making?
"Chapter 11 Review," *a middle school mathematics textbook summary of lessons on displaying and analyzing data (Charles et al., 2010, pp. 572–573)*	Make up a story about the person who displayed data on how many pens or pencils are in a student's backpack.	Each skill review section contains at least one example that relates to school. Pick out two or three of these examples. How do they affect your understanding of mathematics?	What kinds of data would you want to see displayed? How would you want them displayed?
Photograph of Harriet Tubman *(Powelson, n.d.)*	What would change if Tubman had put her signature somewhere else?	Write the dialogue that you imagine occurred between Tubman and Powelson (the photographer) just before this photograph was taken.	How can taking or posing for a photograph be an act of resistance?

continued ⇨

The House on Mango Street, *a novel in vignettes about a young girl's coming of age (Cisneros, 1991)*	If the shoes Esperanza wears in "The Family of Little Feet" are the wrong shoes for her and the shoes she wears in "Chanclas" are the wrong shoes for her, draw the right shoes for her.	Cisneros often incorporates Spanish words and phrases into the text. Pick three or four of these. How do they affect your experience of the story?	What does power look like on Mango Street?
"Types of Water Purifiers" *diagram (Barron's Educational Series, 2005, p. 59)*	According to the diagram, one way to purify wastewater is to pass it through activated sludge. Draw images you associate with the word *activated* and images you associate with *sludge.*	Some parts of the water purification process are *not* shown or explained in this diagram. Find one of these absent parts, and make a list of questions you have about it.	Why not just keep water clean in the first place?
"Avoiding Cross-Contamination" *food safety video (eFoodhandlers, 2014)*	In the section on food storage (1:27–1:46), we learn storage rules to "minimize contamination from accidental drips or other contact." Draw a food storage area that would *maximize* contamination.	The image of a raw chicken and a cook cutting onions in the background appears three times in the video. Why not two times, or four?	Is preventing cross-contamination an act of kindness?

Even though discovery prompts are open-ended and sometimes deliberately weird, and there's never a single right way to approach them, some students will think there *must* be a right way. They'll try to get you to interpret a prompt for them; that way, they won't have to interpret it themselves and risk doing it wrong. They'll ask *do you mean* questions like, "Do you mean make up a story about the shoulder pads?" or *is it OK if* questions like, "Is it OK if I can't think of any ways a body is unruly?" Others will groan, roll their eyes, or stage-whisper, "I'm so confused!" Still others will simply sit there without writing anything.

Unless these behaviors disrupt other students, resist the urge to respond with the answers, attention, or reprieve they seek. Instead, just restate the prompt and remind them that deciding how to approach it is part of their work. You can also try redirecting the student toward the prompt's purpose: "It sounds like you're concerned that you might not know how to respond the right way. There is no right or wrong way."

Even with supports and reassurances, some students will continue to avoid the task itself or the risk taking it requires. But it's possible to have difficult thoughts and feelings without letting them dictate behavior. Students can learn to have the thought "I don't get this," or the feeling of anxiousness, *and* keep writing. Ultimately, they will always be the ones who choose whether to take advantage of opportunities to think more deeply and creatively, or to play it safe.

Getting Ready

Do the following in preparation for the protocol.

- ❑ Choose a text your students will read for your class. (It can be any kind of text, or even an object that they read as if it were a text, such as a microscope or statue.)

- ❑ Write a prompt that draws attention to an odd detail and invites personal connection, play, and speculation.

- ❑ Write a second prompt that asks about a structural or stylistic feature of the writing itself.

- ❑ Write a third prompt that helps students think beyond the text, such as how it connects to other texts, issues in their own lives or communities, current or historical events, or concepts from other units or courses.

- ❑ Make copies of the ways to keep writing when you're stuck handout (figure 4.2) to use if and when students stop writing or avoid making their own decisions about how to proceed.

Ask questions.	"Who . . . ?" "What is (are) . . . ?" "What kind of . . . ?" "When . . . ?" "How many (much) . . . ?"	"Where . . . ?" "How did . . . ?" "Why did . . . ?" "How will . . . ?" "When will . . . ?"	"Why . . . ?" "What if . . . ?" "Would I . . . ?" "Should I . . . ?" "Could I . . . ?"
Make guesses.	"Maybe . . ." "I don't know if this is right, but . . ." "I wonder whether . . ."	"If . . ." "It could be that . . ."	
Argue with yourself.	"But maybe . . ." "On the other hand . . ." "Another way to look at this is . . ."		
Say in another way the same thing you already said.	"Like I said before, . . ." "Another way to put this is . . ."		
Give examples.	"One time when . . ." "This happened when . . ."		
Change the prompt.	"I think the real question is . . ." "What we should be asking is . . ."		

Figure 4.2: Ways to keep writing when you're stuck.

*Visit **go.SolutionTree.com/instruction** for a free reproducible version of this figure.*

Leading the Protocol

The following five steps will help you most effectively lead the protocol.

1. **Explain that your students are about to see a series of writing prompts about a text they've recently read, and that the goal is for them to discover and deepen their thinking.**

   You could say something like, "Today's prompts are intentionally open to interpretation. You might feel pulled to ask what I mean or to express confusion. See if you can hold on to that feeling of uncertainty and respond to the prompts." In school, students are used to planning out what they'll say before they begin writing a draft—for example, by outlining or creating an idea web. These processes teach students to organize their ideas, which is helpful when the ultimate purpose is to communicate clearly and coherently with an audience. But these prompts have a different purpose: discovery. Students don't necessarily know what they think before writing. Creating writing is creating thought.

2. **Give the first prompt (odd detail), and give students time to write a response.**

   Rather than getting all three prompts at once, students see them one at a time and therefore can't avoid a more challenging prompt by moving on to one they find easier. On a test, it's a good strategy to skip hard questions and come back to them at the end, but here, the purpose isn't to demonstrate knowledge and skills; it's to engage in creative struggle.

   While they write, from this prompt and the others, you can encourage students who give up to *un-give up* and say more. They can say the same thing another way, ask questions about what they've already said, have a dialogue with themselves, give another example, or draw and label an illustration of something they said. You could offer suggestions like these to your class, or if necessary, hand out a list of possible writing moves and associated sentence starters, as in figure 4.2 (page 87). If you do use the handout, be sure to tell students that these writing moves are just possible ways for them to say more—not requirements. The only goal is to keep writing so they can see what else they think.

3. **After a few minutes, give the second prompt (stylistic or structural feature). When they're ready, students write a response.**

   You can say, "When you're ready for it, here's the second prompt." Students thus know they can take a few moments, or longer, to come to a satisfying end before moving on.

4. **After a few more minutes, give the third prompt (connection). When they're ready, students write a response.**

   Again, you can remind students that they're allowed and encouraged to finish their thoughts about the second prompt before moving on to the third. You can also give them a bit more time with the third one in case they're still working on the first or second. By this point, they will have been writing for a while and might need continued encouragement or reminders of how else they can proceed.

5. **Let your students know that they'll have one more minute to write.**

Explain that they should find their own stopping point during that minute.

Boosting the Impact

Give students an opportunity to consider their willingness to tolerate confusion, think for themselves, discover new ideas, and struggle. Try asking some of these questions.

- "What did you find hard about this protocol? What did you do at that point?"

- "How do you feel about yourself after doing something hard?"

- "Did you give up at any point? What did it feel like when you gave up? How do you feel about it now?" (You might ask students to consider these questions without sharing responses, since the goal is not to shame them but rather to explore the costs of inaction.)

- "Did anyone *un*-give up? How did *that* feel?"

- "At any point, did you feel like your writing wasn't good enough or smart enough? What did that feeling do for you? What did you do with that feeling?"

- "Was there ever a point when you wondered how much time was left? What did that thought do for you? What did you do with that thought?"

- "Next time we do this, what might you want to try?"

After reflecting on the process, students might simply put away their responses to the prompts, having discovered and deepened their thinking just for themselves. Or they might choose parts to share with a partner or group. You can have them look for points of connection between their responses, in terms of their thoughts, their thought processes, or their underlying assumptions. You can also have them look for points of disconnection—places where they interpreted the question itself differently, had different perspectives, or noticed different things. Or, they might share parts of their responses with the whole class (for example, by using the Track and Acknowledge protocol, page 94, described later in this chapter). By making their thinking visible, students can evaluate the contribution it makes to their own learning, and by sharing that thinking, they can contribute to someone else's learning as well.

We advise against collecting their responses. This work is meant to give students an opportunity for exploration, experimentation, play, and vulnerability. If students know you'll read this work—even if you don't grade it, and even if you have great relationships with your students—they might hold back their genuine thoughts for fear of judgment, or their creativity might shut down. You *could* say something like, "I'd be interested in reading or hearing what you wrote. If any of you would like to share your writing with me, you can leave your notebook on my desk and mark the page where you wrote today." An invitation like this makes space for students to share and feel heard while also leaving them the option to keep their thoughts private.

Using the Protocol Next Time

Discovery Writing works well if used once per unit. Use it too often, and it loses its novelty. But after you use these kinds of prompts enough times, students will believe you when you say the only wrong way to do them is to *not* do them—and avoid the discovering, risk taking, and imagining they're intended to promote. Using Discovery Writing multiple times also shows students that struggling willingly in the service of meaningful thinking is a worthwhile goal that takes practice.

 ## Collaborative Conversations

Students learn how to communicate with a partner in ways that lead to deeper understanding of the material and each other.

Suggested Time:

When students talk to partners, everyone participates in discussion. Unlike in a whole-class or even a small-group discussion, no one can opt out, and everyone has a voice. Many teachers use pair-shares or turn-and-talks, so that after students think or write about their own ideas, they share with each other. Partner conversations give students a chance to deepen their own ideas by talking about them and broaden their perspectives by listening to someone else.

Sometimes, when asked to talk to a partner, a student will simply share a response, wait for the other person to share a response, and be done. This protocol encourages students to listen to each other, continue their conversation, learn from each other, and create ideas together. The discussion structure adapts how professor Jonathan Kanter (2016), at the Center for the Science of Social Connection at the University of Washington, runs partner discussions in his workshops on the psychology of building closer relationships.

Getting Ready

Do the following in preparation for the protocol.

❏ Create a series of three or four discussion questions about the material your students are learning. The questions should require interpretation, speculation, perspective taking, problem solving, storytelling, analogies, or metaphors—something that promotes an interesting, meaningful discussion. Questions about how some aspect of the material connects to the students' lives, other classes and pursuits, community issues, or current events will elicit more active conversations. The sorts of prompts used in Discovery Writing (page 84) stimulate good conversations, too.

Leading the Protocol

The following seven steps will help you most effectively lead the protocol.

1. **Students form pairs and determine who will be partner A and who will be partner B.**

   If you have an odd number of students, either you can create one group of three, or you can participate. A group of three can designate person A, B, and C. You might need to monitor this group so that each person gets a turn to talk while the other two listen and respond.

2. **Pose a question about the material.**

3. **Partner A asks partner B for a response, listens, and responds to B's response.**

   To ask for a response, the student can repeat the question or simply ask, "What do you think?" Although it might seem silly to have students re-ask a question their teacher just asked, their asking means the question is now coming from *them*, not the teacher. If Saskia and Javi turn to each other and Saskia says, "What do you think," Javi doesn't simply answer a teacher's question; he responds to a peer who's just asked for his thoughts. Even if Saskia wouldn't normally care what the student in the next seat thinks of a video about the water cycle, when she practices a behavior associated with curiosity—asking a question—she might discover that she actually is curious!

   After partner B responds, rather than simply firing back a response to the question, partner A has to listen and think about what to say back. Partner A might ask a follow-up question, share a similar experience, express appreciation or empathy—whatever genuine response A has. The goal is for the two students to talk about partner B's ideas before partner A answers the question. Figure 4.3 (page 92) shows steps 3 and 4.

4. **Partner B asks partner A for a response, listens, and responds to A's response.**

   Sometimes, while discussing partner B's response during the previous step, partner A ends up responding to the question. Let's imagine that a science class is studying patterns in the periodic table, and partners get the question, "What is the first time you remember hearing about the elements?" Partner B remembers a song she learned about plants needing oxygen, and partner A says, "That's exactly what I was going to say!" (You can probably imagine the two partners, and maybe the whole class, bursting into song.) If during step 3 partner A ended up sharing a response to the question while discussing partner B's response, partner A can still reiterate that initial response, or A might try to answer the question a different way.

   It's also possible that partner B's response will have shifted partner A's thinking. In that case, partner A might explain the initial thought and how B's response changed that thinking. In that science class, partner A might say, "I was thinking that the first time I heard of an element was when my dad talked about the carbon monoxide alarm in our basement, but actually, I think I heard the oxygen song even before that."

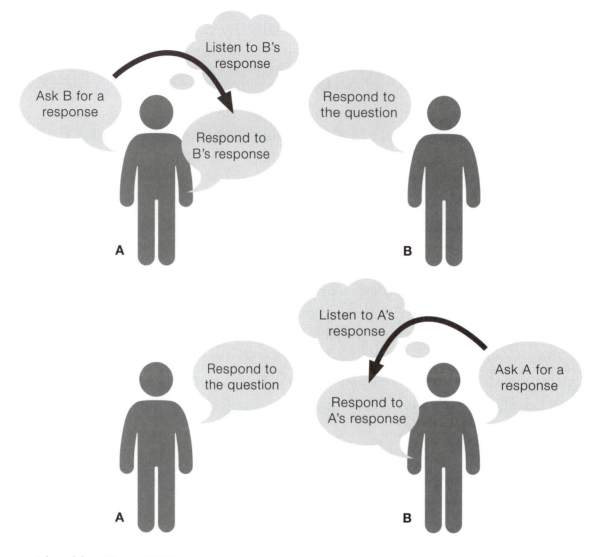

Source: Adapted from Kanter, 2016.

Figure 4.3: Diagram of a collaborative conversation.

5. **The two partners continue a conversation about their ideas.**

   This sometimes takes encouraging if students are used to giving an answer and then being done, or having teachers move discussions along. You can circulate, look for partners who aren't saying much, and ask new questions to get their conversations going again. Even better, ask partners to tell you what they have talked about so far, and then ask them to quickly brainstorm their own questions to continue their conversation. Another option is to let students struggle in their conversations and then debrief those struggles later.

6. **Partners repeat the process with more discussion questions.**

   You could give the questions in immediate succession, or you could intersperse them with didactic teaching so the conversations become a way for students to understand, apply, or otherwise process their learning.

7. **The two partners check in with each other: How did this discussion go? How did it feel to do this work together?**

Asking students to tell each other how their discussion went not only gives them the opportunity to self-assess and get feedback, but also calls their attention to the fact that they've done work *together* and that they might have thoughts and feelings about that togetherness. For a moment, they focus not on themselves, their own learning, or the smartness of their contributions but on their relationship. Something important just happened between them, or had the potential to happen. How they describe what happened (perhaps as deep or smart or interesting) reveals their values. And if they *don't* like how the conversation went or what their partner says about it, then that tells them they might want to approach future conversations differently.

Boosting the Impact

Debriefing the discussion as a whole class can reinforce the academic learning *and* social connecting that just took place. Try asking one or more of these questions.

- "For those of you who responded to the question first, how did that feel?"
- "How did it feel to listen to what your partner said?"
- "What were some of the different ways you responded to your partner's response?"
- "What was the hardest part of listening? Of sharing?"
- "What can you do next time to be a better listener? A better sharer?"
- "What values do you want to bring to your next discussion? For example, what would it mean to respond to a classmate respectfully? Kindly? Attentively? Curiously? Generously? What other values can you bring to a discussion?"
- "Who has some strategies for what to do if your discussion stalls?"
- "What's something you learned from your partner or from having this discussion?"
- "What's a question you and your partner still have?"

Some students might say they went off topic. This may mean they gave up on their discussion and started a new, unrelated one. Other times, going off topic means their genuine response to the question made them think of a different but related topic in their lives. If students say they went off topic, ask them whether that shift in conversation topic was worthwhile to both people involved. Perhaps two students who reminisced about kindergarten haven't learned much chemistry, but they've built a relationship. Maybe that relationship will help them learn chemistry together in the future, and maybe building the relationship is itself worthwhile.

Using the Protocol Next Time

After trying this discussion structure a few times, you might find that your students need help knowing how to respond to each other's responses. Try having your class list different ways to respond to a partner, such as to ask a question, share a related experience, express appreciation for the other person's perspective, or show support if the other person disclosed a difficult or painful experience. You can post this list and refer to it during future discussions. In time, the students might refer to it without your reminders, or stop needing it at all.

If you use this discussion structure frequently, your students will get better at it, but they won't necessarily like it. Those who ordinarily talk a lot might find the artificial limitations frustrating, and those who ordinarily remain silent might feel anxious about having to speak. Although it's always nice when students enjoy a class activity, the point of this structure is not to enjoy it; it's to learn how to have more collaborative conversations and relate to each other more deeply.

Track and Acknowledge

Students learn a large-group discussion structure that helps them listen to one another, express curiosity, build on each other's ideas, and deepen their understanding.

Suggested Time:

Asking students to share their ideas with their class can be a great way to have them honor and learn from each other's thinking, but if you ask for volunteers to share, the same five hands might go up every time. However, if all students put their ideas on paper first, they don't have to compose their thoughts with their peers waiting and watching. When you give students lots of writing time and then ask them to share part of what they wrote, or when you give multiple prompts and then ask students to share only one response, you create the expectation that everyone has something meaningful to contribute while also providing choice in what they contribute.

During whole-class sharing, students sometimes just take turns speaking without listening to each other. Before their turn, they might feel anxious about having to speak and not listen well. After their turn, they might feel satisfied because they've gotten attention and therefore feel less motivated to listen to the rest of the discussion. Or they might simply lack interest in what their classmates have to say. To help students listen to each other, you can have them all write down a little nugget of what each classmate says. The nugget might be a direct quotation or a summary in their own words—whatever they find important to capture.

Finally, with whole-class sharing, the teacher is the one who calls on students and says something about their responses—perhaps appreciating the contribution ("Thank you for that"), correcting a misconception, asking a follow-up question, telling a related story, or pointing out a connection to material the class has previously learned. These moves give the *teacher* good practice in responding but don't give the students that same practice. Meanwhile, the teacher maintains authority in the room, as the one deciding who gets to speak and what, if anything, gets said in response.

Track and Acknowledge shifts that power and responsibility onto the students. After they get a prompt, they all write and share their ideas, listen to each other's responses, write down a nugget of what each classmate says, and choose what to say about one another's responses. The protocol is especially powerful if you, the teacher, participate too. As a fellow participant, you demonstrate your interest in doing the same work your students are doing, as well as your willingness to share your genuine reactions, stories, and questions. You also might have certain ideas you want your students to think about, and if you write and share your own response, you can incorporate those ideas into the discussion without claiming additional authority. You're a learner among learners, contributing your own ideas to the group.

Getting Ready

Do the following in preparation for the protocol.

❑ Create a writing prompt, or a series of writing prompts, that will elicit lots of writing in response to material your students are about to study.

You could have your students write one long response to a single prompt, or give them a series of responses to several prompts (such as the Discovery Writing prompts, page 84). Your prompts could ask them to describe their reactions, questions, inferences, or interpretations of the material; to recall or invent related stories; or to recount their work process, such as how they solved an algebra problem or did a chemistry experiment—what they did, what they noticed, what they now understand as a result, what they might do differently in the future, what they still want to know, how what they learned applies to their lives, or why their new knowledge matters in the world. You could even have your students use other expressive media, such as drawing or sculpting, to respond to material they've learned.

Leading the Protocol

The following six steps will help you most effectively lead the protocol.

1. **Students write at length, responding to new material and each marking off a substantial piece of what they just wrote to read out loud to the class.**

   They could use brackets or a highlighter to make that portion of their work stand out so they can easily come back to it when it's their turn to share.

   Some students might be reluctant to share their most creative thinking, judging that thinking as weird or worrying that their classmates will judge *them* as weird. You can say something like, "In my experience, students hesitate to share what turns out to be their most imaginative and interesting ideas, because they think if an idea is totally different from everyone else's, it must be wrong." Naming the issue might not make a difference right away, but it shows you care about creating a safe environment for sharing thoughts. If over time your class regularly has discussions that validate all kinds of perspectives, your students might become more willing to share them.

2. **Choose a student who will share first.**

   You can either ask for a volunteer to go first and then determine an order, or have a set order for go-arounds so you have no ambiguity. Arranging the chairs in a circle or horseshoe, or putting a number on each desk, allows students to focus on the discussion instead of wondering whose turn it is.

   When students' turn to share the marked-off part of their writing comes, they read it word for word, rather than summarizing, rephrasing, adding to, or qualifying what they wrote. All of them are still working out what they think, and students share these thoughts in progress. Some students might struggle to read their own messy handwriting, or their sentences might not make as much sense as they want them to, or they might feel compelled to explain what they wrote. You'll know who isn't reading word for word because these students will look up and talk rather than look down to read. You don't have to call out this behavior in the moment, but later you can ask the whole class whether anyone felt compelled to revise on the fly, and what thoughts or feelings might be behind that.

3. **While the first person shares, everyone else in the room writes that person's name and some little nugget of what that person says.**

   To ensure that students don't write too much, offer the guideline that whatever they write should fit on one line of their notebook or document. That way, they can listen and decide what to note, rather than scribbling down everything a classmate says without necessarily hearing it. Students do not write anything down during their own turn to share.

4. **As soon as the next person is ready, that person starts to share, and everyone else writes down that person's name and a nugget of what that person says. The process continues until everyone in the room has shared. No one passes.**

   Let's say Dean went first, and Thalía sits next to Dean. If Thalía needs a few extra seconds to write down something Dean said, she takes them, and surely some of her classmates will need those seconds too. As soon as Thalía is ready, she shares. If a few students are still writing what Dean said, it's up to them to make a split-second decision: Will they finish writing what Dean said, or will they listen to Thalía? Outside the classroom, we constantly make decisions about where to focus our attention, so this gives students a small opportunity to practice that skill. Having students share as soon as they're ready allows the class to pace itself and pay attention to the group's needs, rather than waiting for your permission to move on.

   Writing each person's name is a key part of this work. The names remind students that ideas come from someone and that their classmates produce knowledge of value to them. Students also experience each classmate writing down *their* names and contributions. In large schools where students don't all know each other, this gives students an opportunity to relearn each other's names and how to spell and pronounce them. Writing a classmate's name beside that person's thought is a small act of recognition: *I see you. You matter.*

5. **Each student now has a list of everyone else's names and ideas. All students take a moment to read over their notes, reflect on what they heard, and notice what they might want to respond to.**

   You can offer some prompts to help students identify classmates' ideas they want to respond to: "Maybe you have questions about some of your classmates' ideas. Maybe you're noticing connections between responses, or issues that seem important because they keep coming up. Maybe you wouldn't have noticed something if a classmate hadn't mentioned it, or someone had an original way of thinking about the material. Notice anything that stands out for any reason, and just mark it in some way." Even if they don't end up sharing what they notice, just the noticing itself honors their peers' contributions and deepens their own learning.

6. **Choose a student (the *acknowledger*) who will be the first to respond to a classmate's idea. The acknowledger tells the class what thoughts, understandings, observations, questions, or emotions the classmate's response elicited. The classmate whose response was just acknowledged becomes the next acknowledger. This process continues until you stop it.**

   Let's say that in a sixth-grade mathematics class, all the students have just shared how they solved a challenging problem, and now it's time for them to respond to each other. Nico goes first and says something about Wendy's method. It then becomes Wendy's turn to share, and she says something about Vihan's method. Then it's Vihan's turn to respond to a classmate. This continues for as much time as makes sense for the class.

   Some students' ideas might draw multiple responses. For example, if Nico says something about Wendy's response, and Wendy says something about Vihan's, Vihan could say something about Wendy's, and now Wendy has been acknowledged twice. Other ideas might draw no acknowledgments at all, but that doesn't necessarily mean the ideas weren't worth acknowledging. Sometimes classmates won't understand a student's complicated thinking, or the sharing might end before a student who wants to say something about a particular classmate's idea gets a chance. Similarly, some students might get several opportunities to share, and others might get no opportunities. These are all situations to debrief afterward.

   The fact that some students' responses can draw multiple comments and some can draw none is another good reason for you, as the teacher, to participate. When your turn comes, you can say something about the response of a student who hasn't yet had a chance to be the acknowledger. Or you might strategically come back to a response that someone already mentioned in order to amplify the point.

Boosting the Impact

Depending on what happened during the activity, you might ask one or more of the following questions.

- "When it was your turn to share out loud what you wrote, did you actually read what you wrote in your notebook, or did you change or qualify your words? If you read your in-progress thinking word for word, how did that feel? If you didn't read what you wrote word for word, what led you to make that decision?"

- "Did you write down something that each classmate said? Did you ever have to choose between finishing what you were writing and listening to the next person? How did you decide?"

- "If one or more classmates acknowledged your response, how did that acknowledgment feel? If no one acknowledged your response, how did that feel?"

- "Were there responses you wanted to say something about but didn't get a chance to? How did that feel?"

- "Next time we use this discussion format, what do you want to do similarly and differently?"

Any of these discussions brings students awareness to how they want to treat themselves, their ideas, and each other.

The Track and Acknowledge format sometimes creates interesting dynamics, which you can debrief afterward if they occur. Sometimes two or three students will get themselves stuck in a loop. Let's say Dean asks a question about Thalía's idea. Thalía answers Dean's question and then asks a question about Dean's idea, and then it becomes Dean's turn again. Dean responds to Thalía, who responds, and this conversation continues while the rest of the class watches in frustration or amusement. As the teacher, you can always interrupt the exchange by suggesting that other students have ideas worth acknowledging. More importantly, though, you can use this type of behavior as an opportunity to explore what happens when students (or teachers, for that matter) monopolize a discussion. During the debrief, you can ask what that exchange was like for the people involved, what it was like for the people listening, and how the class wants their next discussion to go.

Conversely, you might notice students keeping track of who's participated and intentionally choosing classmates whose responses haven't been acknowledged yet. This is also a behavior worth debriefing later. What motivated students to include more of their classmates? What else can they do to be inclusive, in this or other situations?

At the end of class, you can encourage students who didn't get a chance to share their thoughts to do so as they leave the room. As exciting as it is to get acknowledged in front of the whole class during the discussion, students can find it just as powerful when a classmate takes a moment to come over and say, "I thought you made a really important point" or "I was thinking that exact same thing, but I couldn't put it into words" or "I had no idea how to solve that problem, but your way made total sense."

Using the Protocol Next Time

With practice, students usually get better at all aspects of this activity: writing a response, sharing more of what they wrote, reading it word for word, tracking each other's responses, and saying something meaningful to each other. You might also see certain students always drawing too much or too little attention, not listening unless they're the ones being acknowledged, or making intentionally provocative comments, only acknowledging the same people, or turning an acknowledgment into thinly veiled teasing. You can, of course, stop unhelpful behavior at any point, but you can also use the interesting moments this protocol creates as opportunities for perspective taking and self-reflection.

If, after using this protocol once or twice, you notice that most students share very little, you can specify a minimum amount of writing that they should share. If you notice certain students sharing a lot more than the others, you can quietly give them a maximum. Alternatively, you can decide not to impose any requirements or restrictions on how much they share, and then notice the choice each student makes. You can even take data on how much students share and see if any change occurs over time—for specific individuals or whole classes. If students who are generally quiet or who tend to struggle start to share more, and if students who generally share a lot start to share more judiciously, that provides a good indication that they're learning how to open up and also thinking critically about their contributions.

Values in the Field

Students discover and think critically about how a field trip site's features reflect a set of values. They then identify values they want to bring to their out-of-school learning opportunity.

Suggested Time:

Think of important learning that's relevant to your course yet cannot take place at school. Where can it take place? A field trip might include gathering real-world data, experiencing and analyzing an exhibition or performance, observing and interviewing community members who have knowledge that the academic domain might otherwise undervalue, appreciating a natural or cultural space, or simply creating a new context for students to relate to one another.

Field trips are challenging, not only because we have to address logistics like transportation and budgeting, but because we sometimes find it hard to decide how to structure the trip. Should we provide an activity to ensure students achieve whatever learning outcomes sent us on the field trip in the first place, or will the activity inhibit the students' curiosity? You can imagine how an activity can backfire—on a trip to the National Air and Space Museum, the students barely glance at the actual spacecraft because they're busy copying facts from placards onto worksheets. And you can imagine how the lack of an activity can backfire—at the museum, the students have free rein to see the exhibits, but they use that freedom to browse the gift shop, eat junk food in the café, and hang out with each other.

Informed by the trip's purpose, we can design a more meaningful learning experience. For example, if the purpose is to explore and understand the destination, students can preview the place on websites and make their own guides, for themselves or each other. If the purpose is to research a topic, they can write their genuine questions in advance, and on the trip, they can both look for answers and come up with new questions. Depending on the trip's purpose, students might interview staff members, create art inspired by their destination, perform tests and experiments on site, report their experience live on social media, or sketch redesign proposals for the space. They might serve their destinations instead of being mere consumers.

In addition to designing meaningful field experiences for our students, we can also help them create more meaningful field experiences for themselves. The following protocol helps students notice features of the place, analyze the messages the place sends, and choose how they want to approach the place. You can do the protocol when you first arrive, as a way of orienting your students to the place and to the values they want to bring to it. Alternatively, you can do it midway through the trip, as a way for students to pause and reflect on how the place has shaped their experience so far, and how they can use their own values to shape the rest of their experience.

Getting Ready

Do the following in preparation for the protocol.

- ❑ Get at least one index card per student.

- ❑ In communicating with your students about the field trip, remind them to bring their notebooks and pens. Alternatively, you can supply writing materials at the field trip site.

Leading the Protocol

The following eight steps will help you most effectively lead the protocol.

1. **Students list specific features of the place that catch their attention.**

   They could write these lists in their regular class notebooks or tablets, which they bring along with them to record other observations and data, or you can hand out writing materials just for this protocol.

   Some students will be able to make long lists without much prompting, but others will quickly write down a few things they see and then stop looking. You can help your students continue to look and list by asking questions like these.

   - "What's here? What *else* is here?"

   - "What do you notice about how this space is arranged?"

   - "What materials are used here?"

- "What colors stand out? What shapes?"

- "Where is there light? Darkness?"

- "What do you hear?"

- "Who do you see? What are they doing? What are they wearing or carrying?"

- "What *is not* here that you might expect to see in other spaces like this one?"

- "What *is* here that you hadn't paid much attention to until now?"

Make up your own prompts to help students notice, and notice again, without interpretation or judgment. Giving the prompts about half a minute apart allows students time to think about each one.

2. **Invite a few volunteers to share their lists while the rest of the students keep adding to their own lists.**

   The point is not for everyone to share, but rather for just a few students to read their entire lists so their classmates get a sense of what they, too, might notice. You can make a list too, and share it. As a co-participant, you're not telling your students what they should notice; you're noticing alongside them and inviting them to see what you see.

3. **Students make new lists, this time of their questions about the place or anything in it.**

   They might have questions about things from their first lists or things they heard their classmates share, and they might have questions about new things they notice as they continue to look around. They might have guesses about answers to some of their questions, or they might have no idea. But they shouldn't write down questions they already know the answers to; the point is to express what they genuinely wonder.

4. **Invite a few volunteers to share their lists of questions.**

   The rest of the students keep adding to their own lists.

5. **Students write messages that the place conveys about what it means to be successful there.**

   For example, in an art gallery, what messages do the walls, placards, and lighting send about what *success* means? What do the things people bring to a park tell about a successful experience there? What does the layout of a senior center say about how it defines *success*? Since this question requires analysis, students might need more time and encouragement to write.

6. **Invite a few volunteers to share what they wrote. Then students discuss how they want to approach the place—based on the values it communicates and their own values.**

   This discussion might emerge from the students' written responses. Imagine, for example, that a science class is visiting a local nature preserve to hike around the lake, observe the animals, and do water quality testing. A student notices signs prohibiting fishing, running, and making noise, and she says, "It seems like *success* here means following the rules and not doing anything fun." The teacher could ask questions about why the preserve has these rules in place: "What do the rules protect? What can happen here because these rules are in place? What would you see and do here if these rules didn't exist? What might you see and do here because the rules do exist? Even if that sounds like less fun, what might you find important about the rules?"

More generally, you can ask questions to start a discussion about how the students want to approach the field trip site, based on the space itself and on their own values.

- "What does this space do?"
- "Who is it for? Who isn't it for?"
- "How do social identifiers like race, gender, socioeconomic status, first language, and ability impact our experience of this space?"
- "How does this space empower and subjugate us?"
- "How does this space nurture and diminish things we care about?"
- "How do we want to define what *success* means in this space, according to our own values?"

7. **Give each student one index card. On their cards, the students write statements about the qualities they want to bring to their actions and interactions at the site.**

How will they approach the place itself or those who live or work in it? Or how will they approach each other, themselves, their learning, or their work while in this place? The students begin their statements with the words *I will*.

- "I will listen for frogs."
- "I will be courteous to the museum guards."
- "I will be silent while I watch the play, even if I'm confused."
- "I will stay with my group."
- "I will put my trash in my pocket until we leave the park."
- "I will row as hard as I can, even if I get tired."

Statements that begin with *I will* are personal commitments. They aren't suggestions or predictions, and they don't state what others will do. The statements say what they, the students, will do. You might want to ask volunteers to share their commitments, and if you plan to have your students revisit their commitment statements at the end of the trip or back at school, then you'll probably want to collect the index cards to make sure they don't get lost. But even with no further discussion, the students have now told themselves how they'll bring their values to the site. What they do with that commitment is up to them.

Boosting the Impact

At the end of the trip, or the next time you see your students in class, you can have them look back at their commitment statements and write about their experiences on the trip. For those who kept their commitments, what was that like? How do they feel about themselves as a result of acting in accordance with their values? For those who broke their commitments, what got in the way? The point of asking this isn't to make students feel guilty or embarrassed; it's to help them notice barriers to values-consistent action.

Students can then make new commitments to enact these same values in class. For example, a student who wanted to keep quiet at the lake in order to respect the animals living there might think about how to behave respectfully in science class. A student who asked questions on a trip to an art museum could try asking questions in art class—or any class—that week. Choosing new commitments helps students see how the values they brought to their field trip are also available at school. If they failed to enact their values on the trip, they can re-choose those values now.

Using the Protocol Next Time

If you're lucky enough to go on multiple field trips—or if your colleagues take students on field trips for their subject areas and grade levels—this protocol can provide a familiar structure for students' experiences in new and different settings. Students wouldn't necessarily know what to expect of each new place, but they'd learn to expect this routine. Over time, students would connect each field trip to an overarching set of purposes: noticing their surroundings and choosing for themselves what they want their experiences to mean.

If for any reason you can't do the protocol while on a particular trip, you can take photos at the field trip site (which many teachers do anyway), and then, back at school, your students can analyze the photos: What details do they notice? What questions do they have? What definition of *success* did the place convey, and how did that definition influence them? How did they bring their values to the field trip? How can they enact those same values at school? Questions like these help them notice that their values are always available, wherever they are.

Onward

This chapter's protocols help students explore new academic material as they ask questions, analyze information, evaluate ideas, define problems, imagine solutions, and otherwise investigate new content and practice new skills. In the course of exploring new material, students also clarify the values they want to live by, and choose for themselves how they want to approach their learning.

The next chapter's protocols help students strengthen their understanding of material they've already learned while also strengthening their understanding of their values.

Chapter 5

• • • • •

PROTOCOLS TO REVIEW THE MATERIAL

Review gives students a chance to assemble the details they've learned into a conceptual whole. Only after learning what powers the U.S. Constitution grants the executive, legislative, and judicial branches will history students understand checks and balances in government. Only after studying how different organs function will science students understand how organs work together to form systems. Spanish students might know how to conjugate verbs in the past progressive tense, but at the end of the unit, they'll be able to use those verbs to communicate. Reviewing material doesn't just help students remember all the information they learned; it helps them synthesize, contextualize, and use it.

Often, students demonstrate what they've learned by answering a set of questions, writing an essay, or making a video. Before this demonstration of knowledge and skill (or *unit test*, if you prefer), many teachers devote time to review. Students might color-code their notes based on major concepts, create study guides in which they consolidate and outline what they've learned, or create practice tests so they can anticipate the kinds of questions they'll have to answer and rehearse answering them. In any of these cases, students use some sort of framework to organize the review process. What if review frameworks helped students strengthen and extend their understanding of the material itself *and* how that material matters to them? This chapter's protocols help students synthesize, contextualize, and use recently learned material by connecting it to their values.

- Emotions and Values Audit uses the emotions students felt during the unit to frame review and to build values awareness.

- In Review Tournament, students relate aspects of the content to each other, discovering their values in the process.

- So I Will helps students notice how learning the material has shaped their thinking, and how they want that new thinking to shape their actions.

- Booksploration invites students to extend their learning further, in values-consistent ways.
- Naming Awards helps students remember the content and appreciate their classmates.

Emotions and Values Audit

Students identify moments during the unit when they felt happy, angry, surprised, and other emotions. They learn how those emotions reveal their values.

Suggested Time:

Our emotions give us useful information about the people, places, things, and events we're responding to. If you feel embarrassed after yelling at a student, maybe you value treating students kindly. If you feel scared as you walk into your principal's office for your performance review, maybe you value your work and your autonomy. If you feel depressed when a student you've been helping after school does poorly on his retest, maybe you value your relationship with that student as well as equitable access to the opportunities that academic success provides. Emotions like sadness, fear, embarrassment, frustration, and boredom might feel uncomfortable or even painful, but they're also useful. They give us information. They tell us something important is at stake. Figure 5.1 shows some of the messages our emotions send about our values.

Figure 5.1: How our emotions reveal our values.

Visit go.SolutionTree.com/instruction for a free reproducible version of this figure.

The Emotions and Values Audit protocol has three purposes. First, it structures the review process by attaching course material to emotions that students felt while learning it. Second, it helps students notice that they *have* emotions about what they've learned in class. Third, it teaches students that their emotions are like an *X* marking buried treasure. Dig a little under the surface, and they'll discover something that matters to them.

For the protocol, students receive a blank "Noticing Emotions Chart" (page 216) or your own version with emotion words you write in yourself. When students receive their charts, the first column is labeled *I felt*, the second column is labeled *when*, and the third column is unlabeled. During the protocol, students identify moments throughout the academic unit when they felt each emotion. Only then, they discover that their emotions signal their values, and at that point they write in the heading for the third column: *because I care about*. Finally, they finish their charts by figuring out what was at stake for them when they felt each emotion.

While this protocol's primary purpose is reviewing academic content in terms of students' emotions, you could use it as an opportunity for your class to learn a little bit about emotion itself. You could discuss how emotions have levels of intensity, and how we sometimes give labels to these levels—we call intense anger *rage* and mild anger *annoyance* (Plutchik, 2001). You could also discuss how people can feel a mixture of emotions, and we sometimes label these mixtures. When we feel surprise and joy at the same time, we call that *delight*, or when we feel joy and disgust at the same time, we call that *ambivalence*. Depending on your subject, you could teach your students the physiology and evolution of emotions, or how culture shapes emotion, or how other languages have words for emotions that English doesn't.

Such explorations might feel like detours, but you might discover the detour was worthwhile when your students can describe their feelings more precisely and use those descriptions when discussing the course content. Or you might think learning about emotions is important enough to merit the time simply because your students are capable of having emotions—and of having them in class.

Getting Ready

Do the following in preparation for the protocol.

❑ Make enough copies of the "Noticing Emotions Chart" for each student, or create your own version that better suits your students and subject. Figure 5.2 (page 108) is a filled-out example.

The first column of the noticing emotions chart (figure 5.2) has eight emotions that psychologist Robert Plutchik (2001) identifies as basic, but you might decide to create your own chart with a different set of emotion words. Your chart could have only four or five emotions instead of eight. Your chart could use less intense versions of the emotions: annoyed, curious, content, accepting, nervous, confused, disappointed, and bored. If you teach English, you could create a chart to teach a new vocabulary of emotion words—despondent, contemptuous, serene,

Unit: Chesapeake Bay ecology (science 6)		
I felt . . .	**when . . .**	**because I care about . . .**
angry	I learned how many oysters are left in the Chesapeake Bay	protecting the earth
excited	we collected money to help the bay	people feeling comfortable with how they spend their money
happy	we saw the pictures of the animals that live in the watershed	animals
safe	we read about the scientists restoring submerged aquatic vegetation	protecting the earth
afraid	we went on the canoe trip	staying safe (but it turned out OK)
surprised	I read about forest buffers	stopping pollution
sad	we watched the video about factory farms	animals
disgusted	we learned about pollution from runoff	doing the right thing, and it's not that hard to stop using fertilizer on your lawn

Figure 5.2: Sample noticing emotions chart.

exuberant. If you teach another language, you could make a chart with emotion words in the target language. In any of these cases, you'd fill out the first column with your chosen emotion words. The sample noticing emotions chart in figure 5.2 uses Plutchik's basic emotions and shows how a sixth grader might complete it when reviewing a unit on Chesapeake Bay ecology.

❑ Make enough copies of the how our emotions reveal our values diagram (figure 5.1, page 106) for each student.

You'll notice that the emotion words in this figure match the emotion words on the chart. If you make your own chart with your own emotion words, you could remake this handout, too, but it probably isn't necessary. The point is to help your students see how emotions *in general* reveal what matters.

❑ Decide what, if anything, you'll teach your students about emotion.

Leading the Protocol

The following five steps will help you most effectively lead the protocol.

1. **Review information about emotions.**

   On the board, write the emotion words that your noticing emotions chart (figure 5.2, or your version) includes, and ask your students if they need any of these words defined or pronounced. You can also give a minilesson on emotions at this point, but even if you don't, your students can take this opportunity to expand the vocabulary they use to describe how they feel.

2. **Hand out the "Noticing Emotions" chart reproducible (page 216) or your adapted version. Students search through their notes and resources for times during the unit when they felt each emotion, and they fill out the middle column of their charts accordingly.**

   In some classes, the content might elicit different emotions. Certain moments in a literary work or a historical era might make students feel sadness or disgust or joy. In other classes, the learning process might elicit different emotions; solving problems, looking at graphs, or performing a lab experiment might make students feel nervousness or frustration or satisfaction at various points. If they look back through their notes, handouts, and work, when did they feel each emotion?

   If students say they never felt a particular emotion, you can point out that emotions have degrees. Maybe they didn't feel afraid, but did they ever feel a little worried? Even if the answer is still no, the act of searching through their notes for these moments helps students review the material and better understand their emotions. It also gives you information; if your students felt very little during your last unit, maybe you want to plan a more emotionally engaging unit next time.

   Some students might ask about the third column. Don't reveal its purpose yet. Just tell students to leave it blank for now.

3. **Explain that while some emotions feel unpleasant, all emotions are good because they tell us what we care about. As you explain this, hand out copies of figure 5.1 (page 106) to show students how all emotions can point the way toward what matters to them.**

4. **Students write the words *because I care about* at the top of the third column of their charts. They use what they wrote in the first two columns to identify what they value so they can fill out the third column.**

   When they feel an emotion, *something* important is at stake, but it's still up to them to figure out *what* important thing was at stake for them when they felt each emotion during the unit. Sometimes it won't be obvious. Let's say an eleventh-grade English class has just finished reading *Their Eyes Were Watching God* (Hurston, 1937/2013), and a student says he was sad when the character Janie is forced to shoot her beloved husband after he threatens her in a rabies-induced fit of jealousy. That student might have felt sad because he cares about life or safety or love, or he could have felt sad because he cares about access to health care or equal partnership in marriage—or all of these. If they ask whether they're allowed to write more than one thing they care about, give the question back to them: "What do you think? Is it possible that one emotion can reveal multiple things you care about? Do you actually care about all of those things, or do you think one of them is especially important to you?"

5. **Each student reads aloud one complete sentence from the filled-out chart.**

A complete sentence would sound something like, "I felt excited when I tried using the quadratic formula because I care about getting all the steps right and I made mistakes the first few times," or "I felt surprised when I found out *papas* means 'potatoes' and not 'fathers' because I care about understanding what words mean and not making assumptions," or "I felt angry when Romeo ditched Rosaline for Juliet because I care about women being treated as the human beings they are."

Sharing statements like these can make students feel vulnerable because they're proclaiming what they care about in front of their peers. You can remind them that they get to choose which sentence they read. If you share first, you'll show your students your willingness to be vulnerable too.

Boosting the Impact

Pairs of students can look for any interesting similarities and differences between their emotional responses. The pairs can also talk more about what happened during the unit and use the academic material as a point of connection. Even if a particular moment during the unit made them feel different things, they have the experience of the unit in common, and talking about how it made them feel builds their relationship and shows them how to open up, however tentatively, about what genuinely matters to them.

You can also point out that right this moment, even if they don't feel the emotions listed in the first column, and even if their feelings toward the things in the second column have faded, they probably do still care about the things in the third column. How could the work your students do, right here in your class, connect to some of the things they find important? Even if the content seems unrelated, how could the skills they're learning, or the habits they're cultivating, help them care for the things that matter in their lives? You could make this an ongoing discussion to have as a whole class and with individual students.

Using the Protocol Next Time

After doing Emotions and Values Audit to review a unit, you probably won't need as much direct teaching about the emotions themselves if you use this same protocol to review more units. You can just briefly review the different emotions and then have students go right into filling out their charts. After you do the protocol once, it loses its surprise factor; you can still have students write times when they felt each emotion before writing *because I care about* and filling out the third column, but they'll know it's coming. Still, doing this protocol multiple times gives students practice in noticing how emotions provide information about what matters to them. The stronger the emotion, the more that thing matters. How they decide to behave in the presence of a strong emotion—and to treat the things they care about—is up to them.

Review Tournament

Students receive a tournament bracket with paired concepts from the unit, and they choose winners based on criteria that reflect their values.

Suggested Time:

Our minds constantly make comparisons, judging the things we encounter as better or worse than each other. Which is a better lunch, a kale salad or a pepperoni pizza? Which is a better pet, a dog or a goldfish? Who was a better Hulk, Mark Ruffalo or Lou Ferrigno? We make these sorts of judgments all the time, sometimes just for our own amusement (*Would the Hulk be better in a fight than Luke Skywalker?*) and sometimes with life-altering consequences (*Would it be better to take the administrative job in Annapolis or keep teaching in Baltimore?*).

In all these cases, what we consider *better* depends on our values. We base even seemingly obvious decisions, like whether a spoon or a fork would be better for eating spaghetti, on criteria that reflect our values. Most people would eat spaghetti with a fork because they want to eat their dinner easily so they can enjoy the taste and perhaps the company. But if someone is looking to host an eating contest, then that person might think the spoon would make for a funnier challenge. It all depends on values.

This protocol, Review Tournament, uses the bracket that's so popular among sports enthusiasts and has made its way into competitions of all sorts. In the famous NCAA men's Division I basketball tournament, sixty-four teams play each other, resulting in thirty-two winners advancing to the next round and playing each other, resulting in the Sweet Sixteen who play each other, and so on until one team wins the tournament. The bracket for Review Tournament starts at sixteen.

Different sports leagues have different criteria for pairing teams in tournaments, but some of those criteria include how well the teams played before the tournament, where they're from, and public perception. In Review Tournament, you'll pair academic concepts based on how they relate to each other. In sports, whoever scores the most points wins, but in other kinds of brackets, a judge picks a winner. For example, if you were to put sixteen movies into a bracket, you would have to decide which movie in any given pairing is better—and someone could disagree with you. That's because that someone might have different values and a different perspective than you do. Maybe that person would judge a movie as better if it's funnier, and you'd judge a movie as better if it has more creative direction. Or maybe you'd both judge a movie as better if it's funnier, but you have different ideas of what's funny.

During Review Tournament, students review a set of concepts by judging them against each other—for example, they judge whether N_2O (nitrous oxide) or NH_3 (ammonia) is *better*. They first determine criteria for winning: What could it mean for (in this case) a chemical compound to be *better* than another? Not only do the students review content from the unit, but they also articulate what *better* means, which can tell them something about their values. Then, in groups, they decide together which term wins and advances to the next round. When the students in a group disagree, they have an opportunity to practice taking a stand for the things they care about in a low-stakes context.

Figure 5.3 shows a group's completed bracket in an eighth-grade class reviewing William Shakespeare's (1600/1973a) *A Midsummer Night's Dream*. To advance the characters, this particular group chose different criteria for each of the three rounds: for round one, which character they considered more powerful; for round two, which character they considered kinder; and for round three, which character they considered more loyal.

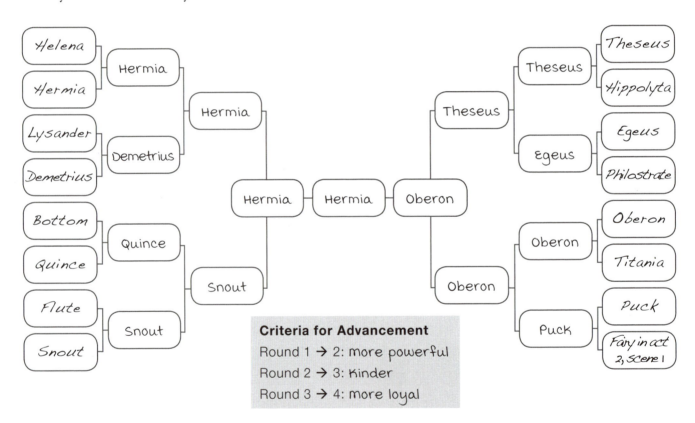

Criteria for Advancement
Round 1 → 2: more powerful
Round 2 → 3: kinder
Round 3 → 4: more loyal

Figure 5.3: Sample Review Tournament bracket—*A Midsummer Night's Dream* (Shakespeare, 1600/1973a).

Getting Ready

Do the following in preparation for the protocol.

❑ Choose sixteen concepts, terms, processes, or works from your unit. These will be the competitors in the bracket.

Sixteen chemical compounds. Sixteen Latin verbs. Sixteen ancient Egyptian inventions. Sixteen polynomial expressions. Sixteen characters from a play. For the sake of simplicity, let's call the sixteen unit-related concepts, terms, processes, or works *competitors*. You could have your students select the sixteen competitors, which gives them an opportunity to go back through their notes and resources, or you could select the competitors yourself.

❑ Make a copy of the "Review Tournament Bracket" reproducible (page 217) for yourself, and arrange the sixteen competitors in it.

In the bracket in figure 5.3, the English teacher grouped the four lovers, the Athenians, the mechanicals, and the fairies to remind the students of relationships in the play. Figure 5.4 has an example bracket for an algebra unit on polynomials, the way it would look when the teacher hands it to students at the beginning of the protocol. This teacher paired the expressions based on their variables, coefficients, exponents, and operations.

As an added challenge to students, you could give them a blank bracket and the sixteen terms, and have groups create brackets themselves and discuss how they decided on their pairings. This gives students yet another way to review by classifying and categorizing what they've learned.

❑ Make copies of your partially filled-out bracket for your students.

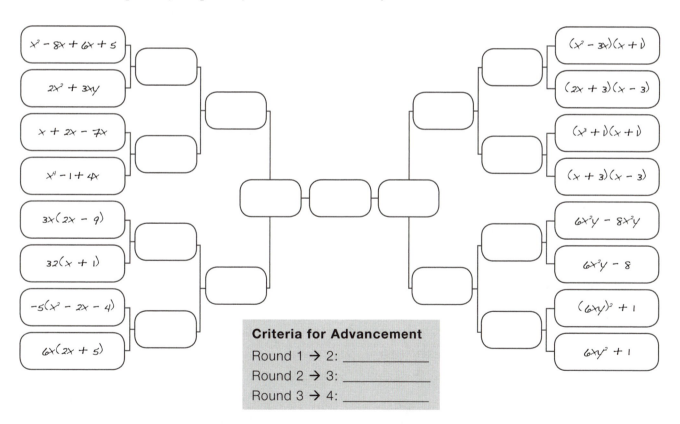

Figure 5.4: Incomplete Review Tournament bracket—polynomials.

Leading the Protocol

The following nine steps will help you most effectively lead the protocol.

1. **Give out copies of the bracket and have students form groups of between three and five.**

   You will have already filled out the bracket with the competitors—sixteen concepts, terms, processes, or works from the unit.

2. **Groups decide on a criterion for advancing competitors to the next round.**

   In comparing ancient Egyptian inventions, *better* could mean which was more essential at the time, which is more commonly used in the 21st century, which would be easiest to make out of duct tape, which would be most helpful in a zombie apocalypse, or which is prettier. Each group decides on its criterion; the group members might come up with some interesting stuff, which in turn tells them about their values. If *better* means more commonly used in the 21st century, maybe they care about practicality or endurance over time. If *better* means most helpful in a zombie apocalypse, maybe having a sense of humor matters to them (or maybe they just want to outlast those zombies).

   Sometimes students will choose criteria that seem obvious or easy. For example, students might decide to advance whichever Latin verb has more letters (so *credere* beats *videre*). Because the students need to come up with different criteria for each round, you can encourage groups that use an easy or obvious criterion to think of a more challenging or creative criterion for the next round.

3. **Groups decide together on one competitor from each pair that will move forward to the next round.**

   Students need to find a way to decide together on a winner. They might try to convince each other and come to a consensus, vote, or give a different group member final say for each round. There isn't a right or wrong way for groups to make decisions, and different groups within the class might develop different decision-making processes. You can debrief these processes later.

4. **For the second round, students decide on a different criterion for advancing four of the remaining competitors to the next round.**

   For example, if a group advanced *A Midsummer Night's Dream* characters in the first round based on how powerful they are, they could advance characters in the second round based on how kind they are. Or if algebra students advanced polynomial expressions in the first round based on how challenging the students found them to simplify, they could advance expressions in the second round based on how many terms they have.

5. **Groups decide together on one competitor from each pair that will move forward to the next round.**

   Again, students need to find a way to decide together on a winner.

6. **For the third round, students decide on yet another different criterion.**

   Two of the remaining competitors advance to the final round.

7. **Groups decide together on one competitor from each pair that will move forward to the final round.**

   Now it's the final round, with only two competitors remaining.

8. **Students use *all three criteria* from the previous rounds to determine a winner.**

   This step gets students to weigh different important criteria against each other. Let's imagine that the group of eighth-grade English students advanced characters from *A Midsummer Night's Dream* based first on how much power they have, then on how kindly they behave, and then on how loyal they are. The group ends up with Oberon, who is very powerful but not particularly kind or loyal, and Hermia, who is much less powerful but somewhat kinder and much more loyal. As the students decide which of these two characters should win, they have to weigh the relative importance of power, kindness, and loyalty. In choosing a winner for their tournament, they're discussing their values.

9. **Each group shares its three criteria, its winner, and why that competitor won.**

   In hearing their peers' choices, students become aware of other values they themselves might have brought to this work. If students nod or say things like, "*Oh*, that's what we should've done," it's a good sign that they've just discovered something that matters to them.

Boosting the Impact

Review Tournament has a lot of steps and tends to elicit interesting thoughts and interactions. To debrief those, try asking a few of the following questions.

- "Did any results surprise you?"

- "What was your group's process for choosing criteria? Was it the same as or different from your process for choosing winners?"

- "What did you say or do to convince your group, or what did your group members say or do to convince you?"

- "Did your group argue at any point? What was the argument about? How did you resolve it?"

- "Were there any terms in the original bracket that you didn't understand? What did you do at that point?"

- "How did your group's discussions help you understand the content better? How could your discussions have resulted in more learning?"

- "During this activity, what's something you learned from a group member?"

- "What did you learn about a group member?"

- "What did you learn about yourself?"

Some classrooms get very loud during this protocol, which might be a sign that students feel invested and are passionately arguing their points. Sometimes, though, a few students pick favorites and defend them no matter what the criteria are, or they use the activity as an excuse to stoke rivalries among themselves. Such behaviors can provide an opportunity for private conversations about whether these students' behaviors match their values: Is this who they want to be? On the other hand, these behaviors might get in the way of their classmates' learning. If that's a concern, you can have students fill out their brackets individually. Doing this protocol individually means the students lose the opportunity to discuss their values in groups and negotiate a decision-making process, but they can still bring their values to the academic content, select decision-making criteria for themselves, and share those criteria with their classmates.

Using the Protocol Next Time

You can use Review Tournament anytime your students are reviewing content, provided that you can come up with sixteen different chunks of content to use. Since the unit content will be different each time, and since the students will come up with new judging criteria each time, the activity retains some novelty. After doing this protocol once, students will understand how it works and be able to spend more time having discussions. They'll also get better at choosing criteria and advocating for winners. Used for every unit, Review Tournament becomes a playful way for students to reinforce what they've learned and revisit their values.

So I Will

Students recall thoughts they had about a topic before studying it, notice what they learned and what they currently think about the topic, and choose actions they'll take as a result.

Suggested Time:

Sometimes, when students learn new material, they ask, "Why do I have to know this?" or "What will I ever use this for?" Unless they're learning a practical life skill, like how to do their taxes or cook a healthy meal, they might not see an obvious connection between school-based learning and real life. A student who plans to go into banking might see the value in learning algebra but maybe not geometry, let alone the meaning of the Queen Mab speech in Shakespeare's (1597/1973b) *Romeo and Juliet*. A student might very reasonably complain, "I'm not going to be a physicist, so why do I need to learn how to calculate angular momentum?" or "Who cares if it's *me and Alvy* or *Alvy and I*?"

When we hear such comments, we might be tempted to recite platitudes like, "Math is everywhere" or "Those who don't learn history are doomed to repeat it," or tell students that others will judge them for lacking such knowledge as the difference between subjective and objective pronouns. In our weakest moments, we might throw up our hands and say, "Even if you don't think this matters, we have to plow through it because it's on the state test."

Instead of convincing our students that the material they've learned will be important one day, we can invite them to choose for themselves what they do with their learning. This protocol, So I Will, helps students observe how recent learning has shifted their thinking and how that new thinking might in turn shift their behavior—not in the future, but right here and now.

Getting Ready

Do the following in preparation for the protocol.

❑ Make enough copies of the thoughts and actions cards (figure 5.5, page 118) for each student. Cut the cards and the strip apart.

❑ Consider how your students will respond to the prompts on the cards and the strip—for example, through writing, discussion, or art. Obtain supplies if necessary.

While the cards have space for students to record their responses, students could first write at greater length in their notebooks; have discussions with a partner; or make drawings, diagrams, living sculptures (*tableau vivant*), LEGO builds, or some other artistic response. Just writing on their cards takes the least time but also allows for the least creativity.

❑ Decide whether your students will discuss the overall unit topic, or they'll brainstorm subtopics and then each choose one subtopic to discuss.

Imagine that a history class is learning about the civil rights movement. During the protocol, when they receive the cards from figure 5.5, the students could simply fill in the blanks on each card with the phrase *the civil rights movement*. Alternatively, students could brainstorm subtopics they learned about during the unit. The brainstorm serves as an additional opportunity for review, and then each student can choose one subtopic that feels particularly interesting and important. In the history class, instead of writing *the civil rights movement* on each card, students might write *Rosa Parks* or *Bayard Rustin* or *protest marches* or *school segregation*. If you do the protocol this way, make sure your students understand that they should fill in all four cards' blanks with the same word or phrase.

Leading the Protocol

The following six steps will help you most effectively lead the protocol.

1. **Give out card 1:** *Images, experiences, assumptions, and associations I had of _____ before this unit.* **Students write the unit topic (or a subtopic they chose) in the blank and respond to the resulting prompt.**

   For some students, the unit might have been the very first time they heard of a given topic. Maybe *Same Sun Here* (House & Vaswani, 2011) was their first time reading a novel in letters, or they'd never had any exposure to sines and cosines before taking trigonometry. In cases like these, the students would have had no previous images, experiences, assumptions,

1 Images, experiences, assumptions, and associations I had of _____ _____ before this unit:	**2** Specific parts of the unit that affected my thinking about _____:
3 How the unit altered or expanded my thinking about _____ _____:	**4** Specific actions I'll take now that my thinking about _____ _____ has changed:

Summary

First I thought _____.

Then I learned _____.

Now I think _____.

So I will _____.

Figure 5.5: Thoughts and actions cards.

*Visit **go.SolutionTree.com/instruction** for a free reproducible version of this figure.*

or associations regarding the topic. For students in this position, you can give an alternative prompt: "Why do you think you hadn't heard about _____ before?"

As always, if your students won't understand the prompt, word it differently. Ask, "What did you know about _____ before this unit?" or "Three weeks ago, if I'd asked you to draw whatever came to mind when I said _____, what would you have drawn?"

2. **Give out card 2:** *Specific parts of the unit that affected my thinking about _____.* **Students write the same topic in the blank as they did before, and they respond to the resulting prompt.**

This step gives students occasion to review their notes and resources to pinpoint moments that influenced their thinking. In an English class, they might identify specific passages in a book that affected how they view a topic or theme. In a history or science class, they might identify specific events, phenomena, or perspectives that impacted their views. In a mathematics or language class, they might look for moments in their own learning process when their thinking shifted.

3. **Give out card 3: *How the unit altered or expanded my thinking about _____. * Students write the same topic in the blank and respond to the resulting prompt.**

   Some students will resist the idea that something they learn in school can change their thinking. They'll ask, "What if my thinking is literally the same as it was?" You can respond by validating their feelings. Not every unit will rock their whole world. Did anything they learned make certain ideas seem more important? Less important? Clearer? More confusing? Do they see connections they didn't notice before? Can they explain something better now? Did the unit give them new reasons to think what they previously thought, or new perspectives on what they thought before? Even small or subtle changes matter.

4. **Give out card 4: *Specific actions I'll take now that my thinking about _____ has changed.* Students write the same topic in the blank and respond to the resulting prompt.**

   Students can consider the following questions to help them determine what actions they might want to take as a result of their learning.

   - "What do I want to think about more?"
   - "What do I want to learn about next?"
   - "What do I want to read?"
   - "What do I want to tell people about?"
   - "What do I want to do in my interactions with others?"
   - "What do I want to do by myself?"
   - "What do I want to do at school? At home?"
   - "What do I want to do in the future? Right now?"

   You can point out that *do* is a very broad verb and can include all kinds of actions, including mental actions. Even the smallest actions count if they're steps toward a meaningful life.

5. **Give out the Summary strips. Students summarize their thinking by writing four sentences, beginning with (1) *First I thought*, (2) *Then I learned*, (3) *Now I think*, and (4) *So I will*.**

   Consider these example summaries.

   > First, I thought Rosa Parks sat in the section of the bus for white people because she was tired. Then, I learned that she actually did not sit in the white section; she refused to give up her seat in what was called the *colored section* to a white person. I also learned that her protest was organized by the NAACP and that she had a leadership role. Now, I think people should recognize and support civil rights leaders beyond Martin Luther King Jr., especially when they're women. So, I will learn more about Opal Tometi, Patrisse Cullors, Alicia Garza, and other women who have leadership roles in today's civil rights movements.

> First, I thought computer programming was kind of nerdy and hard. Then, I learned how to do Scratch. Now, I think it's not that hard, and also it's fun! So, I will keep doing programming in Scratch.

> First, I thought it would be cool to learn how to introduce myself in French so I'd be able to communicate with my grandmother in Haiti. Then, I learned how to say, "Je m'appelle Elizabeth," "Je suis de Chicago," and "J'ai onze ans." Now, I think I need to learn a lot more than how to introduce myself, because my grandmother already knows my name, where I live, and how old I am. So, I will spend more time studying French.

If appropriate, substitute the word *learned* with *discovered*, *tried*, *built*, *made*, *read*, or some other verb that more accurately describes what students did during the unit. Or forgo the sentence starters entirely; the point is to help students consolidate their thinking, not to limit them.

6. **Invite volunteers to share their summary sentences.**

Admitting that their thinking changed might make students feel like they were wrong before, or it might open them up to criticism from their peers. Saying their behavioral commitments out loud might make them fear judgment from their peers if they don't make good on those commitments. When any students share, you can honor the courage it takes to be vulnerable in front of their peers by thanking them for sharing and validating their willingness to grow. A simple comment like, "That sounds hard but definitely worthwhile" or "I never would have thought to do that, but it totally makes sense," shows not just the student who shares but the whole group that your class is a place where they can open up about what matters and get support as they struggle in the service of their values.

Boosting the Impact

Writing their summary sentences on a strip of paper allows students to put them aside (or hand them to you for safekeeping). After a few days or weeks, or even months, you could hand back the paper strips and lead a discussion about whether students took the actions they said they'd take.

- "Don't raise your hand or identify it, but just think about it in your mind: Did you take the action you said you'd take?"

- "For those of you who did take the action you said you'd take—does anyone want to share how it felt? What happened? What's the next step?"

- "For those who didn't take the action, is anyone willing to share what got in the way?"

Students might say they didn't take the action because they didn't actually care about their commitments. In that case, try asking if their learning can shape their behavior in some other way that they do care about. If students say they didn't keep a commitment because it seemed intimidating, you can ask them to try to identify a smaller or lower-stakes version of their commitment. For example, a student who said he'd organize a march to protest mountaintop removal, but quickly found he didn't have the time or resources for such a huge action, could write an email asking his congressional representative to support a bill that would prevent new mountaintop removal projects.

You can then invite all of your students to make new commitments. Let's say that after studying climate change, Daphne committed to eating plant-based meals for a week. Depending on how that went, Daphne could do the same thing she already did (eat plant-based meals for another week), try a bigger version (eat plant-based meals for a month), try a smaller version (eat plant-based lunches for three days), or try something different (walk to friends' houses instead of having her dad drive her). Students can write their new commitments on new strips of paper, and this process of making, discussing, and renewing values-consistent commitments can reoccur as often as makes sense.

An extension of So I Will is for students to write essays about how their thinking changed. Writing an essay takes longer and further reinforces their learning—and any connections between their learning and their values. Figure 5.6 has an essay rubric you can give out to students or adapt based on their needs and your assessment system.

Assignment: Write an essay in which you explain how this unit has affected the way you think about a particular topic—for example, how your learning has clarified, expanded, or complicated your thinking—and what you plan to do as a result of what you learned.			
Elements	**Basic**	**Effective**	**Exemplary**
The essay sticks to a **thesis** about how your learning has affected your thinking about a particular topic.			
Specific **images** help the reader visualize how you thought about the topic before, what specifically you learned, how you think about the topic now, and what you plan to do as a result.			
The essay is thoughtfully **organized**; topics are in an order that makes sense, and transitions help the reader move from one topic to the next.			
The essay is **easy to read**; it has clear sentences, a title, and no errors in capitalization, punctuation, spelling, or grammar.			

Figure 5.6: Example rubric for So I Will essays.

Visit **go.SolutionTree.com/instruction** *for a free reproducible version of this figure.*

Using the Protocol Next Time

If students use this protocol multiple times, they can track how their thinking evolves from one unit to the next. How does each unit build their skills or understandings? What becomes clearer? What becomes less clear as they learn about nuances and exceptions? As their thinking changes over time, how will that affect their day-to-day choices? Each time they do this protocol, they'll practice making a values-based decision about how the material they learn in your class will influence the way they live.

 Booksploration

Students imagine potential benefits of reading more about a topic they've just studied, look at books about that topic, and identify a reason they might choose to read each one.

Suggested Time:

With all that occupies students' time outside school—families, friends, jobs, sports, artistic endeavors, TV shows, games, social media, self-care habits—they don't necessarily consider reading beyond assigned books a priority (McKenna, Conradi, Lawrence, Jang, & Meyer, 2012). Meanwhile, just as our students' academic and personal lives get busier and they have less time to read outside school, they also have less time dedicated to independent reading inside school. Unlike in the elementary grades, middle and high school classes rarely include time to read self-selected books. Like our students' lives, our curricula are packed, and we might not feel we have time to spare for our students to just read.

If neither we as teachers nor the students themselves prioritize reading, they miss out. Professor Vivian Howard (2011) has reviewed literature on independent reading and surveyed adolescents about their reading lives, and she finds that teenagers have a wide range of reasons for reading. It helps them gain knowledge and thinking skills they'll need to succeed in school, imagine their futures and set specific goals, understand the world around them and inside their own skin, treat themselves and others with greater care, develop a stronger sense of social justice, and relax (Howard, 2011). In short, reading can help students discover, develop, and act on their values.

This protocol, Booksploration, helps students extend their knowledge of a topic they recently studied in class, while also discovering how independent reading serves their values. Students first come up with reasons to read, beyond thinking it's fun (since it *isn't* fun for everyone) or having to do it for school. They then look at a variety of books related to the unit topic, and they write down a reason why they'd read each one, according to their own values. Last, they choose one book to read for about twenty minutes, and longer if they'd like.

When you're choosing books related to your unit, think expansively about what it might mean for a book to be *on topic*. Science students learning about climate change could read related nonfiction, realistic fiction, science fiction, fantasy, or poetry. History students learning about the Revolutionary War could read history, biography, or historical fiction about the American Revolution, but they could also read histories of other revolutions, biographies of more recent political actors, or realistic fiction about young change makers. After reading *Brown Girl Dreaming* (Woodson, 2014) in English class, students could read other novels in verse, other books about growing up, or other books with black female characters. If you can't find books at your students' reading level related to the specific unit topic, you could instead use Booksploration to review a larger theme from throughout your course. In any event, aim for diverse genres, styles, and voices, and use this as an opportunity to connect your class to your students' other classes, current events, and issues that come up in their lives.

Getting Ready

Do the following in preparation for the protocol.

❑ Collect lots of books related to the unit topic.

While books are expensive, some districts have book-buying programs, or the parent association might be able to help you collect books or raise the funds to buy them. Better still, see if a group of your students would be interested in organizing a service project to get books for your classroom.

Ideally, during Booksploration, you'll put out enough different books for each student to have a meaningful choice among several alternatives. On the other hand, putting out multiple copies of the same book means creating the potential for students to read together.

❑ Decide how you'll set up the classroom.

Although your students can just pass the books around the room until they've all had a chance to look at each book, you can also spread the books around the classroom and have your students move around. You might notice your students talking to each other about the books they pick up.

❑ Make copies of an article listing various benefits of reading, such as "Why Reading Is Good for Your Health" (https://cnn.it/2mKy3xY; Christensen, 2017), if you think your students will struggle to come up with reasons to read.

Leading the Protocol

The following four steps will help you most effectively lead the protocol.

1. **Lead the class in brainstorming a list of reasons to read independently. Record the list on the board.**

   When asked, "Why read?" students might say early on that they read because it's fun or they're forced to (that is, teachers assign reading, or their parents make privileges contingent on reading). You can acknowledge these as valid reasons many students read. The problem is that students don't have much control over either one. They don't usually create their own assignments, nor do they usually choose whether they find reading pleasurable. They can choose to build their reading stamina and experiment with more books, which might make reading more fun, but it might not, and it takes effort. If they give a book a chance, sometimes they end up liking it more than they expected—although sometimes they end up liking a book *less* than they expected. At any given moment, they like what they like and don't necessarily like to read.

Beyond enjoyment and assignment, why *else* do people read? Students might suggest that reading can help them get information about an important topic, understand perspectives beyond their own, discover how others solve problems similar to theirs, see their own concerns more realistically, learn to relate better to people, and connect with others who are reading the same book. Reading can also help them improve their own writing as they discover new tools and techniques, and it can challenge them just for the challenge. If you think your students will struggle to come up with their own reasons to read, hand out a short article listing benefits of reading. Ask your students whether they agree with each benefit and if they can think of others.

As the class makes suggestions, listen for ones that involve what psychologists call an *emotional control agenda* (Hayes et al., 1999). Often we do things in order to avoid feeling certain emotions, like fear or sadness or surprise. Students might say they read to calm themselves down, relieve themselves from boredom, or mentally escape an upsetting situation. Of course it's understandable that they want to feel less anxious, bored, or upset. The problem is that reading won't necessarily or reliably change their emotions. Reading *might* curb boredom, but not if they read a boring book. Reading *might* be relaxing, but it might not calm someone who's very keyed up. When someone feels anxious, having difficulty concentrating on a book might lead to further anxiety. Or maybe the book's subject provokes anxiety. As much as we try to avoid feeling certain emotions, our emotions are largely outside our control. What *is* in our control is our behavior. If we help students frame their behaviors—like reading—as moving them toward their values rather than away from certain emotions, they will more likely experience an increased sense of satisfaction (Villatte et al., 2016).

If during the brainstorm a student offers a reason to read that comes from an emotional control agenda, start by validating that reason: "Yes, lots of people do read to calm themselves down." Then ask a question like, "Does that always work out the way we want it to? We might read because it calms us down, but *does* it always calm us down?" This sort of question helps students assess how well their emotional control agenda works, which is a first step toward determining if they want to change their behavior to something more consistent with their values. Finally, point out other reasons to read that relate to values that students get to choose, such as expanding their vocabulary, learning new writing techniques, increasing their knowledge, increasing their stamina, understanding experiences they've never had, or discovering new ways to handle a problem in their lives.

2. **Put out a wide variety of books connected to the unit topic or to an overarching course theme. For each book, students copy down the title and author, and then note at least one reason why they would find reading the book worthwhile.**

Rather than only deciding whether they'd enjoy any particular book, they identify a reason that each book would be worth reading. Keep the class's list of reasons to read on the board for students' reference throughout this part of the protocol. Sometimes students will say their reason to read a particular book isn't listed on the board. If that happens, you can just add the new reason to the class's list and announce it so the other students can consider this reason too.

3. **Students each select one book they're willing to read for about fifteen or twenty minutes.**

When students pull a book off a shelf as a potential read, they might spend two seconds looking at the front cover or ten seconds reading the back, or maybe half a minute skimming a few paragraphs, but often not a full twenty minutes actually reading. Sustaining their attention for this long helps them get a better sense of the book's subject and style, and it builds endurance. You can tell your students that they're not committing to finishing this book, but they're giving it a chance and seeing what they think. Sometimes students will ask if they're allowed to take the book home to finish reading it!

4. **Have students form groups of four, such that they're with classmates who chose other books. These groups discuss what they notice in the books they're just getting to know, and whether continuing to read their books would serve their values.**

Post these prompts to guide the discussions or make copies to give to each group.

- In your book, what stands out so far?

- What don't you know yet (for example, about a character, event, or concept)?

- Based on what you've read, does it seem like reading the book will be worthwhile for the reason you identified?

- Are there other reasons you would find your book worth reading?

Since no one has read very much yet, this discussion will feel more like a collective inquiry than a series of book reports. You might notice students asking each other questions, showing each other pages from their books, and starting to read a book they just heard someone else describe. Working in a group of four allows students to hear about three more books and three of their peers' values.

Some students might be more interested in a classmate's book than in the one they happened to pick. You might see students trade books and end up reading each other's. If you have the resources, try to have extra copies on hand in case two or more students want to read the same book at the same time and perhaps discuss it. In any event, students might leave class with a book they're excited to read—whether it is the one they read for the twenty minutes or one a classmate talked about.

Boosting the Impact

This protocol gives students an opportunity to become curious about books and to discover, on their own and within a group, whether reading a particular book is worth their time and energy. We strongly recommend *not* requiring or even urging students to stick with their book so that they can decide for themselves. That said, you can give your students the option of borrowing the book and continuing to read.

After a few days, ask if any students are still reading their book. For those who are, ask how it's going. What do they like and dislike about the book? Even if they don't love it, how does the book serve a purpose they value? How do they feel about themselves as a result of persisting at something that matters to them, even if it isn't fun? To students who stopped reading their books, you can offer help finding other books they might find more rewarding. As the teacher, you always have the power to require students to read; some students will only read if they have that requirement, and some not even then. Regardless of whether you establish requirements, you can keep helping students clarify how reading contributes to a meaningful life.

Using the Protocol Next Time

While you might not be able to find or afford books connected to every unit, or have class time to spare for multiple iterations of this protocol, Booksploration can work after every unit. Done repeatedly, Booksploration reminds students that other people care about every topic they study in your course, enough that all these authors wrote books on the subject. Even students who never read any book beyond the initial twenty minutes will see, repeatedly, that their learning doesn't have to end just because a unit does.

After doing the protocol once, you can skip the step where students list reasons to read, as long as you keep their original list. You can type it onto a slide, or just write it on chart paper, so you can show the list each time you do the protocol. In fact, a student-created list of reasons to read wouldn't be a bad thing to keep on your classroom wall year-round. Each time you start a new Booksploration, ask if your students want to add any new reasons to the list, and then go ahead and look at the new books.

 Naming Awards

Students imagine awards named after various aspects of the content they just studied and give the awards to their peers.

Suggested Time:

Often when we teach new material, we introduce students to new terms. An eighth-grade poetry unit includes *onomatopoeia*, *simile*, *metaphor*, and *personification*. A sixth-grade unit on biomes offers *tundra*, *taiga, deciduous forest, grassland,* and *desert.* And a high school Latin class learns names for the cases: *nominative, genitive, dative, accusative, ablative,* and *vocative.* We sometimes have our students make flash cards, draw pictures, identify examples, or otherwise take time to remember and review what the terms mean and become proficient in using them.

The Naming Awards protocol gives students another way to review and work with terms they've used throughout a unit. After going back through their notes to find terms they learned and writing what they know about each one, students invent awards for their peers based on the terms.

Doing this work requires students to understand what the terms mean, to abstract positive personal qualities from them—deciding, for example, what personal qualities they'd associate with *onomatopoeia*—and then to recognize those qualities in their peers. What would the Onomatopoeia Award entail? What would it take to win it? What about the Simile Award, the Metaphor Award, and the Personification Award? After inventing the awards, students select recipients from among their peers. In doing this work, they think critically and creatively about the content, connect the content to their own experiences and to positive qualities they value, and notice those positive qualities in each other.

Getting Ready

Do the following in preparation for the protocol.

❑ Make enough copies of the examples of positive qualities handout (figure 5.7) for each student.

Accuracy	Determination	Independence	Prudence
Adventure	Efficiency	Innovation	Reliability
Appreciation	Empathy	Integrity	Resilience
Authenticity	Enthusiasm	Joy	Resourcefulness
Awareness	Equity	Justice	Respect
Clarity	Excellence	Kindness	Responsibility
Compassion	Faith	Knowledge	Restraint
Confidence	Flexibility	Leadership	Simplicity
Connectedness	Generosity	Love	Sincerity
Cooperation	Harmony	Loyalty	Sustainability
Courage	Honesty	Modesty	Tact
Creativity	Hope	Openness	Thoroughness
Curiosity	Humor	Patience	Trust
Dedication	Inclusivity	Practicality	Wisdom

Figure 5.7: Examples of positive qualities handout.

*Visit **go.SolutionTree.com/instruction** for a free reproducible version of this figure.*

Leading the Protocol

The following seven steps will help you most effectively lead the protocol.

1. **Lead the class in making a list of terms and their definitions from throughout a unit. Write this list on the board.**

   Working individually or in groups, they can go back through their notes and resources, looking for key terms. These terms might be literary devices, historical figures from a particular era, biomes, organelles, irregular verbs in Spanish, cases in Latin, properties of integers, types of quadrilaterals—it depends on your curriculum.

2. **Ask for examples of existing awards and prizes.**

   Suggest thinking of awards in different fields, such as athletics, arts and entertainment, science, cooking, writing, and academics. Ask a few volunteers to share an award and what someone has to do in order to win it. Try to get the students to say what the award nominee does to merit the nomination, rather than describe that person as being the best. What does an Academy Award–winning director do? What does it mean to win the Heisman Trophy? What does it take for a restaurant to earn a Michelin star? You might hear students naming qualities of award winners' actions, such as creativity, integrity, or precision. Jot down these words on the board if you hear them; they might help your students later as they're coming up with their own awards.

3. **Divide the class into groups, and assign a different term to each group.**

   If students learned seven geometry terms during a unit on the properties of a circle, they'd form seven groups. If the groups end up too large to be able to work productively, you can assign multiple smaller groups the same term.

4. **Each group imagines that there is something called the _____ Award (filling in the blank with that group's assigned term) given out every year to a student at the school. Together, the group members describe what their award criteria would entail.**

   Students will need to think metaphorically so that the award will reflect positive qualities a student can display in a variety of situations. For example, what positive personal qualities can temperate grassland represent? Temperate grasslands have hot summers, cold winters, fertile soil, seasonal drought, and occasional fires. Maybe the Temperate Grassland Award could go to someone who is passionate (like the extreme temperatures and moisture levels of grassland) and supportive (like grassland's fertile soil and hospitable environment to diverse wildlife). The commutative property holds that changing the order of operations in an expression or equation does not change the result: 13 + 6 has the same sum as 6 + 13. Maybe the Commutative Property Award could go to someone who is flexible and doesn't need things to go only one way.

   Some students will think too literally, saying someone who's good at solving addition problems would receive the Commutative Property Award, or a student who likes playing in the grass would get the Temperate Grassland Award. If students need help thinking of qualities their peers have in common with their academic term, give out the list of positive qualities in figure 5.7 (page 127).

5. **Each group shares its criteria for winning its award.**

You could have a member of each group explain the connection between the academic term and the award, or you could see if other groups' members can articulate the connection. Let's say a history class is studying women's rights movements, and one group has designed the Lucretia Mott Award. When sharing, the group could explain that this award goes to a student who takes risks in order to speak up for what's right. The group could go on to explain that this is because Lucretia Mott withstood criticism from within and outside the abolitionist movement for giving speeches as a woman and for allying herself with black activists—or the group could simply state what the award is for and then see if any classmates can make the connection.

As groups share their awards, you can ask the rest of the class for examples of things a student could do to win: "What would it look like for a student to take risks in order to speak up for what's right?"

6. **Lead a class discussion of students' concerns about nominating other students at their school for their awards. Ask for strategies or solutions to address problems that might arise.**

Having to nominate someone currently enrolled at their school (as opposed to a graduate, teacher, staff member, or parent) means they can't avoid noticing positive qualities in the peers they see every day. Students sometimes express concern that people will only nominate their friends, or discomfort that they will have to name a classmate who *isn't* a friend. Reassure your students that these are normal feelings, and then explore possible actions. What might happen if they only nominate their friends? Why might they want to nominate someone who isn't a friend? What happens when they get away from what's comfortable or familiar?

Students also commonly worry that they won't find anyone to nominate. Some will ask, "Can it *please* be someone from outside school?" Or they'll want to change their criteria, saying things like, "I don't think anyone at our school comes close to being as brave as Malala Yousafzai, so can the award be for persistence instead?" Remind these students that the people, places, events, and concepts they learn about in school might seem bigger and more important than the peers they learn alongside, but *their* actions count, too. Ask them to consider, "What happens if we learn how to appreciate these actions? What if we look at each other in new ways? What if we all start to notice actions we haven't noticed before?"

7. **Students nominate peers for their imaginary awards and explain the reasons for their nominations.**

Given the vulnerability inherent in naming a peer to win an award, we recommend having your students nominate others individually, in writing, and share their writing only with you. The point of nominating their peers isn't to discuss, debate, or decide who wins; it's for each individual student to notice and appreciate positive qualities in another.

Boosting the Impact

You can help students think about their work with questions like these.

- "How was it to think about our unit topics in this way?"

- "Did any of your groups argue about how to define your award? What other ideas did you have? How did you decide which idea to go with?"

- "Did any of you nominate someone for your award who isn't a friend? Without saying who you nominated, does anyone want to say how it felt to nominate someone you're not friends with?"

- "Of all the awards we came up with as a class, which one would you most want to win?"

A day or so later, you can ask if any students told the person they nominated that they did so. Again, without having them say whom they nominated, ask, "Does anyone want to share how that conversation went?"

You can extend students' learning—about the academic content and about their values—by having them write essays in which they more fully explicate their term, the criteria for their award, and their reasons for nominating their peer. This essay could serve as a unit assessment task. Figure 5.8 has a suggested rubric for this essay assignment. Feel free to replace the word *term* with something more specific to your unit, such as *poetic device* or *biome*.

Assignment: Write an essay in which you explain: (1) the meaning and features of a term, (2) criteria you could use to select recipients of an award named after your term, and (3) why a current student at this school should receive the award.

Elements	Basic	Effective	Exemplary
The essay sticks to a **thesis**: what it means to win this award.			
Specific, accurate **details** help the reader understand why the award is named for this person, place, thing, event, or idea.			
Specific, accurate **details** help the reader understand what the student did to win the award.			
The essay is thoughtfully **organized**; topics are in an order that makes sense, and transitions help the reader move from one topic to the next.			
The essay is **easy to read**; it has clear sentences, a title, and no errors in capitalization, punctuation, spelling, or grammar.			

Figure 5.8: Example rubric for Naming Awards essays.

*Visit **go.SolutionTree.com/instruction** for a free reproducible version of this figure.*

Regardless of whether they write essays, you can ask a few days or weeks or even months later if students remember their awards. Do they also remember what the terms mean? This gives students a way to recall previous learning, or to relearn material they forgot, by connecting it to their personal experiences.

Using the Protocol Next Time

This protocol has a novelty factor the first time, but creating awards for their peers named after stuff they learned in an academic class might be weird enough that your students will enjoy doing it more than once. After the first time, you can change up the protocol by having all the groups create awards named after all the terms, and then having the whole class vote on which award best captures the person, place, thing, event, or idea it's named for.

Onward

This chapter's protocols help students review academic material so they can understand the content more fully and deeply and use it more skillfully. In reviewing the material, students also become more aware of the values they want to bring to their learning experiences.

In the next chapter, we'll turn from reviewing material to making meaningful pieces of work, and see how that creative process can give students a context to discover and do what matters to them.

• • • • •

Chapter 6

PROTOCOLS TO CREATE WORK PRODUCT

Why bother teaching if our students don't use what they learn? After a unit on landforms, our students should know how to do more than recite the definitions of *canyon* and *peninsula*; they should also be able to visualize these landforms, find examples on maps and in photos, understand what life is like in different kinds of terrain, and develop arguments for why to modify or preserve physical environments.

Students can immediately use what they learn by creating a meaningful piece of work. In an English class studying sonnets, students could recite Shakespearean sonnets, write their own sonnets, or make animations explaining the sonnet form. Physics students learning about magnetism could make toys that use different magnetic field shapes, or they could petition the transportation department to construct maglev trains. In making such products, students apply what they learned in class, continue to learn the content, and practice skills within and beyond the discipline. The work product serves as evidence of that learning that we can use for assessment purposes. Meaningful work gives students an opportunity to explore topics they care about, create things that matter to them personally and in the world, make their own decisions, and bring their own values, such as courage and compassion, to the work process.

Table 6.1 (page 134) features more types of meaningful, real-world work products that students can create.

Some work products are tangible *things* that students can share, take home, and perhaps revisit in the future. Even if they shove their work under a bed, where it collects dust, they might find it again, and it might inspire new thinking about the topic or compel them to make something similar. *Performances* are time-bound experiences that people create for themselves and others.

Students can *approximate* the sorts of things and performances that exist beyond school, such as board games and concerts. Since the students, by definition, are still learning, their board games might not look sellable, and their concerts might not be ready for Carnegie Hall, but they create actual board games and concerts, coming as close as they can at their learning stage, and with their allocated time and resources, to quality standards that exist in the real world.

Table 6.1: Types of Student Work Products

	Things Students create something tangible that they can display and keep.		Performances Students create something that exists for a moment in time.	
Approximated Students come as close as they can to making something that exists in the world beyond school.	• Animation • Board game • Budget • Chart • Collage • Comic • Diagram • Documentary • Field journal • Graph • Letter to an authority	• Map • Model • Personal essay • Photo essay • Picture book • Poetry collection • Review • Script • Toy	• Art exhibition • Banquet • Concert or recital • Guided tour • How-to demonstration • Interactive time line • Interview	• Lab experiment • Play • Poster presentation • Recitation • Re-enactment • Song • Spoken-word performance • Talk
Simulated Students make a mock-up or version of something that exists in the real world.	• Advertisement • Brochure • Business proposal • Catalog • Diary • Letter to a historical or literary figure • Newspaper	• Photo album or stream • Résumé (for a person or thing) • Social media profile • Soundtrack • Travelogue	• Campaign speech • Convention • Crime scene • Eulogy • Focus group • Job interview • Panel discussion	• Podcast • Restorative justice circle • Sales pitch • Talk show • Trial or hearing

Students can also *simulate* real-world work; they make something that exists outside school and that matters to them, but it has an element of playacting or mocking up. If geometry students create advertisements for different methods of finding a line's slope, those methods don't actually go on sale. If history students put 20th century figures on trial for causing the Great Depression, no one is actually convicted. Simulations expose students to real-world situations they wouldn't encounter otherwise.

Simulations create a pretend-yet-serious alternate reality in which students pay a different kind of attention to the content and call on a different skill set. As geometry students, they might use various methods for finding linear slope, but as advertisers, they need to compare and contrast the methods and decide why one is most effective. They also need to decide what *most effective* means; is the most effective method the one that seems most intuitive, the one with the fewest steps, or the one that's easiest to check for accuracy? When creating their advertisements, they'll have to communicate their ideas clearly and vividly enough to convince others. When history students put people on trial, they need to search through primary and secondary resources for evidence of those people's guilt and any mitigating factors. For the trial, they need to construct an argument, listen to each other, and respond on their feet. While the geometry students could just take a test on methods for finding slope, and the history students could just write a paper about factors contributing to the Great Depression, the simulations create a context in which they use content and skills they might not have otherwise used.

Approximated or simulated, thing or performance, meaningful work products can reflect students' interests, capabilities, and values. If students struggle, they struggle in the service of something that matters. This chapter's protocols offer ways to help students turn the creative process into a series of opportunities to discover and do what matters to them.

- In Prototype Analysis, students practice making a smaller version of a product so they can decide where they want to put their effort and time when they do the bigger version.

- Top-Pick Topic helps students choose topics that genuinely and deeply matter to them, as opposed to whatever feels easy or fun in the moment.

- Sandbox Mode gives students a chance to imagine, wonder, and experiment when the stakes are still low so that they have something important to say when the stakes get higher.

- In Exemplar Study, students discover how other makers bring their values to the same type of work the students are making so they can do that too.

- Group Commitments helps students choose personal behavioral guidelines for group work based on their own values.

 ## Prototype Analysis

Before starting a long-term, high-stakes, self-directed project, students do a short-term, lower-stakes, teacher-directed version. They then choose what they want to do similarly and differently for their larger project.

Suggested Time:

We usually associate the word *prototype* with engineering, but people create preliminary, lower-stakes versions of all kinds of work. Sports teams have scrimmages, chefs have test kitchens, pilots have flight simulators, and painters have studies. They create a work product from start to finish, but the work has something less final and costly about it. Prototyping helps them get a feel for their process and see some version of its outcome so they can decide what they want to do when the stakes are higher.

We can imagine prototype versions of almost any school project. Suppose, for example, that a ninth-grade history class will soon get this assignment: "Create a one-page comic in which you explain how an 18th century event has influenced 21st century life." This project involves quite a lot of decision making—which event to choose, what to say about the event, how to combine words and pictures to convey that message, what tone to strike, what comic book elements to use, and how to lay out the panels.

Now suppose that before taking on this complex project, students create preliminary comics, all responding to the same event they recently studied as a class. The teacher gives each student a template with four panels and asks students to illustrate the historical event, a national condition it contributed to, the local effects of that condition, and how the local effects make them feel. Students rough out these prototypes in one class period. The teacher's specifications take some decision making out of their hands, and at the same time, they're getting ideas for what they could include in a comic about history's influence, how words and pictures can go together, and how they can use sequential art to tell a story. When they do the actual comic assignment, they can make these decisions for themselves from a place of greater knowledge.

Students who make a prototype directly experience the consequences of their choices so that they can make better-informed choices in the future. Instead of having a teacher tell them, "You're drawing that figure too small," or "You need to write what the equations represent," they have a chance to make their own choices, notice how those choices impacted the product, and make new choices that lead to a more satisfying outcome.

The Prototype Analysis protocol happens just after students have done the smaller, faster, more teacher-directed version of an upcoming assigned project. During the protocol, they read the assignment and plan how they want to approach it.

Getting Ready

Do the following in preparation for the protocol.

☐ Write up your larger, higher-stakes assignment, and make enough copies for each student.

Your students won't receive this assignment until after making their prototypes, but *you'll* need to know where your students are headed. When you write up this larger assignment, make sure you explain it in enough detail that your students will be able to visualize the work they'll create and understand how it's similar to and different from the prototype.

☐ Have your students create a smaller, lower-stakes version of work they'll soon complete.

When they make the prototype, have your students use the skills that relate to your subject, but take away the decisions that relate to the project itself. Let's imagine that in a mathematics class, sixth graders will soon make travel scrapbooks from the perspectives of exchange students. For the scrapbook, they'll use algebra to make a budget in the currency they're familiar with and in their chosen nation's currency, a map to key local destinations converting distances from miles to kilometers, and a recipe from their imagined home country scaled to feed their class. The project will also involve many decisions unrelated to mathematics, like which country to pretend to be from, which attractions to visit, what recipe to make, and how to lay out the scrapbook. In preparation, the teacher has her students make a prototype for which she chooses the country, the attractions, the recipe, and other elements so that the students focus on solving and displaying their equations.

Leading the Protocol

The following three steps will help you most effectively lead the protocol.

1. **After students complete a prototype, give out the assignment for the larger, longer-term project. Ask students to identify similarities and differences between the two tasks.**

   You can ask them questions like these.

   - "How is this project similar to the work you just did?"
   - "How is the larger project more complex?"
   - "What choices will you have for this project that you didn't have before?"

2. **Students assess their prototypes by observing what aspects make them feel satisfied and dissatisfied.**

   They can describe their observations in T-charts, reflective paragraphs, or group discussions. As they do this work, encourage your students to notice and name how they felt about their prototypes while they were working, and how they feel about the prototypes.

   If a student felt anxious that his comic wouldn't be clear, then clarity matters to him. What will he do to ensure he makes the next comic clear? Or if a student feels disappointed about having solved her equations incorrectly, what can she do differently next time? Students don't have to wallow in any painful feelings, because the prototype isn't the final version. They can simply decide what they want to do next. Their feelings about their prototype can point the way toward what they value in the final version.

3. **Students describe what they want to do again when working on the bigger project, and what they'll do differently.**

   If some students aren't sure how to respond, you can ask guiding questions like "What skills did you learn while doing the smaller version that you can bring to the larger version?" and "What mistakes did you make while doing the smaller version that you can learn from when doing the larger version?"

   Some students might have followed the prototype instructions without considering what the final product would look like. Imagine a student working on the travel scrapbook prototype. Since he's in algebra class, he understands that he's supposed to solve equations correctly, but doesn't picture those equations within a scrapbook. He stuffs all the equations on one page and doesn't include information about the travel experience they represent. On reviewing the larger scrapbook assignment, he has another chance to consider how to display the equations. Encourage your students to look for places where they missed or misunderstood the purpose of an instruction, and ask if they can explain that purpose now.

   The students will have more time for the bigger project, and they can now decide how they want to spend that time. Some might have rushed through all the steps in order to finish their prototypes within the allotted time. They now have a chance to allocate enough time to parts they wish they'd spent more time on. Others might not have finished their prototypes because they meticulously worked on an early step. You can call their attention to the values that led them to work so slowly and carefully. Let's imagine that in the history class, a student did only one panel of her prototype comic and now feels annoyed and embarrassed. To point out the student's values, the teacher could ask, "What did you accomplish in that one panel? What about drawing it was important enough to you that you wanted to put in so much time and care? Now that you have more time, how will you spend it on what's important to you?"

Boosting the Impact

Prototypes reveal opportunities for further growth. If students didn't know to capitalize historical events when making the prototype comic, or if they weren't sure whether to multiply or divide by the conversion rate when making the prototype scrapbook, then doing the larger versions of these projects gives them another chance to learn. Not only does prototyping reveal to you what skills you might need to reteach to which students, but it also gives the students an authentic reason to create learning goals. They have a second chance to do something well, and they get to define for themselves what *well* means.

While your students do the bigger project, check in with them individually or as a class. What choices are they making this time? How satisfied are they with their choices? How satisfied are they with the process? Regularly asking students questions like these helps them stay committed to their values—or at least helps them see how the project presents opportunities for them to stay committed to their values.

Using the Protocol Next Time

Your students can make prototypes for every project. If making prototypes, reflecting on their process, and noticing how they feel about their outcome become regular parts of doing any project, they'll learn how to bring their values to their work when the bigger assignment comes along.

 Top-Pick Topic

Students discuss why a topic they've tentatively chosen is important to them—as opposed to easy, comfortable, or fun in the moment.

Suggested Time:

Meaningful work presents lots of opportunities for students to make choices, and one of the first choices is the topic. Students might wonder, "What will I write my play about?" "What will I teach someone how to do in my French video?" "Which aspect of Sumerian society will I research?" or "What daily problem do I want to collect and graph data on?"

Topic choice can reflect students' values. In the French class making instructional videos, maybe a boy who cares about wildlife makes a video on how to create safe havens for birds in urban areas. Or maybe a girl in the class has a brother who is on the autism spectrum, and she makes a video on how to have play-dates with kids on the autism spectrum. For these two students, the French video becomes an occasion to learn more about something they think is important, share their knowledge and stories, and create a product that could make a difference in an area that matters to them.

We can also imagine students in the French class choosing topics for reasons that don't necessarily serve their values. A girl makes her video about how to make a ham and cheese sandwich because she has the three ingredients in her refrigerator and already knows the French words for *ham*, *cheese*, and *bread*. Another girl makes her video about how to make a video because she thinks it would be funny. Three different boys make videos about how to do a dance that's trending right now. And another boy makes a video about how to feed his pet iguana because he always uses iguanas as his topic for school projects.

There's nothing wrong with choosing an easy, funny, popular, or comfortable topic. But students don't have to choose a topic for only these reasons. Top-Pick Topic gets students to articulate the importance of a topic they've tentatively selected. They answer a series of questions that help them expand their awareness of what could happen if they choose this topic.

Getting Ready

Do the following in preparation for the protocol.

❑ Make enough copies of the perspectives on my topic handout (figure 6.1, or adapt a version) for each student.

Directions: Use the questions to help you talk to your group about the topic you've chosen. You don't have to answer all the questions or answer them in order. Your group members will listen silently and take notes.

- Why am I interested in this topic right now?
- Who else in this class is interested in this topic? How could we collaborate or complement each other's work?
- If I were to work with this topic in another class or outside school, what would be different?
- If I work with this topic, what important things will I be able to do next?
- What would my friends, my family, or other people I trust say to encourage or discourage me from working with this topic?
- What have other students or professionals gotten out of working with this topic?
- When did my past self have an opportunity to work with this topic, and what's changed since then?
- How will my working with this topic impact my community, family, friends, or world?

Figure 6.1: Perspectives on my topic handout.

*Visit **go.SolutionTree.com/instruction** for a free reproducible version of this figure.*

Leading the Protocol

The following five steps will help you most effectively lead the protocol.

1. **Students form groups of three.**

   Three is an ideal number because then students think with multiple classmates about what's important to them, but in a group that still feels intimate. Smaller groups also require less time for everyone to share. However, if students have already been working in pairs or quads throughout the unit (for example, as described in the Unit Partner Meet protocol in chapter 3), and those groups have established a trusting relationship, then you can just leave them in those groups.

2. **One student (the "presenter") talks for a few minutes about a tentatively chosen topic, using the questions in the perspectives on my topic handout (figure 6.1, page 139). The other group members silently listen and take notes.**

   The presenter doesn't have to answer all the questions or answer them in order. Each question helps presenters take a different perspective on what it would mean if they worked on this topic—as themselves versus someone else, here versus somewhere else, and now versus *somewhen* else.

3. **The presenter is silent while the group members say back what they heard. The presenter takes notes.**

   Group members can say back key words or phrases that stood out ("I heard you say…"), or they can offer summaries in their own words ("I noticed that you kept talking about…" or "It seems like you're curious about…" or "To me, it sounds like you care about…"). If your students aren't sure what to say, you can write a few sentence starters like these on the board. If group members aren't sure what the presenter said or meant, they can also ask questions ("Did you mention…?" or "Are you interested in…?"), but rather than answering, the presenter should write down the questions and think further about what it would mean to work with a particular topic.

4. **Groups repeat steps 2 and 3 until each student has had a turn as presenter.**

   Students each commit to a topic—the one they talked about, some variation of it, or a new topic altogether—and tell the group why they're making that choice.

5. **Group members check in with each other on how they feel about the conversation itself.**

   Point out that for the conversation to have gone well, not all group members need to have clarity about which topic to work on. The point of this quick check-in is for students to discuss how they feel about the *process* of discussing their topics together.

Boosting the Impact

You can debrief this protocol in a whole-class discussion, using questions like these.

- "How did that go?"
- "Did any of you discover anything interesting about yourselves or each other?"

- "Of the eight perspective-taking questions, which ones did you find most helpful? Most challenging?"
- "How did you support your classmates after they talked about their topics?"

Don't measure this protocol by what students say about their topics during the debrief. They might announce that they're picking the fun, easy, or familiar topic anyway, but that they feel bad about it. Or they don't feel bad, and they say so, loudly. Or they rampantly insist that the fluffy topic *is* meaningful, the easy topic *is* hard, or the familiar topic *is* novel. Such responses just mean that these students are attempting to avoid feeling anxious and embarrassed about picking topics that don't reflect their values. Rather than trying to change those feelings, just notice them. Notice your own feelings too. Perhaps you feel a little frustrated or annoyed when students don't choose topics they genuinely care about—or triumphant when they do.

Whatever students say, and however they (and you) feel, they've now had the experience of talking (or thinking) about their values. Watch and see what happens next. After they've chosen their topics and created their work products, you can lead another class discussion or have conversations with individual students. How satisfied do they feel with their work product? Their work process? For those who decided to forgo the easy and fun route in favor of a topic that mattered more to them, how do they feel about themselves as a result of that choice? What topic will they choose next time? The time after that? Having follow-up conversations like these helps students discover one of the best things about values: we always have another chance to choose them.

Using the Protocol Next Time

You can reuse this protocol anytime students choose their own topics. To keep the activity from getting stale, you can change the groupings, or encourage students to answer questions they didn't get to last time. To save class time, you can have students use the perspective-taking questions in discussions with their families. Or, you can use the protocol in class but send families the questions so they can repeat the discussions at home. By repeatedly imagining other people's perspectives, other places, and other times, students begin to notice why working with their topic matters to them, right here and now in your class.

 Sandbox Mode

Students respond to playful writing prompts that promote personal and imaginative thinking about topics they've chosen to work with.

Suggested Time:

Online role-playing games involve forming groups, finding and trading resources, building shelters and strongholds, fending off rivals, and dealing with threats to survival. Some games include a *sandbox mode*, a domain separate from the larger game world where players have unlimited access to resources, and no threats, so the player can build things, test features, and otherwise muck about without the limitations and pressures of regular gameplay.

Before we (the authors) begin a draft, and throughout the process of writing one, we muck about. We write ideas with watercolor markers on newsprint. We write ideas on sticky notes on our bathroom mirror. We take walks around our neighborhood, talking about our topic and about other things that sometimes unexpectedly connect back to our topic (like how our daughter's gaming helped us discover an analogous practice to the one we wanted to write about). None of this looks like writing a book, but it's an integral part of the process. It's sandbox mode.

The Sandbox Mode protocol is all about making time for students to play with their ideas. The protocol involves quite a bit of writing (and sometimes drawing), but its purpose is *not* to draft something they'll eventually turn in. English professor Peter Elbow (1989) describes how writing can be a sort of play: "I have a thought, perhaps out of the blue or perhaps in the midst of writing something else, and I give myself permission to pursue it on paper in an uncontrolled way wherever it wants to go" (pp. 47–48). Elbow (1989) calls this *freewriting*, to distinguish it from more controlled writing that results in a draft. We're calling it Sandbox Mode—and not just because we want to sound cool by borrowing a gaming term that is itself borrowed from playgrounds. We want to emphasize the protocol's purpose: for students to have unexpected thoughts, build their ideas, test out ways to express those ideas, and otherwise muck about—all without the limitations and pressures of creating the final work product, whether that's a piece of writing or something else.

During the Sandbox Mode protocol, students get deliberately weird prompts that help them generate ideas about their chosen topic. The weirdness unhooks students from academic ways of knowing and talking about their topic, freeing them to think in more personal, imaginative, and ultimately illuminating ways. But at some point, students might react to the weirdness. They'll laugh, make faces, make comments, groan, or gasp, sarcastically or in earnest. Any reactions usually signal that your students expect classroom questions to have right answers, and using their imaginations makes them uncomfortable. This protocol helps them get comfortable with that discomfort—always in the service of generating work product that matters to them.

Getting Ready

Do the following in preparation for the protocol.

- ❑ Choose about five sandbox prompts from figure 6.2 (page 144), or write your own.

- ❑ Determine a sequence for your prompts. Start with more straightforward ones (like the *One Time I* Story and Genuine Questions prompts), and sequence them such that they demand more creativity but less actual writing over time.

  As the activity goes along, students might become tired of writing, so put the prompts that will elicit more writing at the beginning. Put the weirder ones at the end, so they'll introduce some novelty and humor right when students need it. Most prompts in figure 6.2 have blanks that you can fill in with the general topic your students are learning about (for example, endangered animals) or that the students themselves can fill in with their specific topics (for example, the mountain gorilla).

❑ Create some way to distinguish Sandbox Mode from other writing activities.

Some students will associate *any* writing that takes place in a classroom with the pressure to produce something that the teacher will judge on its merits. You can create a more playful feeling by giving students unusual writing materials (like markers and newsprint), so that physically, the task feels different and the outcome looks different from a typical writing assignment. Or, if you want your students to write in their notebooks so they have access to their ideas later, they could turn their notebooks sideways. You could extend the sandbox metaphor by filling a toy pail with colorful pens that students can use, or (if you can stand it) invite students to take off their shoes as if they were in the sand. Changing something, however small, in the students' physical environment signals that they're about to do a different (and in this case, more playful) sort of work.

Leading the Protocol

The following five steps will help you most effectively lead the protocol.

1. **Tell your students that they're *entering the sandbox*, so to speak, where they will have less pressure and fewer limitations than during usual school activities.**

    If you're handing out special materials (like colorful pens) or giving unusual directions (like to turn their notebooks sideways), do that now. Or just state, "We are now in the sandbox," and tell your students that they're writing only because it helps them think more deeply and because it provides a record of that thinking. If their eventual work product involves writing, as many school work products do, some students might pull bits of their sandbox writing into their drafts. Still, the point is to play.

    If you think students will react to the sandbox prompts in a way that will derail the whole activity, you can let them know they might find some of the coming prompts weird, and warn them again before giving some of the weirder ones. You can also just give the prompts, let any reactions come and go, and debrief later if necessary.

2. **Give the first writing prompt.**

    Giving one prompt at a time prevents students from skipping those they don't immediately have a response to. Since this is just play, giving one prompt at a time is like giving children one toy at a time so they can try it out before turning their attention to something shinier.

3. **When students seem ready, or after a reasonable amount of time has passed, give the next prompt—but tell students they have the option of continuing what they're already writing.**

    Students who struggled with the first prompt or who just feel done might gladly move on, but others, engrossed in what they're working on, might glance up at the next prompt to decide

One Time I Story

Tell a story that relates to ____. Begin with the words *One time I.*

Multisensory Labels

Draw ____, or some part of ____, in detail. Label specific objects, sounds, smells, tastes, and textures in your picture.

Genuine Questions

List your genuine questions—things you genuinely wonder but don't or can't know the answer to when it comes to ____.

"Who . . . ?"   "What kind of . . . ?"
"Where . . . ?"   "How much . . . ?"
"Why . . . ?"   "How did . . . ?"
"When . . . ?"   "Why did . . . ?"
"What is (are) . . . ?" "How will . . . ?"
                       "When will . . . ?"
                       "What if . . . ?"
                       "Would I . . . ?"
                       "Should I . . . ?"
                       "Could I . . . ?"

Montage

Draw assorted images that come to mind when you think about ____.

Lessons

- What can ____ teach you how to do?
- What can ____ teach you about the people in your life?
- What can ____ teach you about how the world works?
- What can ____ teach you about yourself?

Possibilities

Imagine several possible answers to one (or more) of the genuine questions you just wrote about ____. Begin each sentence with *Maybe.*

Fantasies

Imagine several magical answers to one (or more) of the genuine questions you just wrote about ____. Begin each sentence with *Maybe.*

Weird *Ifs*

- If ____ were a meal, what would be on the plate?
- If ____ were music, what instrument would play it?
- If ____ were mathematics, what would the equation be?
- If ____ were an outfit, what would it look like?
- If ____ were a dance move, what would it involve?

Wins and Losses

- How does ____ win?
- How does ____ lose?
- When is there a tie?

Texting

You're texting back and forth with ____. Write the conversation. It can be a group text.

Family Tree

Draw a family tree for ____. Include parents, siblings, grandparents, spouses, children, grandchildren, aunts, uncles, cousins—the whole family.

Superhero

Create a superhero (or supervillain) based on ____. Include this hero or villain's powers, costume, alter ego, nemesis, and origin story.

Perspective Shift

Redo any of the prompts, but this time, write from the perspective of ____, and make yourself the topic that ____ writes about.

Schedule

Make a schedule for a day in the life of ____.

More Weird *Ifs*

- If ____ were weather, what would it be?
- If ____ were art, what materials and colors would it use?
- If ____ were an app, what would it do?
- If ____ were a place, what would the map of it look like?

Pairings

Make a list of things you could pair with ____.

Figure 6.2: Sandbox prompts.

Visit go.SolutionTree.com/instruction for a free reproducible version of this figure.

whether they want to get to it or stick with what they're doing. Still others will just ignore you and stick with the first prompt. All these outcomes are good. Just like children in a sandbox, when they get a new toy, they might immediately start playing with it, or they might finish what they're doing and then play with it, or they might not even notice the new toy because they're so busy. The point isn't to play with all the toys; it's to play.

4. **Continue this process of having students write for a while, giving the next prompt, and having students individually decide whether they want to continue with their writing or try the next prompt.**

   Consider giving your students a break midway through the list of prompts so they can stretch, get water, and potentially talk to each other about what they've written so far. Don't be surprised if some students continue to write when you offer a break.

5. **After students have generated all their sandbox writing, they read through everything and look for running themes or interesting ideas worth pursuing using the prompt, "What does _____ mean to me?" (Students fill in the blank with the topic they have been playing with.)**

   This last prompt helps students consolidate their thinking. Since they might have trouble seeing larger patterns in their own thoughts, you could have your students exchange their writing with a classmate, read through the classmate's responses, and respond to the question, "What does ___ mean to this person?" They fill in the blank with their partner's topic and respond right on their partner's paper. They might notice themes or ideas that their partners didn't see in their own work. Allowing their peers to read and interpret their writing makes them vulnerable, so do this step only if, in your judgment, your class has established the necessary trust.

Boosting the Impact

While students write, you can walk around the room to answer any questions. If students get stuck, sometimes the best way to help is to *resist* the urge to ask more targeted questions and pull their writing out of them, because although that helps them generate material in the moment, in the long term, it teaches them that they can't find their ideas on their own. Let them sit with the discomfort of not knowing what to say. Remind them that these questions are meant to help them generate ideas. If they don't know what to say, they can start with *I don't know*. If they think the prompt is stupid, they can make up a smarter one. Sandbox Mode's purpose isn't for students to give the right response, or even to respond to every prompt, but to play, and in the process, to discover and deepen their thinking about their topic.

Writing about a particular topic will lead some students to discover that they're not actually interested in that topic and don't have much to say about it. If that happens, encourage these students to explore other potential topics.

Some students will simply give up and stop writing. You can encourage them to *un-give up*, and you can also let them choose to give up, and in a later conversation, ask about how that choice worked out for them. When they got stuck, what did they try? How did that work out? If they gave up and wrote nothing, what did that choice cost them? How satisfied are they with the outcome of their sandbox experience? Next time they visit the sandbox, what might they try instead?

After Sandbox Mode, consider sharing all that day's prompts so your students can return to ones they missed if they so choose. Most students won't return to the sandbox, if only because they have other assignments and commitments beyond school. Even though this has been playful work, it's still *work*, and returning to the prompts might feel like extra work. Occasionally, though, a student who worked slowly, or who spent a lot of time on one prompt, will want to spend more time writing.

Using the Protocol Next Time

If you use the Sandbox Mode protocol more than once, try reusing some prompts and also introducing a few new ones each time. Like a child knowing exactly what to do with the same old pail and shovel in the sandbox, students will get better at responding to repeated prompts. Novelty is exciting, like when new kids come to the sandbox with their toys. Responding to new prompts expands students' repertoires and helps them build the willingness to try new things and experience discomfort. If you give five prompts, use two or three that students have seen before and two or three new ones.

You can make Sandbox Mode a regular part of producing work for your class. Eventually, instead of choosing which prompts to give your students, you can create a handout, poster, or slideshow with all the prompts you've used in the past and have students decide for themselves which ones to respond to. You can also invite students to make up their own sandbox prompts to share with their classmates.

 Exemplar Study

Students analyze multiple examples of the type of work product they're about to create, looking for evidence of how the work reflects the values of the person who created it.

Suggested Time:

Anytime you ask your students to create work product, they benefit from seeing a similar piece of work so they can understand and meet expectations. Let's imagine this assignment in a chemistry class: "Choose a chemical compound found in common household products. Create a consumer guide to this compound that includes its chemical structure and properties, products in which consumers might find it, potential benefits and hazards of its use, and alternative products."

Chemistry students might understand why chemical compounds can help and harm people, but that doesn't necessarily mean they'll be able to visualize what a consumer guide to a chemical compound could look like, and why a person would want to read it. For example, how much information will readers find useful? How will the layout draw the reader's attention to the most important points? Would visuals engage or distract readers? The teacher might know the answers to these questions but always has the option of just telling students what their guides should look like—but that would take away their opportunity to discover the elements of good work for themselves, or to imagine creative approaches beyond their teacher's instructions. Rather than telling students exactly what to do, we can give them exemplars—excellent work of the type we ask them to create—so they can see for themselves what's required and what's possible.

Some students can look at a few exemplars and immediately understand how they were made. Looking at several portraits, some art students would extrapolate that the artist's choices regarding color, light, and brushstrokes communicate the subject's feelings and desires, and the artist's as well. They'd further see that in making their own portraits, they get to choose stylistic elements to convey their subjects and selves. Other students wouldn't be able to do this, though. They'd look at the portraits, find a style they like, and copy it. Or they'd look at the portraits, find elements of each that seem easiest to replicate, and go with those. Still others would look at the portraits and say, "So, wait, is a portrait literally just a face?" We might imagine their portraits appearing lifeless and lacking key details.

In Exemplar Study, students look at work of the type that they're being asked to do. This way, they can understand not only what's required and what's possible, but also how these works express their creators' values and how their own work might express their values.

The more varied the exemplars you present, the more options you will make students aware of. If all the consumer guides the chemistry teacher presents are trifold pamphlets, his students will assume they have to make their consumer guides into trifold pamphlets—and if that is indeed the goal, then showing them several trifold pamphlets indicates that this is a requirement, not a choice. However, if they see a trifold pamphlet, a poster, and a video, they'll know they have these options too. Different exemplars will show students the range of topics, audiences, styles, media, and materials they can choose from, as well as aspects where they *don't* have a choice.

Getting Ready

Do the following in preparation for the protocol.

❑ Make enough copies of the looking at exemplars chart (figure 6.3, page 148, or create your own version) for each student.

If you make your own version of the chart, you could substitute *person who created this* with *author, scientist, designer, artist, activist,* or whatever is appropriate. Similarly, substitute *work*

	Work 1	Work 2	Work 3	Work 4
What seems important to the person who created this work?				
What does the creator want the audience to know or do?				
What's something the creator chose to do in this work?				
What's interesting or effective about that choice?				
What's not so effective about that choice?				

Figure 6.3: Looking at exemplars chart.

*Visit **go.SolutionTree.com/instruction** for a free reproducible version of this figure.*

with *article*, *data chart*, *mural*, or whatever the students are making. They'll use these charts to organize their notes about the exemplars.

❑ Collect at least three examples of excellent work of the type you're asking your students to create.

You can include work by diverse practitioners in the field, former students (if you gain their permission), and yourself. If you put out only three exemplars, students just leave a column blank in their charts; if you put out more than four, the students choose which ones they write about in their charts.

Leading the Protocol

The following four steps will help you most effectively lead the protocol.

1. **Place several excellent pieces of work, of the same type that the students are creating, around the room.**

   If the exemplars don't have titles, make sure your students have some way to distinguish and refer to each one. You could do this simply by numbering the exemplars.

2. **Students walk around the room, filling out their looking at exemplars charts (figure 6.3) to track how the works reflect what matters to the people who created them.**

   The chart's first two questions ask about values and goals: (1) What seems important to the person who created this work? and (2) What does the person who created this work want the audience to know or do? In articulating these values and goals, the students make *caring about something* an implicit reason for creating work. The students can create work when *they* care about something—and not only because they have a school assignment.

   The last three questions ask about choices: What's something the creator chose to do in this work? What's interesting or effective about that choice? and What's not so effective about that choice? Often when students look at multiple exemplars, they'll start to compare and contrast them. You'll hear them say things like, "This one's way better," or "I like how this one has pictures, but the other one had more information." Although students can express preferences, encourage them to focus on the values that guided decisions about how to make each one. For example, a student might prefer a pamphlet with more information, but why would someone include less? What does that person want us (the audience) to do? How would including less information achieve that goal? The point isn't to convince students which work is better or even which goal is better; it's to help them connect choices to goals and goals to values.

3. **To help students notice requirements and possibilities of this sort of work, ask, "What are the features of this type of work? What did the people who created these works do that you want to try too? What, if anything, did you see that you don't want to do?" Pause a few minutes between questions so students can respond, either in writing or in a discussion.**

   Although many students will have already started to think about features they do and don't want to borrow from the exemplars, this step helps them organize that thinking. Some students will be inspired by a topic. For example, if they watched several spoken-word performances that happen to include Daniel Beaty's "Knock Knock" (2013) and Hieu Minh Nguyen's "Traffic Jam" (Button Poetry, 2014), both of which are about the poets' relationships with their fathers, a student might also want to write about his father. More often, students will be inspired by a stylistic choice—*how* the person constructed the work, which reflects that person's values.

   Sometimes, if students find an exemplar especially compelling, they'll want to change *their* topic to *its* topic. Instead of simply saying *yes* because you want to encourage this newfound passion, or *no* because you want to encourage your students to stay committed to the topic they already chose, try asking questions to help the student assess why they might keep their original topic or switch to the new one.

- "How did you choose your original topic?"
- "Why is that original topic important to you?"
- "What do you want your audience to know about or do when it comes to that topic?"
- "How about this new one—what about this topic is important to you?"
- "What do you want your audience to know about or do when it comes to this new topic?"

Although it's much faster to give or deny permission (and sometimes that's all you have time for), these questions provide a great opportunity to help students explore how their schoolwork can reflect their values.

4. **Based on their discoveries, students choose a next step for their work.**

Students often do this step spontaneously. As their classmates are still analyzing the exemplars, a few students will come ask you if they can start their work. This is a great opportunity for quick one-on-one conversations about what the students are working on, what they want to do next, and what values guide those choices.

Boosting the Impact

By analyzing the exemplars—not just for their features but for the values that guided the people who made them—students start to see how they can bring their values to their work, too. You still might see students doing whatever seems easiest or most appealing, but even if that's what they choose, it's their choice.

Once your students get to work, try to check in with them all. Often the most vocal students need you the least; they talk because they're charged up about their work (in which case you can get excited with them and then gently redirect them back to *doing* the work they're so excited about). Or they ask you a million questions because they want your permission and validation (in which case you can validate their interest and remind them that they have the power and responsibility to make their own decisions).

The ones who don't approach you might be quietly at work on something they value, in which case you can look over their shoulder, maybe ask about what they're doing, and then leave them alone. But students who don't seek your help might be the very ones who need it. While your class busily works on projects, you have time for one-on-one conversations with students who either don't know what to do next or are avoiding their values because they want to do whatever will be easiest, fastest, or least risky. Try asking them versions of the questions they saw on the Looking at Exemplars chart, but about their work: "What do you want *your* audience to know about your topic? What do you want *your* audience to do? What's important to *you*, and how will you express that through this work?"

Because you care about your students, you might feel pulled to save them from themselves, either by telling them what to do or by pointing out their avoidance moves. You always have these options available to you, especially if your student is working on a high-stakes assignment like a college admissions essay, or if your student lacks the skills and experience to make a meaningful decision. But another option is to let your students make their own decisions, experience the natural consequences, and reflect on what they want to try next time.

Using the Protocol Next Time

Since studying exemplars is so fundamental to learning, you can have your students follow this protocol anytime they create new work. Even if they do the same kind of work over and over (such as in an English class where they write essay after essay), looking at multiple exemplars each time helps them better understand what their work can look like. By repeatedly analyzing how work reflects the values of the person who created it, the students also better understand how they can bring their values to their work. Even if some students keep choosing what's easy or fun in the moment, they're still getting the message, for every assignment, that people can and do make their work matter. They can too.

 ## Group Commitments

Students commit to acting in accordance with their values when working in a group.

Suggested Time:

Sometimes our students create work products in groups. Benefiting from multiple perspectives, groups can come up with ideas that no one person would have thought of. Members can divide burdensome tasks and contribute according to their strengths. Working in groups, students can learn to listen to each other, honor all voices, build consensus, and resolve disagreements respectfully—all while strengthening relationships, having fun, and making something that becomes a source of pride for all.

Despite these benefits, group work doesn't always go so well. Groups have trouble making decisions when no one is willing to compromise, and conflict-averse groups make decisions no one actually wants. Anxious group members take over out of fear that others won't do a good enough job, those with low motivation slack off, and those with low skills back off. Those who don't know how to assert themselves feel frustrated. Those used to getting their own way retreat. Friends distract one another and leave out group members who aren't their friends. The group produces work that's worse than what any member would have produced alone, and no one wants to work together again. No wonder some students come to dread group work.

Knowing all of this, some teachers avoid assigning group projects. Others attempt to engineer their way around these unhelpful behaviors. They carefully decide whom to put together and whom to keep apart—only to be frustrated when the groups still don't collaborate well. Or they jigsaw the project so that each student has responsibility for a self-contained piece: one of three subtopics in a speech, two of eight paragraphs in an essay, ten of fifty trading cards in a deck. Splitting up a project minimizes potential for conflict, keeps students from doing too much or too little work, and clarifies who should get what grade. But it *also* lowers the stake students have in each other's success. Individuals can make their own decisions without having to listen deeply, challenge their own thinking, explain their ideas more clearly, or think creatively about how to integrate multiple perspectives.

This protocol, Group Commitments, empowers students to notice for themselves how people tend to behave in groups, and then choose how *they* want to behave. Use it on the first day of a group project. Instead of hearing the rules from you (or telling you rules they've heard a million times), they derive behavioral guidelines from their own values and then commit to those behaviors—not because a teacher told them to, and not because they're trying to behave politely or get a good grade, but because these behaviors are important parts of who they want to be.

Getting Ready

Do the following in preparation for the protocol.

❑ Make groups for an upcoming project.

Some teachers allow students to form their own groups, and others assign students to groups themselves. Any group requires trust, so students usually prefer to choose group members they already feel comfortable with. However, asking students to organize themselves into groups could put those who are less outgoing or confident at a disadvantage, and students might choose to work with friends they already know instead of with peers who will challenge them and whose strengths will complement their own. To provide some choice while also ensuring diverse and effective groups, you can give out slips of paper and have students write the names of classmates they'd most want to work with. Tell them from the outset that you're not bound by their requests and that your goal is to place all students with classmates whose perspectives they'll benefit from hearing.

❑ Make enough copies of the group commitments flowchart (figure 6.4) and the group membership rubric (figure 6.5, page 154) for each student.

Group Commitments uses a flowchart to help students derive values-consistent actions they can take in their groups. After they fill out the flowchart, they choose three behaviors they want to commit to and create rubrics for themselves with these three behaviors. Each day throughout the project, they can use the rubric to evaluate their own behaviors and recommit to their values.

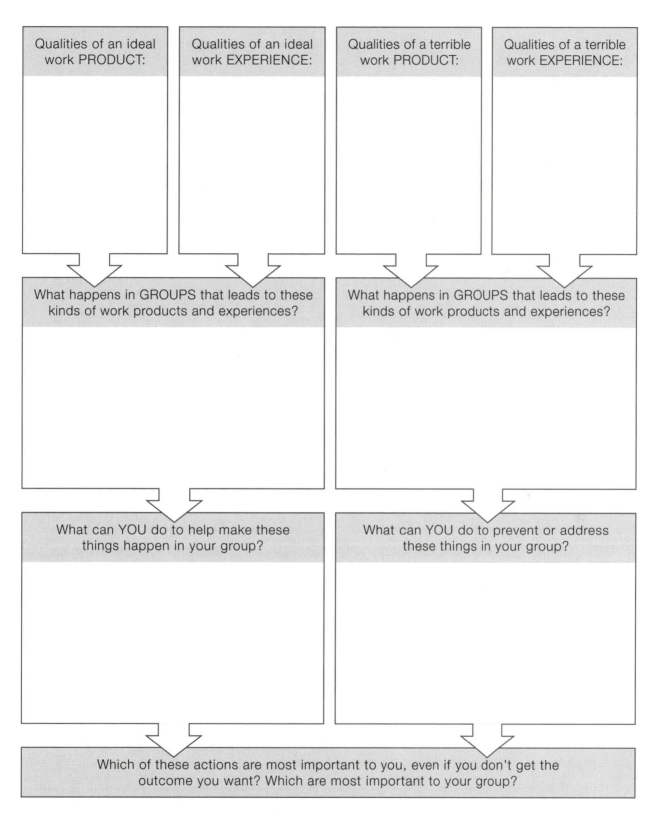

Figure 6.4: Group commitments flowchart.

*Visit **go.SolutionTree.com/instruction** for a free reproducible version of this figure.*

You chose three actions to help maximize the benefits and minimize the drawbacks of group work. List them below, underneath where it says Actions. For each, check a box to indicate how you think your group members would rate your behavior today.

Actions	Basic	Effective	Exemplary
1.			
2.			
3.			

Figure 6.5: Group membership rubric.

*Visit **go.SolutionTree.com/instruction** for a free reproducible version of this figure.*

Leading the Protocol

The following seven steps will help you most effectively lead the protocol.

1. **Ask your students to recall times when they did work that went well, and times when they did work that went poorly.**

    Have students close their eyes if that helps them remember and take themselves back to work they think went especially well or especially poorly. The work doesn't have to be schoolwork. It could be artistic work, like a clay sculpture or a cello recital. It could be athletic work, like the time they ran their first mile or scored a game-tying run. It could be when they built a block tower in preK or recreated a hairstyle they saw online. It could involve gardening or engineering or fundraising or pet care or activism—any memorable work, as long as it went especially well or poorly. Have students spend a few minutes just listing good and bad work they did.

    Emphasize that they, the students, get to judge whether work went well or poorly. If they knit a hat nobody liked but they loved, they might still judge their work product as positive, and if they sang a solo for which they received a standing ovation but they didn't like how they sounded, they might judge the experience as negative.

2. **Hand out copies of the group commitments flowchart (figure 6.4, page 153). Students fill out the top row.**

    Based on their own experiences and values, what would they say are the qualities of ideal work products and experiences? Maybe an ideal cake uses a creative recipe that no one thought of before, or maybe a cake is ideal when it comes out exactly the way it did in the recipe video.

The flowchart differentiates between qualities of an ideal work *product* and qualities of an ideal work *experience*. Don't worry about whether students correctly make this distinction. For example, they might say that the ideal work product is fun to make. You might quibble that *fun to make* is a quality of the work experience, not the product, and you'd be right. For this exercise, though, it doesn't matter whether students call something a quality of the product or of the experience. The flowchart makes the distinction so that students will consider qualities of products and experiences, rather than only one or the other.

Some students might say the qualities of terrible products or experiences are just the opposites of the qualities of good ones. Encourage them to think about how else work might go poorly. Again, the point isn't so much what they say; it is for them to become aware of the values they bring to their work.

3. **Students fill out the second row: What happens in groups that leads to work products and experiences with these qualities?**

Some students might say that when they were thinking about ideal and terrible work, they thought of work they did alone. That may very well be, but when they look at the qualities themselves, which they have now identified as *ideal* and *terrible*, what do they think can happen in a group to make those qualities more likely? For example, let's say Catrice writes that ideal work is creative. Even if Catrice made her most creative work products alone, what happens in groups that leads to creative work? Or let's say Raviv writes that work experiences are terrible when they take a long time. Even if the groups he's worked in have quickly finished their tasks, what happens in groups that makes a task drag out?

Thinking about group experiences can make students want to tell stories about their triumphs and ordeals. Instead of having them share these stories, ask them to just notice any emotions that come up and continue silently filling out their charts.

4. **Students fill out the third row: What can they do to promote helpful group dynamics, and either prevent or address unhelpful ones?**

Here, students distinguish between what groups do and what they as individuals have the power to do to impact the group.

Maybe Catrice writes that when groups share many different ideas, that leads to a creative work product. What things can she do to help her group share many different ideas? Maybe she can share her own ideas, or notice moments when her group quickly comes to a decision after hearing only one or two ideas and encourage the group to brainstorm more.

Or maybe Raviv writes that groups can have arguments and get off topic, and that can make the work process take longer. Although he can't control what other people do, what can he do to help his group stay on topic? Maybe he can listen for times when the conversation strays and compassionately direct his peers back toward their purpose. What can he do to prevent destructive and time-consuming arguments in his group? Maybe he can model asking questions, making concessions, and validating other people's points. He might not be able to prevent or solve every problem, but he can contribute to a more productive and efficient dynamic—because he values productivity and efficiency. Even if his group continues to fight and waste time, and even if he's not satisfied with that particular experience or its outcome, he can still feel satisfied with his own choices. He can also learn something about who he wants to be and what matters to him in groups. Sometimes that's the best we can do.

5. **Tell your students their groups for an upcoming project.**

   Your students should move into their groups once you've announced them.

6. **Once groups have come together, students take turns sharing behaviors they listed in the third row of their flowcharts. While sharing, they identify and mark behaviors they think are most important. They also ask which behaviors their group members find most important, and they mark those too.**

   Some students might say everything on their list is important, and at this point, that's fine. The goal is for group members who will soon be working together to talk about their values.

7. **Give out blank copies of the group membership rubric (figure 6.5, page 154). From the behaviors students marked during the last step—the ones they themselves think are important, and the ones their group members think are important—they choose three behaviors they will commit to throughout the project. They write these three behaviors in the Actions column of their group membership rubrics.**

   Students might choose behaviors because they matter to them personally or because they matter to their group. Either way, encourage your students to choose behaviors they might find challenging. Let's say Catrice thinks it's important to contribute many ideas to her group, but she already does that. She also thinks it's important to encourage her group members to spend more time generating ideas when they come to a decision too quickly, but that behavior comes less readily to her. That more challenging behavior would be something she could put on her rubric.

Boosting the Impact

Once they've filled out the Actions column, have students hand in their rubrics so you can photocopy them all. That way, students each have a copy for each day they're working on the project. Save the master copies just in case the project goes on longer than you expect. Better yet, create an electronic rubric template that students can fill out and copy for themselves.

To end each class period during the project, your students can take one minute to fill out their rubrics. Over time, they can track their progress as group members. How are they growing with respect to each behavior? To be a more effective group member, what can they do more, the same, and less? What can they learn from each of their group members—about their group's topic, about the work process, or about being in a group? Asking students questions like these—whether individually or in a whole-class discussion—helps them assess how well their past behaviors have served their values and choose behaviors that will better serve their values in the future.

They can also track their own levels of commitment. If they struggled some days, did they then give up, or were they able to recommit the next day? How do they feel about themselves as a result of committing, and recommitting, to their values? Such questions remind students that even if they break their commitments, they always have the power to turn back toward their values.

Using the Protocol Next Time

After using this protocol once to help students identify behaviors that lead to optimal group experiences, you don't need to go through the protocol for every group project. Instead, have students take out their original flowcharts and re-evaluate which behaviors they think are most important—to themselves at this point in time, and to their new groups. When they choose which behaviors to put on their rubrics the second or third time around, you can reference previous projects in your class by asking, "What was challenging for you last time that you want to work on this time around?" Often if something really matters to us, we want to keep working on it, so encourage students to choose some or all of the same behaviors if they still feel important. Students can also feel free to choose new commitments. Either way, each group project becomes a new opportunity for students to consider the values they want to bring to their learning, their work, and their relationships.

If you regularly give group projects, consider repeating the entire protocol every so often. As students make more work products and have more work experiences, their definitions of *ideal work* might change, and they'll better understand how groups operate. Redoing the full protocol helps students see how their values and skills have developed.

Onward

Creating academic work product helps students develop and demonstrate fluency with content and skills, and with the creative process itself. This chapter's protocols empower students to make their schoolwork about more than just completing assignments; it's about becoming the people they want to be.

In the next chapter, we'll see how to help students refine their work product, not only because a teacher told them to or it helps them get a better grade but also because that work reflects their values.

Chapter 7

• • • • •

PROTOCOLS TO REFINE WORK PRODUCT

Students rarely find refining work product—studying it, evaluating it, and deciding what to add, cut, replace, rearrange, and keep—as fun as making it. Let's imagine students writing historical fiction set during the Industrial Age. The fun part, if there is one, is creating the story: inventing a character, imagining the character's voice, making up a conflict that's both personal for that character and related to the Industrial Age. Some students might find all of that fascinating and enjoy the process of writing their stories. Others, less excited about writing historical fiction, only feel satisfied when they finish and sigh with relief that they've gotten another assignment out of the way.

But they're *not* finished yet! They still have to, for example, add more historical detail, explain why the character was afraid to open the letter she received in the first paragraph, check their bibliographies, check their commas, and give the story a title. Revision is dreadful for a student who didn't feel excited about the work in the first place and felt relief on finishing, and even students who did enjoy the creative process feel a whole lot less excited about revision. We might frog-march them through it, handing out checklists and meeting with individual students, and then *we* get frustrated when they revise minimally.

The term *adaptive peak* describes situations when doing something that feels good reduces our motivation to do other things that would serve our values (Villatte et al., 2016). If you take the croutons off your salad at lunch, you might tell yourself it's OK that you didn't exercise. Or if you recycle the container your salad came in, you might feel good enough about that action and not do the harder but potentially more satisfying work of starting a compost pile for your uneaten lettuce, or joining a group that works for environmental justice. Each of these is an adaptive peak: an "approach toward a positively reinforcing consequence which leaves us stuck, away from more meaningful goals" (Villatte et al., 2016, p. 51).

Finishing a first iteration can leave some students stranded on an adaptive peak. They feel happy enough with what they created, and that happy feeling keeps them from doing more work that would lead to a more satisfying outcome. That outcome might feel distant and not worth the additional work. This chapter's protocols make the revision process slightly less daunting by organizing it into defined tasks, or by helping students define those tasks for themselves. The protocols also dignify revision—the rougher climb to a higher peak—by helping students associate the peak itself and the act of climbing it with their values.

- Rubric Response helps students discover values they can bring to the revision process.

- Strategy Selection empowers students to draw on revision strategies they've learned in the past and to choose a strategy based on what matters to them, as opposed to whatever feels easy or familiar.

- During Nonjudgmental Peer Review, students share their experiences of each other's work to help each other make values-conscious decisions for how to refine the work.

- Considerate Editing reframes the final and often most painful stage of a project as showing kindness toward others.

- Testing for Doneness helps students decide whether they've truly finished their work, based on their values.

 Rubric Response

Students analyze their assignment's rubric and make values-conscious plans for how they'll continue to work.

Suggested Time:

While an assignment describes the task, and exemplars show what excellent outcomes look like, a rubric outlines elements of excellent work. If you evaluate students' work, then it seems only fair that you tell them what criteria you'll use. But these criteria shouldn't come as a surprise; by the time students get a rubric, they should have already seen multiple exemplars so they understand what success means and learned the skills they'll need to meet all criteria for success. After a student hands in the finished work, the teacher fills out the rubric and explains what the student did that worked well, what was less effective, and what the student can work on next time.

Analytic rubrics (Nitko & Brookhart, 2007) are usually charts, with the columns representing performance levels (such as a number of points) and the rows representing performance criteria for the assignment. In the boxes, the teacher describes each performance level for each criterion. Some teachers like how analytic rubrics provide detailed breakdowns of what it means to do well and poorly. In practice, though, it's hard to anticipate and categorize the many ways students might stumble or excel, and defining excellence too narrowly risks limiting students' creativity. Also, while analytic rubrics help teachers justify grades given *after* students finish their work, the differences between levels can be too subtle and subjective to help students revise *before* turning their work in.

Instead of trying to anticipate and categorize everything a student could do, your rubric could only describe what it would look like to do well. This is called a *single-point rubric* (Fluckiger, 2010) because it describes one point the students could reach: proficiency. All the rubric examples in this book are single-point rubrics. The rubric in figure 7.1 is for a tenth-grade history assignment for which students interview people about their Cold War memories and then write articles comparing life during the Cold War to life now. By the time students receive it, they presumably will have learned about the Cold War era, as well as how to interview someone, write and organize an article, and incorporate quotations. Rubrics describe outcomes; they don't teach students how to get there.

Assignment: Interview someone who experienced the Cold War, and write an article comparing and contrasting life during the Cold War to life now.			
Elements	**Basic**	**Effective**	**Exemplary**
Specific **images** help the reader visualize the subject's life during the Cold War.			
Thoughtful **explanations** help the reader understand key similarities and differences between the Cold War era and today.			
Properly attributed **quotations** from the interview show the subject's thoughts, feelings, and experiences.			
The article is thoughtfully **organized**. Topics are in an order that makes sense, and textual features (such as subheadings, numbers, or bullets) help the reader move from one topic to the next.			
The article is **easy to read**. It has clear sentences, a title, properly cited sources, and no errors in capitalization, punctuation, spelling, or grammar.			

Figure 7.1: Cold War interview rubric.

Some students might have a heavy feeling as they read a list of expectations they'll have to meet. They might feel frustrated: *I can't do all of this.* They might feel apathetic: *I don't want to do all of this.* They might feel exhausted: *I've already done all of this.* A rubric helps students imagine and achieve success—according to *our* values. The Rubric Response protocol helps them choose what success will mean to *them.*

Rubric Response begins with students anticipating what will appear on the rubric. Then, when they receive the rubric, they imagine it from four perspectives: (1) their curious selves, (2) their grateful selves, (3) their responsible selves, and (4) their kind selves. Instead of asking students to be curious, grateful, responsible, or kind, the protocol invites them to embody capacities they already have (such as the capacity for gratitude), and to see how it feels to approach the assignment that way. After imagining how each version of themselves would approach the task, they choose a next step. They might still feel frustrated, apathetic, or exhausted, and they still don't get to choose the assignment or your expectations. But they *always* get to choose how they approach their work—curiously, gratefully, responsibly, kindly, or in accordance with other values they choose.

Make sure you pace this protocol so you leave class time for your students to do some revision work immediately after finishing it. Even if they only have time to take a small step toward further work they'll do at home or during the next class, getting that momentum will make it much easier for them to continue working in the direction of their values.

Getting Ready

Do the following in preparation for the protocol.

❑ Create a rubric for a project that students are working on, and make enough copies of the rubric for each student.

We strongly recommend using a single-point rubric, but this protocol will still work if you use an analytic rubric.

Leading the Protocol

The following seven steps will help you most effectively lead the protocol.

1. **Tell your students their assignment, but before giving out the rubric, ask students to make a list of performance expectations they anticipate seeing on it.**

   Encourage them to review their resources, such as exemplars and notes from throughout the unit. For this type of work product, what does success mean? What skills have the students learned that they'll need to do this work successfully? Also ask them to consider their past experiences with similar assignments. Even if they've never, say, written an article before, they have done other writing assignments. What were the expectations then? Which ones apply now?

2. **Give out the rubric. Ask students which elements they expected and which surprised them.**

   Some students will want to have accurately predicted what is on the rubric. The point is not to have read their teacher's mind but rather to have noticed what they've learned so far, in and beyond this class, about the content and skills they'll need to access when they do this work.

   You can also ask students what they think should be on the rubric that isn't. This gives your students a chance to articulate elements they value. Let's imagine an assignment to make an interactive poster about home energy use. One student thinks the poster should have a fun game someone can play to learn about energy consumption, and another thinks the poster should be made from energy-efficient materials. Even if these criteria aren't on the rubric, they reflect these students' values. Their teacher might say back these values: "It sounds like playfulness is really important to you," and "I'm hearing you say that sustainability matters. Does anyone else think so?" When you ask your students to share elements they think the rubric should include, you help them and their classmates see new ways they can incorporate their values into their work.

3. **Students imagine their most curious selves, who ask lots of questions and are fascinated by everything. They write what their curious selves would say about the rubric.**

What does the rubric make their curious selves wonder about? What questions do they have— about the project's design, its topic, the work process, the potential audience, or any other aspect? What's new or different about this task? What does it ask them to explore—in the world, in their memories, or in their imaginations?

You can help your students take the perspective of their most curious selves by inviting them to close their eyes and imagine a time when they were especially curious. Where were they? How old were they? How did they feel in their bodies? What did they say and do? Rather than asking them to be curious about expectations they didn't design, you take them back to a time when they were genuinely curious and ask them to bring this curious self to your classroom.

4. **Students imagine their most grateful selves, who see everything in life as a golden opportunity. They write what their grateful selves would say about the rubric.**

Students might groan at the idea of being grateful for someone else's expectations—and the work they entail. You can acknowledge this and even mention expectations you find difficult to meet. You might not enjoy the work of meeting these high expectations, but how are you grateful for them? Sharing a quick story of gratitude for someone's expectations of you might help your students understand the concept. Imagining their grateful selves helps them see this project as an opportunity rather than a burden. They might notice, for example, that they'll learn important skills from refining their work, or that the work will improve in ways that matter to them.

5. **Students imagine their most responsible selves, who manage time wisely and do what needs to be done. They write what their responsible selves would say about the rubric.**

Imagining their responsible selves helps students notice that meeting expectations will take planning and follow-through. Which details need their attention? Why is that attention worthwhile? Seeing the rubric this way reminds students that they're capable of noticing and doing seemingly small and tedious parts of the job, because ultimately those parts will serve their values.

6. **Students imagine their kindest selves, who genuinely want to be warm, thoughtful, and helpful toward others. They write what their kindest selves would say about the rubric.**

Students might think about this in different ways depending on what they're making. If they're creating something that could help their community, like a neighborhood guide for Chinese speakers, they might consider how their work could make a bigger difference. If their projects aren't necessarily meant to *help* an audience but they still *have* an audience, students might consider how that audience will receive their work. If, for example, students need to make a speech a certain length or they must organize a poster a certain way, how can they read these requirements as opportunities to be kind to their audience?

Finally, they might consider how to be kind to their classmates during the work process. Which requirement on the rubric is a strength for them, and how can they offer their peers useful strategies or feedback for that requirement? Which requirement on the rubric is a weakness for them, and how can they meet that requirement without distracting their classmates or monopolizing the teacher?

7. **Now that they've considered the rubric from the perspectives of their curious, grateful, responsible, and kind selves, students choose a next step for their work.**

Most students will see curiosity, gratitude, responsibility, and kindness as positive and desirable qualities. That doesn't necessarily mean they'll be excited to take the next step in their work. They might feel overwhelmed by the many possibilities and tasks ahead. Ask them to take a moment to notice how they feel. Whether they feel excitement, dread, or something in between, why is the next step worthwhile? How does it build curiosity, gratitude, responsibility, kindness, or some other quality that matters to them? Such considerations help students connect the next step of their work to their values.

Boosting the Impact

By the end of the protocol, your students have identified a next step in their work process. As they do that next step, you can circulate and ask students questions about their choices.

- "What are you working on?"
- "Why do this today?"
- "What's important to you about this?"
- "What will this help you accomplish?"
- "If it doesn't work out, what else can you try?"
- "If it does work out, what happens next?"

In asking such questions, you'll give your students opportunities to describe how well their chosen actions serve their values. Of course you can offer your own suggestions, but when students observe for themselves how well their actions are working for them, and use their own words to describe these observations, they learn how to make decisions based on their own experiences rather than yours.

Using the Protocol Next Time

You can have students do the first two steps of this protocol—(1) anticipating what will appear on the rubric and (2) comparing their expectations to what's actually there—every time they have a new assignment. If they get an assignment that's at all similar to one they've had before, they'll grow more familiar with criteria for success.

You can ask the same perspective-taking questions each time, but you can also have your students explore other values. How would their *courageous* selves see this new rubric? Their *inventive* selves? Their *hopeful* selves? Imagining how these versions of themselves would see their rubrics helps them notice new possibilities for their work while also experimenting with different values they might want to embody.

 Strategy Selection

Students decide which revision strategies will best move them toward an outcome they value.

Suggested Time:

Revision isn't intuitive. Students need to learn strategies for figuring out what changes to make. In a seventh-grade English class, for example, students would need to learn strategies for adding more detail, cutting unnecessary sentences, organizing and reorganizing their paragraphs, and finding grammatical errors in order to fix them. Figure 7.2 has a list of revision strategies that this English class has learned to use while working on writing projects. It's here only as an example of strategies that one teacher has taught her students. A list of revision strategies suitable for your subject, students, and assignments would most likely look different.

- **Thirds (adapted from Moore, 2009):** Divide your draft into three roughly equal parts. Can you find a beginning somewhere near the dividing line between part 1 and part 2? Make that the new beginning, and cut everything that came before it. Can you find an ending somewhere near the dividing line between part 2 and part 3? Make that the new ending, and cut everything that came after it.

- **Color highlighting (adapted from Christensen, 2009):** Get two highlighters in different colors. Use the first to highlight in-the-world things and actions, and the second to highlight in-the-head thoughts or feelings. Do you have a balance between the two, or do you need more of one or the other? Is there an alternating pattern, or do you have clumps you need to break up?

- **Reverse outlining:** Write each paragraph's topic and purpose on a sticky note. Explain (out loud to a partner or in writing) why the paragraphs are in that order. Move your sticky notes into a different order, and now explain that order. Choose the order that makes the most sense, and move paragraphs in your draft if necessary to match that order.

Figure 7.2: Example revision strategy list.

continued ⇨

- **Noun circling:** Circle all the concrete nouns in your draft (or in part of your draft). Does the draft have a place where the nouns are very sparse? That part has no people, places, or things for your reader to visualize—no imagery. Add more.

- **17 things:** Make a list called "17 Things I Know About _____" (filling in the blank with the topic of your draft). When you make your list, write in complete sentences so you're stating complete facts or opinions. When you finish your list, choose a statement you can tell a story about, and add that story into your draft. Choose another statement you haven't thought about before, think about it, and add your thoughts into your draft. Choose a third statement that's about something particularly important to you, write about why you find it important, and add that text into your draft. If you can't finish your list of seventeen things you know about your topic, do more research.

- **Find the acorn:** Find your favorite sentence (or group of sentences) in your draft. Imagine that you've found the best acorn from the oak of your draft, and now you're growing a new tree. Copy and paste the sentence (or group of sentences) into a new document. Now create an entirely new piece of writing, with this as your opening.

- **80–20:** Find the word count of your draft. Calculate what 80 percent of that word count would be. Cut unnecessary words, sentences, or paragraphs from your draft until you reach a number close to the one you calculated, but don't aim for that exact number.

- **Simile build:** Find something you want your reader to notice and understand. List adjectives that describe it. Choose an adjective that names a quality you want your reader to notice and understand. List lots of other things that adjective describes. Pick something off this list that is totally different from and not an obvious comparison for the original thing you want your reader to notice and understand, and that creates the mood you're going for. Use it to create a simile that you incorporate into your draft.

- **Solo read-aloud:** Read your draft very slowly and out loud, listening to each sentence. Does it make sense? Does it sound like you? Can you find any mistakes?

- **Partner read-aloud:** Have a partner read your draft out loud to you. Does your partner ever stumble, seem confused, or read a sentence the wrong way? Consider changing those sentences.

Source: Adapted from Christensen, 2009; Moore, 2009.

The Strategy Selection protocol relies on three assumptions: (1) your students have already created their work product, but the work is still very much in progress; (2) you have allocated class time for your students to do the work and reach the expected level of quality; and (3) you've taught your students a variety of revision strategies they can use to make that class time productive. Once your students have built up a repertoire of revision strategies—because you've demonstrated new strategies, guided your students in practicing them together, and reviewed strategies they've learned elsewhere—they can learn to notice for themselves what they need to accomplish, take stock of their resources, and choose a strategy that serves their values in that context.

Getting Ready

Do the following in preparation for the protocol.

❑ Create a list of revision strategies your students have used before (like figure 7.2, pages 165–166). Post the list as a wall chart in the classroom, or make enough copies of the list for each student.

Alternatively, you can have your students brainstorm strategies they've used in the past—in your class, in their other subjects, and in previous years. Although this takes significantly longer, it helps your students recall and apply strategies they've learned beyond your class.

Leading the Protocol

The following six steps will help you most effectively lead the protocol.

1. **Give out a list of revision strategies your students have previously learned, and briefly review each one.**

    Your strategies will vary based on your students; they won't be the same as those in figure 7.2.

2. **Ask, "Which strategy sounds most appealing—something you most feel like doing right now? Mark it on your list."**

    If any students say none of the strategies seem appealing, just ask them to mark the one that seems the least unappealing.

3. **Ask, "Which strategy sounds most useful—something you think you need to do at this point in order to make your work better? Mark it on your list."**

    Asking about what's useful *after* asking about what's appealing honors students' preferences and helps them notice that what's meaningful isn't always what they'd prefer. If any students ask whether they can identify the strategy they marked as most appealing as most useful too, try asking them to name an activity they find appealing but not so useful (like playing video games), one they find useful but not so appealing (like doing laundry), and one they find both appealing and useful (like jogging on a beach). Coming up with such examples shows them that the same strategy can be both appealing and useful, but that it's not necessarily useful just because it appeals to them.

4. **Ask, "Which strategy sounds most different from what you usually do at this stage of your work process or when creating this type of work product? Mark it on your list."**

    Urging students to try something new can elicit their resistance or make them feel like their usual choices are wrong. Asking them to identify a strategy that differs from what they usually do gets them curious about new possibilities.

5. **Have students write, *Today I will _____ because _____*. They fill in the first blank with one of the three strategies they just marked; they fill in the second blank with why they chose that strategy.**

Examples follow.

- *Today I will reverse outline my essay because I want to make sure I put my points in an order that makes sense.*

- *Today I will use 80–20 because I think I might have too many slides and I don't want my presentation to be boring.*

- *Today I will rewatch the video about air resistance because I want to get more ideas for how to make my mousetrap car go faster.*

6. **Students take turns reading their resulting statements out loud to the class.**

Having your students read their statements out loud serves three purposes. First, they feel what it's like to make values-based commitments in front of their peers. Second, when students hear each other's reasoning, they might notice actions they want to take, too. For example, Connie might not realize her long presentation could be boring until she hears Greg's plan to cut 20 percent of his slides for that very reason. Third, when you hear your students' choices, you can coach them on using certain strategies effectively or help them notice that other strategies might serve them better. Maybe Greg's presentation seems long to him, but his teacher knows his work tends to be underdeveloped. The teacher now knows to check in with Greg about his strategy choice. What makes him think he has too many slides? If engaging his audience is important to him, he might consider how he can make his presentation more interactive, informative, or humorous.

Boosting the Impact

Even with this protocol, some students will pick whichever strategy seems easy, familiar, or fun. When they avoid the challenge of meaningful revision, you can ask questions one-on-one, while the rest of your class is busy revising. Let's say a student always chooses to reverse outline his essays, and his English teacher suspects he's just comfortable with that strategy and unwilling to try others. The teacher could say something like, "Tell me about how you decided to reverse outline today. Where have you struggled in the past? How will reverse outlining help?" If the student says he usually struggles with organization and that reverse outlining helps him see if his drafts make sense, then maybe he should continue to use the strategy. But if he says he just likes reverse outlining, or if he can't say why he's using the strategy, he might be avoiding choosing something that would work better.

Some students won't have any idea which strategy to pick, especially if they haven't practiced certain ones enough to know how or why they work. If some students ask you what they should do, or if they seem to be picking a strategy at random or copying their neighbor, you can ask them to look at feedback on past work so they can identify their growth areas. That way, if they're not ready to choose a strategy and you have to suggest one, you can connect it to something they say while reviewing their own feedback: "You mentioned that you're working on proofreading, so it sounds like you need a strategy for that. How about reading your draft out loud?"

Still others, after choosing a strategy, might ask you to approve every tiny decision they make, saying things like, "Is it OK if one of my paragraphs takes up half a page but the rest are only a few lines long?", "Is it OK if my thesis is in my last paragraph?", "Is it OK if I don't reverse outline?", and "Actually, I'm going to reverse outline—is that OK?" *Is it OK if* questions (and their cousins, *Will you take off points if* questions) signal that the student is focused on pleasing you and getting a good grade rather than developing an effective work process.

When students repeatedly seek your approval, you might feel tempted to tell them, "Yes, it's OK," just so they'll do their work and you can focus on students who actually need your help. But when possible, respond to approval-seeking students with your own questions that get them to make the decisions themselves: "How long are the paragraphs in the exemplar?" "How does each paragraph lead to your thesis?" "If you do reverse outline, how will it help you?" If they make a choice, something good will happen. Either they'll choose a strategy that effectively improves their work product, or they'll choose a strategy that doesn't improve their work product much, but then they'll learn what's not effective.

When a few minutes remain in the period, have your students copy this sentence starter: *Today I _____ because _____.* They fill in the first blank with whatever they actually did (as opposed to what they *said* they'd do) and complete the sentence by saying why they made that choice. Then, ask questions to help them reflect on how it went: "How did this help you as a learner? How did it improve your work? What will you try next time?" After assessing their choices, they often make better ones during future work periods.

Using the Protocol Next Time

You can use Strategy Selection at the beginning of every revision work period, for every project, adding more strategies to your master list as your students learn them. Like every other skill, noticing how their work could improve and choosing strategies that will lead to that improvement takes practice.

 # Nonjudgmental Peer Review

Students learn to offer their observations, questions, and interpretations instead of making suggestions; they also learn to use their peers' feedback to figure out how to revise their work.

Suggested Time:

Often, people equate *feedback* with *judgment*, whether it's praise ("This is good"), criticism ("This could be better"), or suggestions ("Add this," "Move this," "Take this away"). Praise, criticism, and suggestions can help students improve their work, but they also position reviewers as authorities. Some students, uncomfortable with that authority, will qualify their comments—"This is just my opinion" or "I hope this helps"—or they'll withhold their honest critical feedback. Everyone might feel happier this way, but the work won't get any better.

But even in situations where the reviewer gives genuine praise, compassionate criticism, and thoughtful suggestions, students then base any revisions on how much they please someone else. If the reviewer is pleased, students can assume they're finished. If the reviewer isn't pleased, they can remove displeasing elements and add more pleasing ones. If the reviewer gives a suggestion—something that would please the reviewer more—students can take or leave it, based on whether they think their work will be more pleasing to others as a result.

Sometimes our goal is to please others, in which case praise, criticism, and suggestions can really help us. When we (the authors) cook dinner for our children, we're extremely receptive to their praise ("I like the string beans"), criticism ("Kale—ugh"), and suggestions ("More garlic") because if our food pleases them, they'll eat it. When students make something for school, though, their goal is not necessarily or exclusively to please others. It's also to explore possibilities, test options, solve problems, and understand how their work impacts others beyond whether it pleases them.

Nonjudgmental Peer Review elicits a different kind of feedback. Based on English teacher Ted Nellen's (n.d.) I Heard, I Noticed, I Wondered approach, Nonjudgmental Peer Review asks reviewers to share their experiences of the work, rather than judgments they've made about it. From the reviewer's observations, students learn what stands out in their work and what reactions their work elicits. Students then get to decide whether that's the reaction they want, and if not, they can make changes. From the reviewer's questions, students learn how their work makes someone curious or confused; they can then add more detail and clarify their explanations. From the reviewer's interpretations, students learn what larger messages their work communicates and then get to decide how to amplify or change that message. A reviewer's observations, questions, and interpretations empower students to make decisions about their work based on the experience they want their work to create.

During the protocol, students trade cards (like those in figure 7.4, page 172) so they know what kind of feedback to give (observations, questions, or interpretations). When they trade these peer review direction cards, they don't have to get the same kind of card they give. For example, Orly could trade her observations card for Shaun's interpretations card, her questions card for Frank's interpretations card, and her interpretations card for Robyn's observations card. She's now traded away all three of her cards, which means she'll get all three kinds of feedback on her work. She's gotten cards from three different classmates, which means she'll give feedback to each of them (interpretations to Shaun and to Frank, and observations to Robyn). Figure 7.3 diagrams Orly's three trades, using O for observation, Q for question, and I for interpretation. During the protocol, each student ends up getting all three kinds of feedback but will not necessarily give all three kinds.

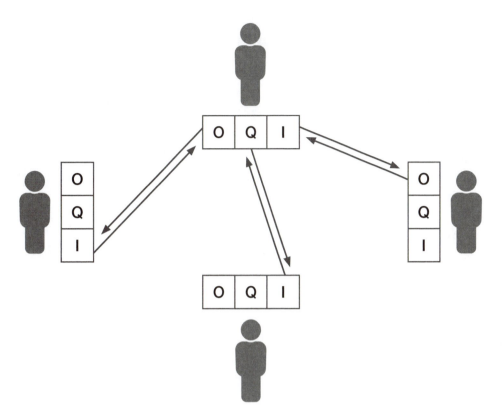

Figure 7.3: Example of students trading reaction, question, and interpretation cards.

Getting Ready

Do the following in preparation for the protocol.

☐ Decide how students will record their feedback (for example, on sheets of paper or sticky notes, or on the work itself). Obtain any necessary supplies.

☐ Make enough two-sided copies of the "Peer Review Direction Cards" reproducible (page 218–219) for each student. Cut up the cards.

The Peer Review Direction cards, shown in figure 7.4 (page 172), are designed to be two-sided. (You can accomplish this by making double-sided copies or by making single-sided copies and folding the cards down the middle line.) On the front of the resulting cards will be directions for reviewers to use during this protocol, written from the feedback receiver's perspective. The reviewers respond to the prompts—whether on a separate sheet of paper, on sticky notes, or on the work itself—and then return the card and any notes to the peer whose work they reviewed. After students receive the feedback, they use it to help them make decisions about their work. The thought clouds on the *back* of each card guide the students in using their peers' feedback.

Feedback Giver: Feedback Receiver:

Tell me your OBSERVATIONS.

What stands out to you? Point out specific details or moments that get your attention, and use just a word or two to show me what these parts make you think or feel (*cool*, *whoa*, *hmm*, *been there*, and so on).

Are the details that stood out the ones I think are most important? If not, what will I add or cut? Did I get the reactions I wanted? If not, what will I change?

Tell me your QUESTIONS.

What makes you curious or confused? Ask me lots of questions. Questions beginning with *What*, *Which*, or *What kind of* will help me most.

Based on the questions I got, what details can I add? Where can I be more specific? What can I explain more fully or clearly?

Tell me your INTERPRETATIONS.

What seems important to me? What does it seem like I'm trying to get you to think about or do? Help me see what's getting across in my work.

What matters to me? Is that what's getting across in my work? If not, what can I expand or clarify?

Figure 7.4: Peer review direction cards.

Leading the Protocol

The following six steps will help you most effectively lead the protocol.

1. **Lead a brief discussion about students' previous experiences with feedback.**

   Most likely, when you bring up the topic of feedback, students will mention experiences with praise, criticism, and suggestions. Use this opportunity to distinguish judgmental feedback—even if that judgment is positive—from the nonjudgmental feedback they'll offer each other today. Try asking questions like these.

   - "How does it feel to get criticism?"

   - "When is criticism helpful? When does it get it the way?"

   - "How does it feel to get praise?"

   - "Are there times when praise isn't actually helpful?"

   - "When are suggestions helpful?"

   - "Can a good suggestion ever be unhelpful?"

Students might notice that even helpful criticism can hurt, praise can feel hollow or fake, and even genuine praise can reduce motivation to further improve their work. They might also notice—or you can point out—that suggestions can keep people from coming up with their own ideas.

2. **Give out the two-sided cards you made from the "Peer Review Direction Cards" reproducible (page 218–219), along with any supplies students will need to record their feedback (such as sticky notes).**

   Students write their name on each direction card, where it says Feedback Receiver.

3. **Students trade each of their three cards with a different classmate. They write their names on their classmates' cards, where it says Feedback Giver.**

   By the end of the trading, students will have three cards again, but now each card is from a different classmate.

   Make sure students understand that in a trade, they don't have to get the same type of card they give away. (For example, Orly can trade her observations card for Shaun's interpretations card.) They also can't trade away someone else's card. (For example, if Orly has Shaun's interpretations card, she can't then trade Shaun's card for one of Frank's cards; she's only allowed to trade away her own.) Finally, students shouldn't trade more than one card with the same classmate. (For example, if Orly already traded cards with Shaun once, she shouldn't make another trade with him.)

   Seeking feedback makes students vulnerable, so it's important that they choose their reviewers. You might instruct your students to keep their own cards in hand but immediately put their classmates' cards on their desks so they don't accidentally trade them away. Once they've traded away their own cards, they can return to their seats and wait for the next step. This allows you to see who still has cards and help them find classmates to trade with.

4. **Students review their three classmates' work by writing their observations, questions, or interpretations, using the prompts on the cards to guide their responses.**

   For a writing project, students might find it easier to make notes in the margins of each other's drafts. In that case, ask reviewers to initial their feedback to clarify who wrote what.

   Some students will blurt out judgmental comments, whether positive ("This is so good") or negative ("This makes no sense"). They'll thinly disguise their judgments as self-judgments ("I think I'm too dumb to understand what you're talking about") or questions ("Why is this picture even here?"). Remind your students that while it's impossible, and often unhelpful, to silence their inner critics, the prompts suggest other kinds of feedback they should give that will help their classmates improve their work.

5. **As soon as a student finishes reviewing a peer's work, that student hands the card back to its owner.**

   This way, students can keep track of whether their work is still under review. When they get back all three cards, they can move on.

6. **Students read through the feedback they received and use the prompts on the backs of the cards to help them decide what to add, cut, replace, rearrange, and keep in their work product.**

Some students might want to ask their reviewers follow-up questions or further discuss their work, but caution them to try not to defend their work if the reviewer misunderstood it. At this stage, all students can assume their work is still in progress, and all feedback is information they can use.

Boosting the Impact

Once students have all given and received their feedback, you can lead a brief discussion about the process.

- "How did it feel to offer your observations, questions, and interpretations to your classmates?"

- "How did it feel to hear your classmates' observations, questions, and interpretations?"

- "What are some of the most helpful comments or questions you received?"

Asking for examples of helpful feedback gives students occasion to acknowledge their peers' contributions. It also allows students who are less skilled at giving feedback to hear what helpful feedback sounds like. You can even give feedback on their feedback, using a rubric like the one in figure 7.5.

Assignment: Read your peer's work, and give the kind of feedback that your peer asks for. Your goal is to help your peer improve the work by sharing your observations, questions, and interpretations.			
Elements	**Basic**	**Effective**	**Exemplary**
Observations: Your responses show your peer which parts of the work stand out most and why. You show how you reacted to ideas, examples, stylistic choices, and anything else that got your attention.			
Questions: Your questions prompt your peer to add more specific detail and explanation. You ask lots of questions, including questions that begin with *What*, *Which*, and *What kind of*, to help your peer think of more details to add.			
Interpretations: Your interpretations clarify the deeper meanings under the surface. You don't simply state the topic; you explain what seems important to the person who created this work and what bigger ideas or messages get across.			
Withheld Judgment: You offer only observations, questions, and interpretations. Regardless of how much you like or dislike the work, you do not praise or criticize it, and even if you have ideas for what you'd do differently, you do not make suggestions.			

Figure 7.5: Peer feedback rubric.

*Visit **go.SolutionTree.com/instruction** for a free reproducible version of this figure.*

You can also ask your students questions about how they plan to use the feedback they got.

- "What if the details your reviewer noticed aren't that important? Are these details distractions? Does that mean you should cut those details or add more detail to the important parts—or both?"

- "How will you use the questions your reviewers asked?"

- "If a peer didn't understand the message you were trying to get across, what will you do?"

You might ask a few volunteers to share their revision plans with the class, and you can also ask individual students these kinds of questions as they revise.

Using the Protocol Next Time

Once your students understand how to give and use each kind of feedback, they can request it more strategically. For example, a student who often struggles to add enough detail could start giving out questions cards to multiple reviewers.

After students have peer reviewed a few times, you can encourage them to trade at least one card with a classmate they've never peer reviewed with before. Trading nonjudgmental feedback is a great way to start building a relationship with a classmate and to appreciate that person's perspective. If some students choose the same reviewers again and again, you can help them explore that choice with questions such as, "What are the benefits of having the same person get to know your work over time?" and "What are the drawbacks of seeking the same perspectives every time?"

Another variation is to have students work in groups of four, trade cards within their groups, and give spoken instead of written feedback. Having the class talk in groups instead of write often creates a livelier and more intimate atmosphere, which can lead to deeper conversations about the work. But in a group, not every member necessarily trusts every other member. Orly could feel comfortable sharing her work with Shaun, Frank, and Robyn, and they might all feel comfortable sharing their work with her, but that doesn't mean they feel comfortable sharing their work with each other. Also, peer review group discussions can have all the usual problems of group work; groups might get off topic, one student might dominate the discussion, three students might gang up on the remaining one, and the room might get so loud that students who are ready to apply their feedback won't be able to focus. If you think your class can handle talking in groups, try it. You can always go back to written feedback the next time.

You don't have to limit nonjudgmental review to your classroom. Try emailing parents the feedback prompts and encouraging them to choose one type—observations, questions, or interpretations—to give to their child about a work in progress. Some students avoid showing their work to their parents because they don't want their parents to judge it. Some students do show their work to their parents, and the parents simply correct all their mistakes. Nonjudgmental feedback allows parents to see their child's work, provide another perspective on it, and avoid well-intentioned behaviors that might interfere with the student's learning. The review might even create a context for conversations at home about what matters to the student.

Considerate Editing

Rather than framing editing as just what's done or as a necessity for looking smart and being taken seriously, students frame editing as an act of consideration for the project's audience.

Suggested Time:

In trying to get students to edit, some teachers tell them that spelling, grammar, capitalization, and punctuation mistakes might not seem like a big deal but will cause readers to judge the students as uneducated or stupid. The teacher says things like, "If you don't proofread, it looks like you don't care about your work, so why should anyone else care?" or "You should learn how to proofread now, because even one tiny mistake on an application might cost you the job you want."

For sure, some people do harshly judge writers who misplace an apostrophe or use *there* when they mean *their*, and those judgments might make a difference as students pursue their goals. But rather than encouraging them to act out of fear of judgment or in pursuit of status, or to just obey a rule, you can invoke your students' values. Editing shows they care about their audience and their work, and if they make a mistake, that's because everyone does.

During the protocol, your students will discuss the impact of various editing decisions on readers or audience members. To illustrate these impacts, you could create exaggerated examples of what *not* to do. Show a slide with magenta words on a red background. Speak to the class as if to someone next to you at a ballet performance. Hand out a single-spaced article with no paragraph breaks, and ask how students like reading it. Show them work with no title, or a label instead of a title (like *Ancient Egypt Poster* or *Science Homework*), and ask how the reader might experience these. Project a paragraph with mistakes in spelling, grammar, punctuation, and capitalization, and ask your students how they feel as they read. Your students probably won't experience such a demonstration as inconsiderate—they'll more likely think it's funny. But you can ask them to imagine how they'd feel if they encountered similar problems in a book, movie, podcast, poster, or other works they expected to learn from and enjoy.

Considerate Editing helps students think about their work as a communicative act. A person will read, listen to, or otherwise experience their work. Stylistic choices like the line spacing in a report, the font size on a slide, the construction of a sentence, or the volume of their speaking voice aren't just conventions; they're acts of empathy.

Getting Ready

Do the following in preparation for the protocol.

❑ Identify three editing decisions for your students to focus on.

Choosing only three editing decisions helps you keep the discussion focused and brief, and it prevents your students from feeling overwhelmed during the protocol. (That doesn't mean you can't mention other editing decisions later!) In choosing your three, consider which editing decisions would most impact a reader or listener for this particular project. For example, if your students are creating websites, you could have them think about text density, font combinations, and links. More generally, if your students are working on a writing project, you might have them think about font, line spacing, paragraphing, titles and subtitles, references, links, or proofreading. If they're working on a presentation, you might have them think about any of those writing decisions, or the amount of information on a slide, their slides' color scheme, the volume and speed of their delivery, or their overall pacing, tone, and interactivity.

You might also use this protocol as an opportunity to have students examine rigid rules of style they've learned in the past, so they can approach these editing decisions more flexibly and in the service of their values. For example, many teachers make the rule that students must double space all papers, without necessarily telling students why. This protocol could give students occasion to think about the fact that teachers usually write comments on student work, and double spacing leaves room for those comments. However, teachers who read student papers in electronic documents that have comment functions don't need room to write between lines and might find the paper more readable in 1.15 spacing. Rather than following a rigid rule like "always double space," the student can learn to make editing decisions based on the reader's needs.

❑ Consider making exaggerated examples of *inconsiderate* editing in the three areas of focus for your students to analyze.

❑ Make enough copies of the blank "Considerate Editing Chart" reproducible (page 220) for each student. Figure 7.6 shows what the chart might look like after a student has filled it out.

Editing Decision	Most Considerate Options
Font	• Big enough to read but not so big it's distracting • Posters and slides—make information easy to find • Essays—make paragraphs easy to read
Line spacing	• Printed—leave room to write comments • On screen—let the reader see the whole paragraph
Paragraphing	• Help the reader know which sentences go together or are part of the same idea • Short paragraphs—not too overwhelming

Figure 7.6: Sample considerate editing chart.

Leading the Protocol

The following four steps will help you most effectively lead the protocol.

1. **Ask what it means to be considerate.**

   Ask for examples and tentative definitions, and then either come to a consensus definition or post one yourself. We define *considerate* as showing awareness for other people's experiences and feelings, and giving careful thought to how you do things.

2. **Ask what it means to be considerate as a writer or presenter.**

   Again ask for examples, and create a writing-specific or presentation-specific version of your class's general definition of *considerate*. If being considerate in general means showing awareness for other people's experiences and feelings, being a considerate writer would mean showing awareness for the reader's experiences and feelings. If being considerate in general means giving careful thought to how you do things, being a considerate presenter would mean giving careful thought to how you deliver ideas.

   While this protocol will ask students about how style (color scheme, spacing, punctuation, speaking volume, and so on) makes the reading or listening experience easier, students might first bring up ways to be considerate in terms of their work's content. They might say, for example, that being a considerate writer means avoiding offensive language, imagining diverse viewpoints, and maintaining the dignity of people they write or talk about. Being a considerate presenter means avoiding jokes only some people in the room will understand and using culturally relevant examples.

3. **Give out copies of the "Considerate Editing Chart" reproducible (page 220). Lead a discussion of three specific editing decisions, framing each one in terms of what would show consideration for the students' audience. Students take notes on the discussion in their charts.**

   Ask questions that help your students think about their audience. For example, if they want to be considerate of their reader, what kind of font will they choose? Rather than telling them, as many teachers do, that they must use twelve-point Times New Roman, have them look through the font gallery on their word processing program and identify which ones they like, versus which ones they think people will find easiest to read for pages at a time. Some students will continue to ask you whether they've chosen a good font, and others will struggle to take the reader's perspective. If a student doesn't get it, you can always say, "Just use twelve-point Times New Roman," but even then, you can add, "Teachers and publishers ask for that font because it's easy for most people to read."

   Continue asking questions about different considerations. Paragraphs and slide breaks signal new topics and break up information to keep the audience from feeling overwhelmed. Titles prepare the audience to understand the text or presentation. References give other authors credit for their ideas, and they also help curious, confused, or skeptical readers track down further information; links make that process even easier. A loud yet modulated speaking voice ensures listeners can hear but don't feel like they're getting yelled at, and a slow yet lively pace ensure listeners can process new information but don't get bored. Rather than simply telling students this information for each editing decision, ask about the audience's experience.

4. **Based on the three discussions, the class creates a considerate editing checklist for all students to use every time they write or present.**

   Have your students write the checklist in their notebooks and mark the page so they can easily find it whenever they edit. You can also post a copy of the checklist in the classroom or online for future reference. Figure 7.7 has an example of what a considerate editing checklist might look like.

☐ Choose a **font size and style** that is easy to read.

☐ Use **line spacing** that helps the reader. For reading on screen, 1.15 is usually easiest to read. If your reader needs a printed copy to comment on, 2.0 is best.

☐ Use **paragraphing** to break up the text and signal new ideas.

Figure 7.7: Sample considerate editing checklist.

Boosting the Impact

After doing this protocol, you can remind your students to use the considerate editing checklist every time they write or present. As they edit, you might find that some students need to review certain decisions, like how big a font to use or how loudly to speak. But instead of just telling these students, "That font is too small," or cupping your hand around your ear to indicate that their voice is too soft, you can ask questions about the audience.

- "Who's reading (or listening to) this?"

- "What will their experience be like?"

- "What do you want your readers (or listeners) to pay attention to?"

- "What do you want the experience of reading your work (or hearing your presentation) to be like?"

- "How can you honor the time and effort your audience spends reading (or hearing) and thinking about your work?"

- "How can you honor the time and effort you spent making your work?"

When you ask these questions, tone matters. You can probably imagine asking, "How do you think your reader will experience this?" in a shaming way. These questions aren't meant to shame your students into editing. They'll most likely want to avoid anything they associate with shame—proofreading, writing, speaking, sharing their work, and you. But asked with curiosity and compassion, a question like, "How do you think your reader will experience this?" can help students notice that when they write or present, they're communicating with another human being. Who is that human being? How do your students want to treat the people who will experience their work? Even if students typically associate editing with boredom, frustration, and embarrassment, they can also learn to bring their values to the different ways they communicate.

Using the Protocol Next Time

You can use this protocol over the course of several successive projects. Each time, you can review editing decisions students have discussed in the past and add new ones to focus on. Instead of making a new considerate editing checklist each time, they can add new items to the original one. Figure 7.8 has an example of what a cumulative considerate editing checklist might look like. This example focuses on presenting.

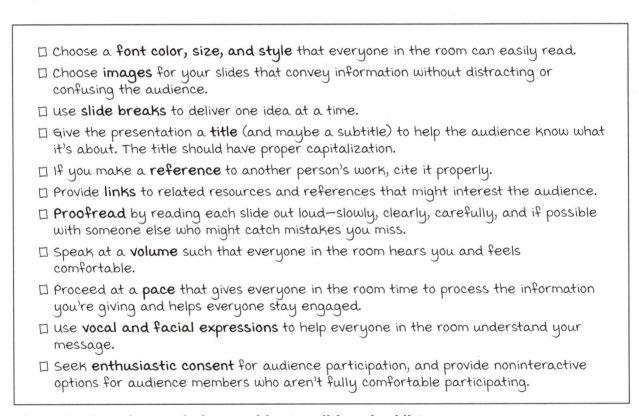

☐ Choose a **font color, size, and style** that everyone in the room can easily read.

☐ Choose **images** for your slides that convey information without distracting or confusing the audience.

☐ Use **slide breaks** to deliver one idea at a time.

☐ Give the presentation a **title** (and maybe a subtitle) to help the audience know what it's about. The title should have proper capitalization.

☐ If you make a **reference** to another person's work, cite it properly.

☐ Provide **links** to related resources and references that might interest the audience.

☐ **Proofread** by reading each slide out loud—slowly, clearly, carefully, and if possible with someone else who might catch mistakes you miss.

☐ Speak at a **volume** such that everyone in the room hears you and feels comfortable.

☐ Proceed at a **pace** that gives everyone in the room time to process the information you're giving and helps everyone stay engaged.

☐ Use **vocal and facial expressions** to help everyone in the room understand your message.

☐ Seek **enthusiastic consent** for audience participation, and provide noninteractive options for audience members who aren't fully comfortable participating.

Figure 7.8: Sample cumulative considerate editing checklist.

If your students build a long checklist, try quizzing them on it. Don't collect or grade the quiz; just let them see what they know. Ask questions like, "What makes a font considerate?" "What's the difference between a title and a label?" or "What's the ideal speaking volume when you present?" Have your students write and then discuss their responses, just to remind themselves how they can edit their work with their audience in mind.

In between projects, you can share your own considerate editing choices. When you make a handout or slideshow for your students, how do you take their needs into account? When you choose colors for a wall chart, or when you lay out text on a syllabus, how are you being considerate? For that matter, how are tasks like rearranging the classroom furniture, setting up lab equipment, or creating art stations *editing*, and how are you considerate of your students in these instances? Of course you'll need to protect students' privacy and dignity when sharing your decisions; don't tell your whole class that you use a certain font because one student has dyslexia, or that you changed your classroom lighting to accommodate a trauma survivor. But to the extent that you can share your editing decisions with your students, see what happens if you do. You might garner an eye roll or a sarcastic "Thank you so much," but you might get genuine thanks too, and you'll be modeling the considerate behaviors you want to evoke.

Testing for Doneness

Students imagine showing their work to a person they admire in the present, decide whether it honors the memory of someone who struggled for their sake in the past, and picture themselves rediscovering the work in the future. From these perspectives, they decide whether their work is done or they want to change something.

Suggested Time:

The maxim attributed to writer Paul Valéry (as cited in Auden, 1966, p. 16), "A poem is never finished, only abandoned," seems true not just for poetry but for all kinds of work products, from reports to slideshows to maps. The student creates an iteration, tinkers, and tinkers some more. How does *anyone* know when a work is done, let alone a student, who by definition is still learning?

Sometimes students try to figure out whether they're done by asking us. They show us their work, usually asking some version of "Is it good?" But they really want to know whether their work product currently meets our expectations and will garner them an *A*, or they need to do something else to it, and if so, what. On one hand, if we will evaluate their work, it's only fair that we tell them what will meet our expectations. On the other hand, if we tell them what to do, they don't figure out for themselves whether or how they could improve their work. To get them to decide for themselves, we might refer them back to the project rubric or have them see what their peers are doing. Even in these situations, though, the students decide whether they're done according to the teacher's expectations or their peers' actions. How can students use their *own* standards of excellence to decide whether their work is done?

Cooks know that it's hard to tell whether certain foods are done, so they have ways to test for doneness. If they put a skewer into a cake and it comes back with just a few crumbs clinging to it, they know the cake is done. They know a chicken breast is done when the internal temperature reaches 165 degrees Fahrenheit. In Testing for Doneness, students look at their work from three different perspectives: a person whose work they admire in the present, that of a person who struggled for their sake in the past, and the person they'll become in the future. Seeing their work from these three perspectives reveals possible ways they can improve it—or helps them decide that their work meets their own standards of excellence and is therefore *done*.

You can use this protocol with your whole class once some students reach the point where they don't know what else they can do to improve their project. Alternatively, while the rest of your class continues working on the project, you can do this protocol with individual students or small groups who are wondering whether they're done.

Getting Ready

Do the following in preparation for the protocol.

❑ Decide how your students will respond to this protocol's three prompts—in writing, in conversations with partners, in a whole-class discussion, or some other way.

Leading the Protocol

The following four steps will help you most effectively lead the protocol.

1. **Give the first prompt: "Think of a well-known person, alive today, whose work you admire. If this person saw your work as it is right now, would you feel proud? Is there something you'd want to change so you would feel even prouder to show this person your work?"**

   The person can do any kind of work—as a musician, dancer, artist, athlete, political figure, activist, writer, inventor, business leader, chef, YouTuber—as long as the student has seen or experienced the person's *work*, as opposed to just the person's celebrity. Imagining someone who's alive helps students more easily visualize how that person would react to their work product. Imagining someone famous means the students don't have a relationship with this person and are unlikely to in the future, so any emotions they feel when they picture this person seeing their work aren't entangled with emotions they've felt toward that person in direct interactions.

2. **Give the second prompt: "Now think of someone from the past whose struggle made it possible for you to be here today. Does your work, as it is right now, honor that person's memory? Is there something you'd change so your work would better honor that person's memory?"**

   Students can think of any person or group who took action that made it possible for them to exist, come to school, and do this learning. They might imagine their ancestors, or the inventor of something they need for survival, or people whose political work gave the students access to certain resources. It's not necessary for students to know the people's names.

3. **Give the final prompt: "Now think of your future self, ten years from today. Would future you be glad to rediscover your work, and remember making it, as it is right now? Is there something you'd want to change so that future you would feel more satisfied?"**

Students might say something like, "I don't think I'll really care about this ten years from now," or "I doubt I'm going to save this." If they express apathy about their work, ask, "How could you change this so you *would* care about it ten years from now?" or "What changes could you make so you *would* want to save it?" If they dig in ("Absolutely nothing would make me want to save this"), that's a choice too.

4. **Based on their responses to the three prompts, students declare their work *done* or create a plan for revising it.**

   Sometimes all you can do is remind students that they're making a choice and help them make a different one next time.

Boosting the Impact

If you do this protocol with an individual or a small group, you might not get all the way through it before the students figure out what further revisions they want to make. For example, when a student imagines his favorite movie director reading his essay, he might say, "Yeah, I'm gonna go proofread this again."

You might also get students who say they'd very proudly show their work to the famous person they admire, the work indeed honors the memory of those who struggled before them, and their future self would be excited to rediscover it—but *you* think it still needs revision. You can always just tell these students what they should do ("I'm glad you feel good about it, and I think it needs another round of proofreading"). You can also have a one-on-one conversation about why they think their work is done. As they talk to you, they might realize that they can do more. But even if you end up telling them to revise further, you'll learn what excellence means to these students, and you can build on that later.

Using the Protocol Next Time

This protocol has emotional impact when students visualize the three people looking at their work. If you use it more than once, help your students fully bring the three people to mind so they feel the associated emotions—rather than just answering the same three questions. You can invite them to close their eyes and imagine each person, or make quick drawings of each person, or describe each person to a partner. Visualizing the three people helps students take those people's perspectives, but what students really see is how well their work matches their own values.

Onward

This chapter's protocols help students refine their academic work product, not only to meet the teacher's expectations, but also to live up to their own values. While none of these protocols will necessarily make revision more fun, they just might make it more meaningful.

The next chapter has ways to help students reflect on their work, not only by noticing where they succeeded and where they have room for growth, but also by redefining what *success* and *growth* mean based on their own values.

Chapter 8

• • • • •

PROTOCOLS TO REFLECT ON LEARNING

During a unit, students have various goals that orient their attention—writing an essay, studying for a test, sitting next to a friend, or just getting through a forty-five-minute lesson. When people are pursuing a particular goal, their attention tends to focus narrowly on achieving that goal (Gilbert, 2010). This makes good evolutionary sense; if our ancestors, hungry for dinner, had focused on anything but finding edible berries, we wouldn't be here. Faced with a goal, we become singularly focused on pursuing and achieving that goal, whether it's finding a berry or finishing an assignment.

Learning also presents all kinds of challenges—difficult concepts, looming due dates, confusing directions, distracting peers, or just the tediously repetitive tasks students need to complete in order to achieve mastery. These daily challenges can threaten students' sense of competence and control, and when people feel threatened, their attention tends to focus solely on avoiding the threat (Wilson & DuFrene, 2009; Wilson & Murrell, 2004). This again makes sense; if our ancestors, encountering poisonous snakes, had focused on anything but getting away, we wouldn't be here. Faced with a threat, we become singularly focused on removing or escaping that threat (Gilbert, 2010), whether it's a poisonous snake, a difficult assignment, or an annoying classmate.

When we have a goal, our minds say, "Get it!" and under threat, our minds say, "Get it away!" We focus on that *it*, and nothing else. But when we feel safe and contented, our attention tends to widen, and we become more open, curious, and connected (Gilbert, 2010). At the end of a unit, with fewer immediate goals and threats to capture their energy, students' attention can expand. They can have more curiosity about how they approached their learning, work, and classmates. They can have more openness to new approaches they can try next time. They can connect with each other, with you, and with themselves.

During dedicated reflection time, students can attend to more of the factors that influence their behavior: their thoughts and emotions, their past actions and current desires, the external circumstances that affect their success, and what *success* even means. With that awareness, students are empowered to make choices—*they* are the ones having all these experiences at school, and *they* get to choose how they approach each one.

Typical reflection activities have people ask themselves, "What did I do well?" (strengths), "What could I have done better?" (weaknesses), "What do I want to work on?" (goals), and "What steps can I take?" (plans). At school, *doing well* usually means getting high grades or scores, reaching a next level, or in some other way meeting someone else's standards. This chapter's protocols ask students to define *doing well* in terms of their own values, and to formulate values-consistent goals and plans, so they can bring those values to their future work and make school a source of meaning and vitality in their lives.

- In Concentric Self-Portraits, students take time to notice what they did during a unit, how they feel about their actions, what they plan to do next, and how their actions connect them to their classmates.

- Sentence Expanding helps students step back from their self-judgments and choose how they approach future assignments.

- In Support-Push-Inspire, students consider how their classmates positively influenced their learning.

- Upcycling helps students imagine new possibilities for their work, based on what matters to them.

- In Values-Based Portfolios, students reflect on what makes their work meaningful, celebrate times when they've chosen to make their work meaningful, and discover how they can make their work more meaningful in the future.

Concentric Self-Portraits

Students bring more awareness to their experiences during a unit by drawing what they did and how they feel about their actions now. Then, they write how they plan to use their learning, and they share their finished self-portraits as a way to connect with their fellow learners.

Suggested Time:

In day-to-day lessons and work periods, students are so busy *doing*—listening, taking notes, thinking, asking questions, making posters, telling stories, giving speeches, staring out the window, asking to borrow a pencil, opening their laptops, opening their documents, having side conversations, building mousetrap cars, proofreading, filling in the bubble next to the best answer. As a result, they don't necessarily *notice* what they're doing or why. During Concentric Self-Portraits, students pay attention to what they did during a unit so they can choose what they do next.

To start the protocol, students draw something they experienced during the unit and how they feel about it now. Drawing allows students to bring the memories and emotions that are inside them into the outside world. They literally gain a new view of their psychological experiences, and in the process, they gain some agency because they're the artists. From this empowered perspective, they get to decide how they want to relate to their internal experiences and what they want to do in the outside world—which they write in the outer oval. The separate concentric ovals help them see that they can have thoughts and emotions in response to past experiences, *and* they can choose what they do next time. After drawing and writing, pairs of students look together at how their self-portraits reveal interesting differences and similarities between them. Finally, students share how they want to bring their values to future learning.

Getting Ready

Do the following in preparation for the protocol.

❏ Make enough copies of the "Concentric Self-Portraits" reproducible (page 221) for each student. Figure 8.1 is a filled-out example.

❏ Gather markers or other art materials (optional).

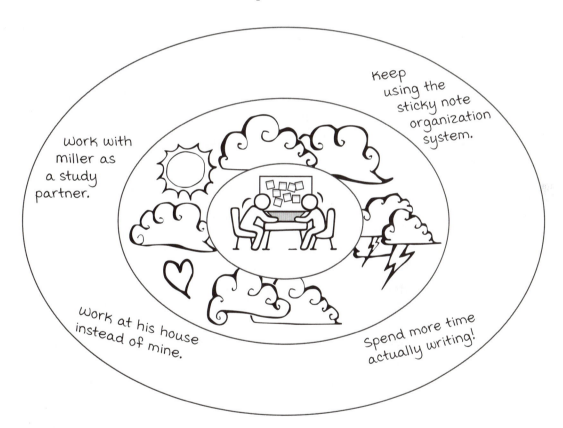

Figure 8.1: Sample finished concentric self-portrait.

Figure 8.1 represents the finished self-portrait of a student who did a research project with her best friend. In the middle, she drew herself and her friend organizing their findings using sticky notes. She has mixed feelings about her experience, which she represented with different kinds of weather, as well as a heart to indicate her love for her friend. She plans to keep using some of the same strategies and to change others.

Leading the Protocol

The following seven steps will help you most effectively lead the protocol.

1. **Give each student a copy of the "Concentric Self-Portraits" template reproducible (page 221). Let them know they're about to do an activity that will involve making some very basic drawings and doing a little bit of writing, and tell them how much time they'll have for each step.**

   There is no right or wrong amount of time to work on the drawings; students could make one- or two-minute drawings, or they could draw for longer, but knowing in advance how long they have will help artistic students rein themselves in and those who dread art push themselves, knowing there's an end in sight.

2. **In the innermost oval, students draw themselves learning, working on, or experiencing something during the unit.**

   These innermost drawings should represent reality. Students can draw stick figures and such, but they shouldn't exaggerate elements or put anything in their drawings that wasn't physically there, like a speech bubble or sound effect. For example, if they got frustrated, they could draw a frustrated expression but not steam coming out of their ears. The point is for the students to take themselves back to the moment when they were doing this work and bring more of their awareness to the experience by drawing it.

   As they draw, prompt them to remember details by asking questions like the following.

   * "What were you wearing?"
   * "What were you holding?"
   * "What was around you as you worked?"
   * "Who, if anyone, was there?"

3. **In the middle oval, students draw any feelings that come up now as they consider the outcome of the experience they drew, or of the unit as a whole.**

   They should make these drawings symbolic or abstract. Tell them to avoid writing any words and instead use lines, shapes, shading, and (if practical) color to represent their emotions. People often mislabel their internal experiences—they say they're mad when they're hurt, bored when they're frustrated, and confused when they're distracted—or no word seems right. Drawing symbols or abstract shapes may help them identify and express their feelings even if they can't find the words for them.

4. **In the outermost oval, students write their thoughts, plans, and ideas for the future as a result of this learning experience.**

   Students don't have much space to write, which means they'll have to condense their thoughts to a few words, phrases, or brief sentences. This isn't a time to elaborate; rather, they're capturing their ideas so they can put them into action later.

5. **Students share their completed self-portraits with partners.**

   They can explain their work or let it speak for itself.

6. **Partners reflect collaboratively on differences and similarities between them.**

   Try asking these questions.

   - "What does learning look like for your partner?"
   - "How does that learning look different than learning looks for you?"
   - "Even with your differences, how do your learning experiences reveal similarities between you?"

   That last question doesn't necessarily ask students how their *experiences* are similar; rather, it asks them how their experiences reveal similarities between *themselves*. For example, let's say that a Chinese class has just finished a unit on finding one's way around. Although one student drew himself studying vocabulary with a friend and his partner drew herself giving her dad directions in Chinese, both students notice that they find learning satisfying when they work with someone.

7. **Invite volunteers to share with the class anything they learned just now, or how they want to approach their next learning experience.**

   Students might identify something they learned about themselves ("I learned that I'm a little hard on myself"), about their partners ("Randall and I both really care about our work and sometimes have trouble trusting the people we work with, but we also like working with other people"), or about an academic skill ("I learned about Frida and Miller's sticky note organization system"). Anything they learned can have implications for their future behaviors. Even if they're not excited about the next topic or assignment, they still can choose how they want to approach their learning.

Boosting the Impact

After the protocol, you could post the self-portraits around the room so that students get an even broader sense of what their classmates did, felt, and planned. Seeing their peers' responses will give them more ideas for values-consistent behaviors they can choose during the next unit. Just make sure you give students the option to keep their drawings private, or don't post them at all.

Even if you don't post the self-portraits, you can still collect them, and at some point during the next unit, you can hand them back and ask your students whether they've followed through with their plans. If they have followed through, ask how it's going. If they haven't, ask what's getting in the way. These quick check-ins will help you see which students are intentionally growing from their past experiences, and which students might need longer one-on-one conversations about their learning.

Using the Protocol Next Time

If your students do Concentric Self-Portraits for several units in a row, they can use their portraits to track the effectiveness of their actions. Do they use the same strategies over and over, regardless of how well those strategies work? You can't force them to change what they do, but you can keep helping them explore the costs of *not* changing. Over time, the students will also get better at depicting their emotions and making plans. Students who are able to recognize their own emotions tend to have better social support networks (Rowsell, Ciarrochi, Deane, & Heaven, 2016), seek the help they need more readily (Ciarrochi, Deane, Wilson, & Rickwood, 2002), and experience increased well-being (Ciarrochi, Kashdan, Leeson, Heaven, & Jordan, 2011). We think that beyond any of these benefits, the opportunity to notice their emotions and make values-guided choices is reason enough to repeat this activity.

Sentence Expanding

After receiving evaluative feedback, students notice and step back from their self-judgments so they can focus on what the feedback suggests they might try next time.

Suggested Time:

Evaluative feedback tells students how well they did so that they can do more of what worked and less of what didn't. Just as a thermometer tells us how hot it is so we can decide what to wear, grades and narrative comments inform our students about what they did well or poorly so they can decide what to do next time. They're just information.

However, students don't usually see evaluative feedback as mere information that can help them make decisions. Otherwise, they wouldn't get so caught up in what their grades are or what our comments say. After receiving evaluative feedback, students have all kinds of judgmental thoughts—not just about the grade but about the project ("I hate writing"), the subject ("I hate science"), and the teacher ("She hates me"). Worst of all, they have judgmental thoughts about themselves. No matter how much we insist that this assignment represents only one moment within their larger academic experience, which is only one part of their larger lives, some students very quickly turn "I got a 79" to "I did badly on the history test" to "I'm bad at history" to "I'm bad."

Self-judging thoughts powerfully influence students' actions. Imagine a history class just got tests back. Martha got an 82, which she considers pretty good. She's happy she did well, but she sees herself as being bad at history, so she thinks she just got lucky with the 82. "The test was on the stuff I happened to study," she thinks, "and it must have been an easy test that everyone did well on." Stanley also got an 82, but he considers that bad, and he thought he was good at history. His friends tell him he just had an off day and his grade isn't bad, but he feels like maybe he's not as smart as he thought. Omar got a 98, which he thinks is great. He already thought he was good at history, and this confirmation makes him a little arrogant about it. It also makes him complacent; he doesn't think he needs to study that much. Right now, he can get good grades without studying, but that could change, and he also might feel more satisfied if he learned the material more deeply and took more risks in his work. Finally, there's Ray, who got a 64, which he thinks is bad. He already thought he was bad at history, and this latest score just reinforces that belief. Despite the fact that he correctly answered well over half the questions and learned quite a bit during the unit, he feels like a loser and thinks he shouldn't bother studying for history tests any more. He also feels indignant, thinking, "This stupid school is forcing me to take this stupid class with this stupid teacher, and who cares, because I'm not going to open a history store." All four students focus on their academic status as opposed to what they've learned about history, what skills they've developed, and why any of it matters.

None of these reactions is inevitable. Many students push themselves beyond what they need to do to get good grades, take setbacks in stride, attribute their successes to their own efforts, and persist in areas where they're weak. But we all have the potential to get stuck in our self-concepts (like "I'm smart" or "I'm bad at history") and are prone to self-defeating behaviors as a result (Hayes et al., 2012). Figure 8.2 summarizes just some of the ways we can get caught up in self-judgment.

Self-Concept

		"I am GOOD at this subject."	"I am BAD at this subject."
Performance Judgment	"I did WELL on this assignment."	• Arrogant • Complacent	• Dismissive • Distrustful
		Possible Reactions	
	"I did POORLY on this assignment."	• Disoriented • Defeated	• Hopeless • Resentful

Figure 8.2: Ways that self-judgments can lead to self-defeating reactions.

It's not practical, and perhaps not even possible, to prevent self-judgmental thoughts from forming. We can, however, undermine the influence of judgmental thoughts over our actions (Hayes et al., 2012). Instead of letting negative or even positive self-judgments dictate what we do, we can notice our self-judgments. When we choose to pause and notice a thought occurring in our minds, in that moment we have more freedom from that thought's influence. If students notice themselves having a thought—as in, "*I'm having the thought that* I did badly on the history test" as opposed to "I did badly on the history test"—then they don't have to succumb to defeat or resentment. They can instead just notice the thought and then choose what to do.

In the Sentence Expanding protocol, students learn how to see self-judgments like, "I did well on the test" or "I'm bad at history," as what they are: thoughts. By seeing a thought as a thought, the students take away some of that thought's power, and they have more power to choose how they want to approach their future learning.

Getting Ready

Do the following in preparation for the protocol.

❑ Make enough copies of the blank "Sentence Strips" reproducible (page 222) so each student and yourself get one strip. Figure 8.3 has a single filled-out example, but the reproducible in the appendix has multiple blank strips.

I notice	I'm making the judgment that	I did meh	and	next time I can	Keep my notes organized and clear all my other stuff off my desk.
1	2	3	4	5	6

Figure 8.3: Sample completed sentence strip.

❑ Cut the strips apart.

Leading the Protocol

The following eight steps will help you most effectively lead the protocol.

1. **After your students have seen evaluative feedback (such as a test score or your comments on a paper), hand each student a blank sentence strip. In box 3, they write a brief sentence to say how they think they did.**

   You might need to put the sentence starter *I did _____* on the board and give examples of how your students might fill in the blank—with *well, OK, horribly, awesome, meh,* and so on. Don't use teacher language here; use words you hear students say about their performance.

   Sometimes students will want you to characterize their performance. They'll ask, "Is a 91 good?" or "What was the class average?" We advise against posting averages or ranges, since it breeds competition and masks biases that account for how well students did. This activity's purpose isn't for students to compare themselves to each other or to find out what you think *good* is. It's to notice judgments they make about themselves. You can tell your students to write how *they* think they did. If they're thinking, "I don't know if I did well or not," then that's what they should write in box 3.

   Since this protocol's steps don't follow the numerical order of the boxes, students sometimes get confused about where to write. Try drawing your own sentence strip on the board and filling it out alongside the students. Not only will this help them know which box to write in, but if you fill out your sentence strip with your self-judgment (say, how well you think you did teaching yesterday's lesson), you'll model the courage it takes to be honest with yourself about your own thoughts. Then your students will know they can be honest, too.

2. **In box 2, students write *I'm making the judgment that.***

   This adds to what they wrote in box 3, as figure 8.3 shows: *I'm making the judgment that I did meh.* Ask students if, without sharing their sentences, any of them want to share what happens when they add *I'm making the judgment that* to their sentences. They might notice a sense of detachment, that it makes what they wrote in box 3 just a thought. Or they might get defensive of their thought: "I still think I did meh." Fine, they agree with their thought. But how does it feel to see that they're *having* the thought?

3. **In box 1, students write *I notice.***

   I notice I'm making the judgment that I did meh. Ask students what happens when they add *I notice* to their sentences. Who is this person, noticing that they're noticing? Does the person who is noticing the thought have to listen to the thought?

   When they notice something happening in their minds, the thought is no longer in charge. They are.

4. **In box 4, students write the word *and.***

   The *and* means there can be more to the story than whatever their judgments tell them. It suggests that other possibilities exist, and that they get to choose what they do.

5. **In box 5, students write *next time I can.***

   Now that they've acknowledged their self-judgments, they can consider possible actions for next time.

6. **In box 6, students finish the sentence with a specific action that the feedback suggests they try the next time they have a similar assignment.**

   If they felt happy with the feedback, that's a sign that their actions worked for them. In that case, what do they want to keep doing? Is there also room for growth, or more creative risks? If they felt upset with the feedback, that's a sign that their actions didn't work out for them. What do they want to try instead? What do they want to do more or less of? Despite their disappointment, what is working for them that they want to keep doing?

   If your feedback includes comments that offer specific strategies to try in the future, refer your students to them. They don't have to follow your suggestions, but you gave them a good place to start. If you don't write comments with suggested strategies, your students might struggle to come up with ones to try. In fact, the weakest students will have the most trouble thinking of strategies; if they knew what to do, they'd do it, and then they'd be stronger students! You could lead a quick sharing of strategies, or you could offer a few yourself.

7. **Students read their completed sentences silently to themselves.**

   I notice I'm making the judgment that I did meh, and next time I can keep my notes organized and clear all my other stuff off my desk. Read your own sentence aloud. Invite your students to share how it felt to write and read their sentences—again without sharing the actual sentences.

8. **Tell your students to fold their sentence strips in half, right through box 4, and then open their papers again.**

Point out that everything on the left half involves thoughts inside their heads, and everything on the right half involves actions in the world. The *and* in the middle shows that they can have the thoughts without necessarily acting on them; they can act on their values.

Boosting the Impact

Ask if anyone would like to share just that right-side sentence (that is, everything after the *and*), which involves actions in the world, such as, "Next time I can keep my notes organized and clear all my other stuff off my desk." For those who shared, how did it feel to make the statement out loud? For the others, how did it feel to hear their classmates' sentences?

You can collect the sentence strips, and the next time you give a similar assignment, you can hand them back and lead a discussion about whether they tried their strategies. First, ask if anyone wants to describe what it was like to try the strategies they wrote in their sentences. Ask these students to share how they feel about themselves as a result of trying new actions, or continuing to act in ways that work for them. Then, ask if anyone who hasn't used the strategies yet, but plans to, would be willing to share about that. Depending on the responses, you might follow up by asking when they'll start, what might get in the way, and what they'll do if they encounter those obstacles. If it seems appropriate, conclude the discussion with a class brainstorm of more strategies that might work better. This way, students discover that they can recommit to their values in new ways, and that they have useful ideas to offer each other as a community of learners.

Using the Protocol Next Time

Sentence Expanding works in part because of its gradual reveal: students express a judgment, then notice it *as* a judgment, then notice *they* are the ones making it, and finally realize they can have that thought while *also* choosing to act in a way that serves their values. After doing the protocol once, you'll lose the element of gradual discovery. However, you can use the protocol's language anytime you hear a student making a self-judgmental statement like, "I did OK on the test" or "I'm not really a math person" or "I'm not that good a proofreader" or "I'm so disorganized" or even "I'm such a bad friend." You can help students notice these thoughts *as* thoughts by saying something like, "It sounds like you're having the thought that you're not a math person." Then ask questions like, "What is that thought telling you to do about your math assignment? Do you have to listen to your thought? How do you want to approach math?" Over time, you can keep guiding your students to notice their self-judgments, and notice themselves noticing their self-judgments, which gives them more power to choose what they do.

Support-Push-Inspire

Students acknowledge classmates who positively impacted their learning.

Suggested Time:

Even though students learn as part of a class, and even though some of their classmates might be their close friends or people they've known since early childhood, they don't necessarily notice how their classmates influence their learning. They might notice when a classmate's behavior disrupts their learning ("Can you *please* tell him to stop tapping his pencil?"), but they don't always see their classmates' positive impacts.

Maybe that's because, despite the fact that students learn in groups, education remains an astoundingly individualistic enterprise. Students usually work independently (except for the occasional group project), and they're usually assessed independently. Sometimes they're not allowed to talk to each other while learning or working, and certainly not while testing. In some classrooms, the students' desks are separated like islands in an archipelago; students receive the same information, do the same work at the same time, and interact with the same teacher, but they have limited interactions with each other. Of course there are reasons for these practices, but they send a message that classmates learn next to each other, not together, and certainly not because of each other. Even the language they use to describe classmates—"She's in my class," as opposed to "We're learning together"—suggests merely being in the same place at the same time rather than having a stake in each other's learning.

But even if students don't recognize how they contribute to each other's learning, they are part of each other's learning context and necessarily have an influence. During the Support-Push-Inspire protocol, students identify classmates who helped them during the unit by supporting them, by pushing them to think differently or more deeply, and by inspiring them through positive example. Students also think about how they want to support, push, and inspire their classmates. Thus students reflect on not only what they themselves learned, did, and achieved, but also how their classmates impacted their learning—and how they want to impact their classmates.

Getting Ready

Do the following in preparation for the protocol.

❑ Think about the colleagues who have supported, pushed, and inspired you.

   You might decide to tell your students how some of their other teachers have contributed to your learning. But even if you don't share your experiences, appreciating your colleagues will probably be as worthwhile an activity for you as it will be for your students.

Leading the Protocol

The following five steps will help you most effectively lead the protocol.

1. **Give the first writing prompt: "During this unit, who in this class supported you in an important way? What did the person do to support you?"**

   Students will sometimes ask if they're allowed to write their own names (as if they only received meaningful support from themselves), or if they're allowed to write that you, the teacher, supported them. Or they'll claim they can't think of anyone. If your students struggle to identify a supportive peer, they might need help expanding their concept of *support*. Try eliciting ideas from your class and then adding any of your own. For example, *support* could mean helping classmates understand the material, giving feedback on their work, showing them how to do something, suggesting a good resource, catching them up after an absence, offering encouragement, or just listening when they express frustration or anxiousness.

   Sometimes students will ask if they can write more than one person. Throw that question back to your class: "What do we think? Can we acknowledge more than one person who supported us?" If the class doesn't come to a consensus, then individual students can make their own decisions about what's allowed.

2. **Give the second writing prompt: "Who in this class pushed you to think differently or more deeply? What did the person do? What changed for you as a result?"**

   Here, too, students might need help noticing the many ways a classmate might push their thinking. Maybe someone pushed them to think differently or more deeply about the content, their work process, or how they relate to others. Maybe a classmate debated their ideas or pointed out their assumptions. Or maybe their classmate offered creative interpretations, or introduced a perspective they hadn't thought of. Pushing someone doesn't necessarily mean being confrontational.

3. **Give the third writing prompt: "Who in this class inspired you by setting a positive example? What did the person do that inspired you?"**

   Explain that what they consider a positive example depends on their values. A student who values creativity might find inspiration in a classmate who has creative ideas about the material. A classmate who checks over each assignment might inspire a student who cares about thoroughness. If students think kindness is important, a classmate who's especially kind to them or to others might inspire them.

   Note, too, that inspiration is different from admiration. When we admire someone, we think that person is doing something great, but that doesn't necessarily mean we want to do that great thing. When we allow someone to inspire us, we think that person is doing something great that we want to try doing, too.

Sometimes students won't know why someone inspires them. Thinking about what that person does might help them clarify their values. A student could set a positive example as a learner, thinker, worker, citizen, helper, leader, change maker, or friend. In thinking expansively about how their classmates set positive examples, students notice what matters to them and begin to consider the various roles *they* play in class.

4. **Invite volunteers to share one or more of their responses with the class.**

   Noticing how their classmates support, push, and inspire them is hard enough. Saying it out loud invokes even more vulnerability. You might notice that students only acknowledge their friends, or that after students acknowledge a particular classmate, that classmate acknowledges them back (perhaps even if the classmate didn't write about them). Sometimes, though, students will share how a classmate who isn't their friend supported, pushed, or inspired them. Some awkward giggling or slightly sarcastic comments might follow. If that happens, say something like, "We're not doing that." Then, acknowledge that thinking about people in a new way can be uncomfortable, and that saying it out loud can be even more uncomfortable. Ask your students why that discomfort is worthwhile.

   You can also share how your colleagues support, push, and inspire you. Students might enjoy hearing how their other teachers have impacted you, or become curious about teachers and staff members they don't know. In any case, you're showing that you're a learner too and that you're willing to open up in the same way you ask of them.

5. **Give the last writing prompt: "What will you do to support, push, and inspire your classmates?"**

   This last question brings students' focus back to themselves. Even if they don't get to choose what they learn about, who is in their class, or how their peers behave, they can always choose how they want to approach their learning, their work, and their classmates.

Boosting the Impact

You'll know how successful this protocol is by your students' behavior. If they willingly share diverse, meaningful ways their classmates impacted their learning, and they acknowledge peers who aren't their friends and don't share their interests and affinities, all you need to ask is, "How did that feel?" or "How was that?" They'll say, "Good," or nod or give a thumbs-up, and you can leave it at that. Not everything requires analysis.

If the protocol doesn't go so well, that's when you might ask questions to help students explore the costs of missing a chance to notice how their peers impact them, and what they might try instead.

- "Did you take this opportunity to notice and appreciate meaningful ways your classmates supported, pushed, and inspired you?"

- "Does anyone think you might have played it safe—maybe by mentioning only your friends, or by naming impacts that aren't all that important to you?"

- "Did you choose for yourself how to define *supporting*, *pushing*, and *inspiring*, or did you feel like you had to ask if your definitions were OK?"

- "Is there anyone who avoided the task entirely?"

- "How do you feel about yourself as a result of the choices you made?"

- "Is there something different you want to try next time?"

- "Is there something different you can try right now?"

Depending on the relationships your students have established with each other and with you, and the kinds of discussions you regularly have, you might ask students to journal privately, write their thoughts on index cards they give you, or just reflect in their heads. Or, rather than asking questions that might make students feel like they were wrong to avoid making themselves vulnerable, you could instead just notice these reactions for yourself. What do they tell you about your classroom environment? What, if anything, do you want to change?

Using the Protocol Next Time

If Support-Push-Inspire goes well, with lots of students warmly and earnestly acknowledging each other's contributions to their meaningful learning, you might want to do it every day! But we would suggest the opposite. If the protocol goes well, don't do it again until a few units have gone by. Give your students an opportunity to support, push, and inspire each other in new ways, and to notice the contributions of classmates they hadn't fully noticed before.

If it goes poorly—students don't take it seriously, no one wants to share, the people who do share only talk about their friends—you might not feel like trying it again. But give your students another chance soon, maybe after the very next unit, or maybe even sooner, after some reflection on how they've approached this class and what they might want to do differently. If and when you do the protocol again, begin by sharing important ways your colleagues have supported, pushed, and inspired you, rather than waiting until the sharing step to talk about your experiences. Without calling out your students for understandably refusing to take risks, you can take the first risk.

 Upcycling

Students imagine their previous work products as raw material for future work products, thus seeing the value in what they created and discovering the values they want to bring to their work.

Suggested Time:

Our son Jason's favorite pajamas were made by taking two old New York Mets T-shirts, one orange and one blue, to create a top with an orange front and a blue back and pants with one orange leg and one blue leg. Besides giving Jason some pro-Mets indoctrination, the pajamas show how something just OK (like old T-shirts) can become something better, in a process known as *upcycling* (McDonough & Braungart, 2002). You can see upcycling at craft fairs and online—old magazines made into beads, old wine bottles made into chandeliers, old vinyl records made into clocks, old bicycle chains made into jewelry.

Upcycling involves taking something that already has worth and transforming it so it has more worth. But worth is not an inherent property of a thing; it depends on personal values. The person who made Jason's Mets pajamas decided that while the T-shirts had some worth, the pajamas would be worth more.

Too often, after students get back their classwork, they ask something like, "Do we still need this?" They see their finished work as even more worthless than an old T-shirt; they certainly won't keep revising it now that we've graded it, so they bury it in a drawer, donate it to us as an exemplar for future students, recycle it, or throw it out.

This Upcycling protocol helps students revalue their work by imagining how they could use it as raw material to make new work products. During the protocol, students imagine upcycling their work in various ways. They don't actually *make* the new products; this is a reflective exercise that helps them notice what their work means to them now, what it could mean to them if they kept or repurposed it, what those meanings tell them about their values, and how they can bring those values to future assignments in your class.

Getting Ready

Do the following in preparation for the protocol.

❑ Choose five upcycling writing prompts from figure 8.3 (pages 192–193), or write your own.

For almost any piece of work, students can repurpose the work's ideas.

- If you told a story inspired by this work, what would the story be about? What medium would you use to tell it? (Children's book? Series of poems? Short film? TV series? Graphic novel? Song? Ballet?)

- If you used an excerpt from this work in a speech, at what occasion would you give the speech? What else would you talk about in your speech?

- If you did a research study using this work as data, what would your research question be? What would your hypothesis be? What other data would you collect?

- If you used this work to demonstrate a social justice issue, what issue would it be? How does this work reflect inequalities with respect to ethnicity, first language, socioeconomic class, gender, ability, age, religion, or another social identifier? What would your thesis be? How would you present this work in defending the thesis?

- If you developed a dish based on this work, what would it be? What ingredients would you need? What cooking style would you use? At what occasion would you serve this meal?

- If you created a line of merchandise—tote bags, mugs, stickers, pens, hats, T-shirts, and so on—based on this work, what images or phrases would you select from it? What color scheme would you use for your merchandise? What would some of the merchandise look like?

Figure 8.3: Upcycling protocol prompts.

continued ⇨

If the work is a tangible thing—such as a poster, model, or test paper—students can imagine repurposing the physical material.

- If you used this work as art materials, what kind of art would you make? What would the subject of your artwork be? It wouldn't need to have the same topic as the original work.

- If you could use this work as a building or decorative material, what would you build with it or use it to decorate? How would you use it? How do you imagine people reacting to it?

- If you made something wearable out of this work, what article of clothing or accessory would you make? What other materials would you need? What would the rest of the outfit look like? Who would wear it? Where would they go in it?

- If you turned this work into a toy or game, what would it be? How would someone play with it? Who would play with it? Would the game be cooperative or competitive?

If the work is a time-bound performance—such as a poetry recitation or simulated convention—students can imagine repurposing its sounds, its imagery, and other aspects of the experience.

- If you turned this work into an audio track for a film or animation, what would be happening on screen? The film or animation wouldn't necessarily need to have the same topic as the original work.

- If you filmed this performance to use in a music video, what song would it be a video for? Which parts of the performance would you use in the video? What else would appear in the video? What statement would you try to make with the video?

Leading the Protocol

The following five steps will help you most effectively lead the protocol.

1. **Students silently examine or recall a recently completed piece of work.**

   If the work is a tangible object (like a printed essay) or electronic (like a slideshow), they should take it out or pull it up so they can notice its features and remember making it. If the work is something they performed, like a skit or a tableau, you can help them remember it better by describing how they made it or referring them to any notes or materials they still have.

2. **Verbally give a set of writing prompts to help students notice that their relationship to their work might have changed, and might continue to change: "What value did this work have while you were creating it? What's its value now? What value might it have in two years?"**

   Pause for a minute or two after each question so students have time to write a response before thinking about the next one. When students are thinking about the value of their work, they might consider its value to them (as the person who created it) or to others who might interact with it.

3. **Give five different Upcycling prompts (figure 8.4, page 199–200).**

Pause for several minutes after each one so students have time to imagine and write about each new way to repurpose their work.

4. **Students look back over their various reimaginings and identify the one they'd find most satisfying to make. Each student shares that one idea with the class.**

At this point, you might need to remind your students that you won't require them to make the thing. Still, you might see some students get excited about their own ideas or about each other's. That's a good sign that something meaningful is at stake.

5. **Give a final set writing prompts to help students notice the values they want to bring to their future work—regardless of whether they actually upcycle their past work product.**

The prompt could be "Of all the works you imagined, which would you find most meaningful to create? What does that tell you about your values? How can you bring those values to your future work in this class?" Pause for a minute or two after each question so students have time to write a response before thinking about the next one.

Students might have trouble answering the last question, if only because they don't know what their future classwork will entail, or because they can't picture how they'd bring their values to it. Even if they can't think of an answer, the question reminds students that they can bring their values to their work, and when they get new assignments, they might realize how.

If you have your students share their responses, you'll know more about the values they want to bring to their work, and you can make suggestions if and when appropriate. Let's say Elodie chooses the merchandising line as the product she'd find most satisfying to make out of her Sumer research paper. As she thinks about why, she realizes she wants to challenge stereotypes of Iraq. She might not be able to imagine how she can use future history essays to challenge stereotypes, but now that her teacher knows that's what matters to her, he can point out opportunities.

Boosting the Impact

After this protocol, students might ask, "*Now* are we done with this?" and gleefully toss their work in the trash when you say *yes*. Similarly, even if your students get excited about upcycling their old work, they probably won't do it. They have other schoolwork and out-of-school commitments. But you don't have to measure this protocol's success by how many students create the work product they imagined. Instead, you can see whether they expand their thinking about *future* work. Do they start to bring any values they identified to their future assignments, within and beyond your class? As they do new work, do they come up with their own ideas for repurposing it? Look for any kind of change in how students approach their work, because that flexibility is a good sign they're creating space to make their work meaningful for themselves, not just to fulfill an assignment.

Using the Protocol Next Time

Upcycling is not a protocol you'd use after every unit—its novelty would wear off—but you can reuse it with a different type of work product and different prompts. As a year-end project, you could possibly have your students try making the things they envision. But even if it remains an imaginative exercise, the Upcycling protocol gives students a reason to reassess their creations, refine their thinking, and bring their values to their work.

 # Values-Based Portfolios

Students create academic portfolios based on their own definitions of what's meaningful at school.

Suggested Time:

Academic portfolios provide students with a tangible record of their learning, with the associated struggles, opportunities, discoveries, risks, and triumphs. But what should go into an academic portfolio? When teachers ask students to make portfolios of their best work, the students tend to include work because they got a good grade on it, and not necessarily because they feel satisfied with what they created or learned. Even if we ask them to identify work they feel proud of, they have trouble getting past academic status as measured in our terms.

Rather than asking for *best* work, some teachers ask students to make work portfolios that demonstrate specific achievements. For example, they'll ask students to identify work they put effort into making, work they did in collaboration with a partner or group, work that shows their ability to problem solve, or work that demonstrates their study skills. While such prompts help the students consider their successes beyond grades, the teacher is still the one defining *success*—in this case, as effort, collaboration, problem solving, or study skill development.

Instead of creating academic portfolios based on what matters to *us*, what if our students created portfolios based on what matters to *them*? During this protocol, Values-Based Portfolios, students first identify the top three factors that make an assignment meaningful to them. Then, they create a portfolio of work that represents times when they succeeded *and* failed to make their work meaningful in each way they identified. They can use their portfolio to start conversations with teachers, parents, and peers about how they can make their work more meaningful in the future.

Getting Ready

Do the following in preparation for the protocol.

❑ Decide on a format for your students' portfolios.

They can put together a physical binder or folder of work samples, or they can use an online platform so they can share their portfolios with their teachers of other subjects or from previous years, as well as their families and friends.

Some work will be easy to include; students can just print or upload a copy. If the work is too big to include, such as a large poster, students can take a photo of it and print or upload that. If the work has no tangible product, such as a tableau vivant they performed in class one day or an online study group they led, then they can write about it or draw it for the portfolio.

❑ Decide how long your students will need to collect their work to put into their portfolios.

Unless students' work is very easily accessible in the classroom, they'll need to spend time collecting it and can do so over the course of several days. Bringing work products back from home (or even their lockers) can be a homework assignment.

❑ Make enough copies of the making assignments meaningful checklist (figure 8.4) and the creating a values-based portfolio chart (figure 8.5, page 204) for each student.

Directions: Below are some factors that make assignments meaningful to some students. What makes an assignment meaningful to you? Please choose three factors that you find most important for an assignment to be meaningful to you. If the wording doesn't quite work for you, change the words so they do work—or write your own factors!

To me, an assignment is meaningful when it provides opportunities for me to:

- ☐ Explore, experiment, and ask questions
- ☐ Imagine new and different ways to do things
- ☐ Bring energy and excitement to my work
- ☐ Take a playful approach
- ☐ Make connections to topics and issues I've learned about before
- ☐ Build closer relationships
- ☐ Belong to a community
- ☐ Make sure everyone gets a fair chance
- ☐ Give others what they need most
- ☐ Seek solutions and work toward them
- ☐ Seek new perspectives and develop empathy
- ☐ Appreciate the good things in life
- ☐ Appreciate beauty and excellence
- ☐ Develop skills I can use in my other classes or outside school
- ☐ Develop skills I'll need as an adult
- ☐ Use what I learn to understand myself and my place in the world
- ☐ Use what I learn to make a positive difference in my community
- ☐ Challenge myself
- ☐ _____
- ☐ _____
- ☐ _____

Figure 8.4: Making assignments meaningful.

Visit go.SolutionTree.com/instruction for a free reproducible version of this figure.

To me, an assignment is meaningful when it provides opportunities for me to:

1. _____

2. _____

3. _____

I was very able to _____ when . . . (1)	I didn't really _____ when . . . (1)
I was very able to _____ when . . . (2)	I didn't really _____ when . . . (2)
I was very able to _____ when . . . (3)	I didn't really _____ when . . . (3)

Figure 8.5: Creating a values-based portfolio chart.

*Visit **go.SolutionTree.com/instruction** for a free reproducible version of this figure.*

Leading the Protocol

The following six steps will help you most effectively lead the protocol.

1. **Hand out copies of making assignments meaningful (figure 8.5). Students identify three factors that are most important to them in making work meaningful.**

   Students might have thought about what makes an assignment fun, but not necessarily what makes it meaningful to them. The checklist provides some language they can use to express what they find meaningful, but they should feel free to add, eliminate, or change words, or to write their own factors. Maybe Gia finds work meaningful when it gives her the opportunity to use her creativity, challenge herself, and develop closer relationships with her teachers. Maybe for Russell, work is meaningful when he can ask lots of questions, show kindness to his peers, and understand his place in the world.

   Choosing three different factors helps students notice multiple ways to make work meaningful; choosing *only* three helps them prioritize what's most important to them at this time.

2. **Hand out the creating a values-based portfolio (figure 8.5). Students copy their three criteria for meaningful work onto the top lines.**

They don't have to put the factors in any particular order; the numbers are just for reference. Copying the factors gives them another chance to tweak the wording so it fits their sense of what makes work meaningful.

3. **Reflecting on the past term in their class, students identify specific times when they were able to make their work meaningful in each way they identified. They fill out the chart's left column accordingly.**

They might write about lessons, homework assignments, class activities, discussions, field trips, study sessions, work sessions, work products—anything they did or made for the course.

Imagine that Russell and Gia are in the same mathematics class. Since Russell finds work meaningful when he shows kindness to his peers, he writes about a time when he encouraged a friend while they studied for a challenging test together. Since Gia finds work meaningful when she's creative, she writes about the color-coded study guide she made for that same test. Even if Russell and Gia didn't particularly enjoy taking this test or get good grades on it—and even if their teacher thinks they should have focused more energy on learning the material than on helping a classmate or turning the study guide into an art project—these two students did use their assignment as an opportunity to enact their values.

4. **Students identify specific times during the past term when either they didn't have opportunities to make their work meaningful in each of the three ways, or they failed to take advantage of those opportunities. They fill out the chart's right column accordingly.**

For example, Gia writes about a graphing activity that she found easy and couldn't make challenging for herself because she had to do the steps exactly as instructed. Russell remembers a mini poster comparing airplane speeds, which he made using only information he found in his textbook, when he could have asked more questions about airplanes or chosen a topic he was more curious about. Even if these two students found the activities fun and got good grades on them, the activities weren't as meaningful as they could have been.

5. **Students create a portfolio of meaningful work based on their own definition of *meaningful*.**

These can be physical or electronic portfolios, and the students can make them right then or over time.

6. **Students share their portfolios with one another in small groups.**

They might discover that they found the same assignments meaningful for different reasons, or that they share similar ideas of what makes work meaningful but found meaning in different assignments. In any case, they'll each share their experiences of meaningful work, and they'll hear what makes work meaningful to their peers.

Boosting the Impact

In later discussions or through writing, your students can consider how the work in their portfolios reflects their values. Try asking questions such as these.

- "How are the topics of these pieces of work important to you?"

- "If you'd had another week to work on these, what would you have done to make them even better?"

- "If you were to redo one of these assignments, which one would you redo, and what would you do differently?"

- "What skills did you learn from doing these assignments?"

- "What did you learn about yourself from doing these assignments?"

In one-on-one conversations, you can ask more specific questions about how the work in students' portfolios aligns with their values. Russell's teacher might ask, "What were some of the questions you asked during the measurement unit? If you could redo your mini poster project, what questions would you ask this time? What are you working on now that you can ask more questions about? What are some questions you could ask? What can you do that might help you think of more questions? In the future, when you get an assignment and can't think of questions, how else can you make that work meaningful?"

Such discussions help students notice how their behaviors match their values and choose for themselves what they want to do next. For Gia, color-coding notes might be an act of creativity, but it might also take time away from studying. Instead of telling Gia to spend less time coloring and more time doing practice problems, her teacher could ask whether doing practice problems gives her an opportunity to challenge herself—which is another way she finds work meaningful. If so, how does Gia want to allocate her time when she's studying for her next test?

Values-based portfolios can also structure family conferences. Instead of only reporting the student's achievement, you can invite the parent and student into a conversation about making school more meaningful in the future. Imagine if Russell, his mathematics teacher, and his parents all used his portfolio to help him think of ways to ask more questions about mathematics, show kindness to his mathematics classmates, and consider the role of mathematics as he discovers his place in the world. Russell could continue these discussions at home with his parents and in class with his peers, and he could start similar conversations in his other classes with his other teachers, and at his cello lessons and wrestling practices, this year and throughout his life.

Using the Protocol Next Time

If students create portfolios every term, they can track changes in what makes their work meaningful. As Gia matures, she might discover that developing relationships with her teachers becomes less important, and that working for gender equity becomes more important. Noticing this change might help Gia choose topics and projects—in and beyond her mathematics class—based on the extent to which they enable her to do equity work. More generally, revisiting what makes work meaningful can help students approach their assignments more flexibly, instead of picking the same topics and strategies every time.

Eventually, you might coordinate with colleagues who teach other subjects so that students make multidisciplinary portfolios. Now that Russell has identified what makes his work meaningful, he could find times when he succeeded and failed to make his history, English, science, Latin, art, and ethics assignments meaningful in those same ways—and maybe notice connections among these disciplines. Your students' multidisciplinary portfolios would show you what they do in other classes that they find meaningful so you can help them make their work in your class more meaningful. Maybe if Gia's history teacher sees her creative study guide from mathematics, he can help her set up her history notes more creatively.

When it's based on a student's definition of *meaningful*, the portfolio becomes more than just another assignment students have to complete. It becomes a way for students to discover and do what matters to them.

Onward

This chapter's protocols help students reflect on their academic learning, reinforce workable learning behaviors, and change unworkable ones. But what *workable* means depends not only on external definitions of success, like standards and benchmarks, but also on students' own values. In the course of reflecting on their learning, students become more aware of the values they bring to school, so they can choose what they want school to mean.

Although this marks the end of the unit—and the last chapter of this book—it isn't the end of students' learning. Reflecting on past learning empowers them to notice what matters and choose to do what serves their values during the next unit, the next year, and the next phase of their lives.

Conclusion

• • • • •

CREATING LEARNING MOMENTS THAT MATTER

You've now seen how teachers can turn every stage of an academic unit into a context for values work. This book described a total of thirty protocols that help students notice and choose opportunities to act on their values as they prepare for learning, explore and review new material, create and refine a work product, and reflect on their learning. Each protocol included a step-by-step description of what to do, ways to boost students' commitment to their values, and ideas for how to use the protocol in the future.

You can think of the protocols as recipes. It's possible to mess up a recipe; you might miss a step, misunderstand the directions, omit an ingredient, or measure wrong and end up with an oozy mess where your lemon meringue pie was supposed to be. Sometimes, when people get enough bad-tasting results in the kitchen, they declare themselves bad cooks and stop trying. Others know that cooking is hard, even with a recipe to follow, but they find cooking worthwhile and try again. Maybe they try to follow the same pie recipe more carefully, or maybe they find a different recipe that serves a similar function— say, for chocolate chip cookies. We hope that if you don't get the results you want from a protocol, you'll reread it and try again, or you'll find a different protocol to try instead.

Sometimes following a recipe to the letter won't get you the results you want. A barbecue sauce recipe calls for a teaspoon of chili powder, but that would make it too spicy for your kids. A frittata recipe includes ham, but you don't eat meat. A salad recipe mentions watercress, which isn't available at your local market. When you see a recipe—or a protocol—that you don't think will work for you as written, you can adapt it. Put in more or less of something. Add something, or leave something out. Replace something that won't work with something that will. We wrote the protocols as we did because we think each part is important, and we hope you'll consider each part, but we also hope you'll question and change parts that you don't think will work for your students, subject, and time frame.

If the protocols don't get you the results you want, we hope you'll reread chapter 1 (page 15) of this book. Chapter 1 explained how teachers can create the conditions for students to explore and enact their values by designing relevant learning tasks, delivering tasks to foster psychological presence, giving empowering feedback on student work, managing the power dynamics in the room, and responding to student avoidance. If you were to change some aspect of your students' learning environment to make it more conducive to values work, which aspect would it be? What change would you make? What would be your first step?

Some cooks, after following enough recipes, discover the underlying principles. They notice, for example, that they can knead all kinds of ingredients into bread dough, or that many soup recipes begin with sautéing aromatic vegetables. An experienced cook can riff off a recipe for olive-rosemary bread to make apricot-tarragon bread, which tastes completely different but uses many of the same ingredients and the same basic procedure. Experienced cooks can also make soup from whatever they find fresh at the market, not following any recipe but abstracting general principles from recipes they've followed in the past. After trying some of the protocols in this book, we hope you'll make up your own.

If you decide to make up your own protocols, we would encourage you to reread chapter 2 (page 35), which described how deictic, analogical, and hierarchical framing help people notice new possibilities for themselves and freely choose actions that make their lives meaningful. All this book's protocols use one or more of these framings. Once you've tried some of the protocols, see if you can use the science behind them to more creatively and flexibly help your students discover and do what matters.

We began this book by asking you to recall a classroom experience you had in each grade from kindergarten to your senior year in high school, and to consider the kinds of learning moments you want to create for your students. Returning to memories of your own school experiences, you might also remember when those experiences inevitably came to an end. Whether it meant transitioning from kindergarten to first grade or graduating from college, everyone has confronted a last day. And on that day, you might have looked around at your peers and teachers, wondering what would remain of your experiences together as you moved forward into the unknown.

As teachers ourselves, when the last day of school approaches, we've sometimes felt stumped trying to produce an appropriate gesture that honors, appreciates, and commemorates the work we've done with our students. Some years, we've tried making cards or giving speeches or telling stories. Other years, we've simply shared a final good-bye or hug as our students filed out the door. When we end a year of living by our values at school, we attempt to honor the hard work our students did throughout the year, not just in learning the academic content, but also in developing an awareness of their values, sharing their emotions, and building authentic relationships. We have one last moment when we can notice and name the fact that something meaningful happened to us, between us, and because of us. When we reflect on these experiences, we feel a sense of reverence.

As we reach the end of our work with our students, we also hope that their academic learning, their relationships, and their commitment to their values will continue to grow without our careful attention. At the same time, we often feel a sense of loss that our work with our classes has culminated. We may have missed opportunities and glimpsed but never fully realized possibilities. This, too, is part of saying good-bye, as we make peace with what can no longer be.

Ending offers us one last moment to recognize where we've gone together. We have now arrived at that moment with you, our reader. While we don't know you, we hope that your experience of reading this book has allowed us to travel along the same byways of values work and student empowerment. Our fondest hope is that you feel empowered to design learning experiences for your students that culminate in moments of reverence like we have felt toward our students, and now, toward you.

Appendix

• • • • •

REPRODUCIBLES

Unit Task Organizer

Unit:

Outcome:

Prepare for learning

Explore new material

Review the material

Create work product

Refine work product

Reflect on learning

Intention Icons

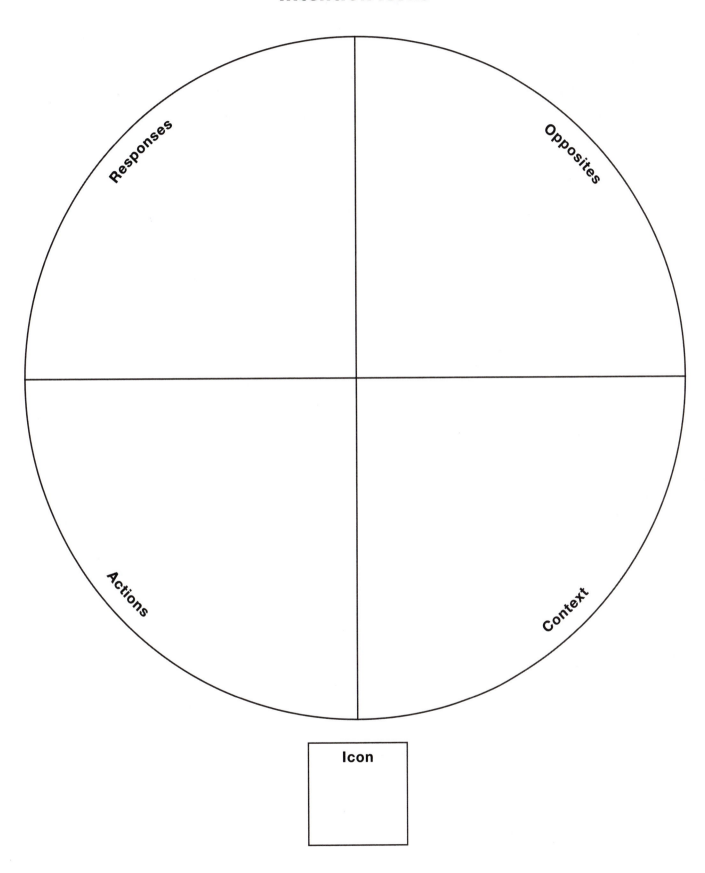

Responses

Opposites

Actions

Context

Icon

Noticing Emotions Chart

Unit:		
I felt . . .	**when . . .**	
angry		
excited		
happy		
safe		
afraid		
surprised		
sad		
disgusted		

Review Tournament Bracket

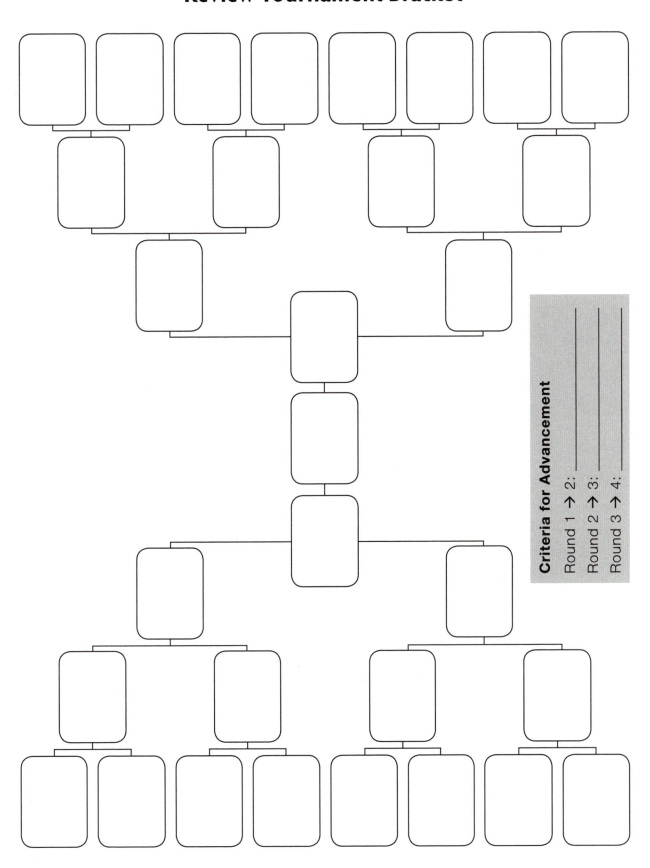

Criteria for Advancement

Round 1 → 2: _____

Round 2 → 3: _____

Round 3 → 4: _____

Peer Review Direction Cards

This is the front page; the next page is the back. Print out the cards two-sided. Then cut out the cards.

Front (Feedback Giver)

Tell me your OBSERVATIONS.

What stands out to you? Point out specific details or moments that get your attention, and use just a word or two to show me what these parts make you think or feel (*cool*, *whoa*, *hmm*, *been there*, and so on).

Tell me your QUESTIONS.

What makes you curious or confused?
Ask me lots of questions. Questions beginning with *What*, *Which*, or *What kind of* will help me most.

Tell me your INTERPRETATIONS.

What seems important to me?
What does it seem like I'm trying to get you to think about or do? Help me see what's getting across in my work.

Back (Feedback Receiver)

Are the details that stood out the ones I think are most important? If not, what will I add or cut? Did I get the reactions I wanted? If not, what will I change?

Based on the questions I got, what details can I add?
Where can I be more specific?
What can I explain more fully or clearly?

What matters to me?
Is that what's getting across in my work?
If not, what can I expand or clarify?

Considerate Editing Chart

Editing Decision	Most Considerate Options

Concentric Self-Portrait

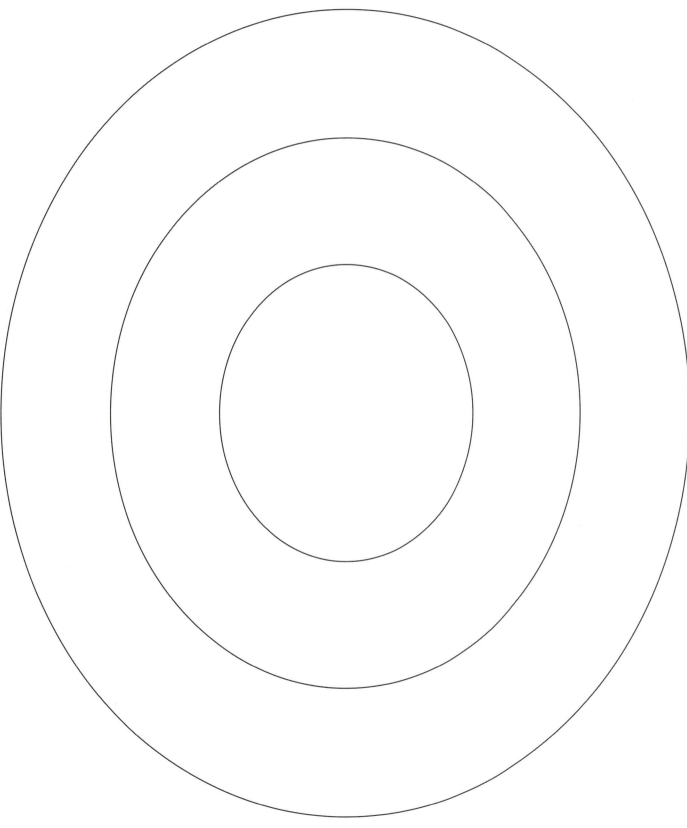

Two-for-One Teaching © 2020 Solution Tree Press • SolutionTree.com
Visit **go.SolutionTree.com/instruction** to download this free reproducible.

Sentence Strips

6	5	4	3	2	1
6	5	4	3	2	1
6	5	4	3	2	1
6	5	4	3	2	1

References & Resources

• • • • •

Aronson, B., & Laughter, J. (2016). The theory and practice of culturally relevant education: A synthesis of research across content areas. *Review of Educational Research, 86*(1), 163–206.

Auden, W. H. (1966). *Collected shorter poems, 1927–1957*. London: Faber & Faber.

Banks, J. A., & Banks, C. A. M. (2010). *Multicultural education: Issues and perspectives* (7th ed.). Hoboken, NJ: Wiley.

Barron's Educational Series. (2005). *Essential atlas of ecology*. Hauppauge, NY: Author.

Beaty, D. (2013, December 17). *Knock knock* [Video file]. Accessed at www.youtube.com/watch?v=L0jTeuBpn5s on August 3, 2018.

Berens, N. M., & Hayes, S. C. (2007). Arbitrarily applicable comparative relations: Experimental evidence for a relational operant. *Journal of Applied Behavior Analysis, 40*(1), 45–71.

Bergman, S. B. (2018, April 3). Conformation: The body no longer policed by gender. *Medium.* Accessed at https://medium.com/s/unrulybodies/the-body-no-longer-policed-by-gender-c92d6163de9b on April 16, 2018.

Boud, D., Keogh, R., & Walker, D. (Eds.). (2013). *Reflection: Turning experience into learning*. Abingdon, UK: Routledge.

Brackett, M. A., Rivers, S. E., Reyes, M. R., & Salovey, P. (2012). Enhancing academic performance and social and emotional competence with the RULER feeling words curriculum. *Learning and Individual Differences, 22*(2), 218–224.

Bradbury, R. (1953). *Fahrenheit 451*. New York: Ballantine Books.

Button Poetry. (2014, May 21). *Hieu Minh Nguyen—"Traffic jam"* [Video file]. Accessed at www.youtube.com /watch?v=Q7RHM1xQMiw on August 3, 2018.

Camus, A. (1946). *The stranger* (S. Gilbert, Trans.). New York: Knopf.

Carlsen, A. & Patel, J.K. (2018, March 22). March for Our Lives: Maps of the more than 800 protests around the world. *The New York Times.* Accessed at www.nytimes.com/interactive/2018/03/22/us/politics/march-for -lives-demonstrations.html on April 14, 2019.

Charles, R. I., Illingworth, M., McNemar, B., Mills, D., Ramirez, A., & Reeves, A. (2010). *Prentice hall mathematics: Course 2*. Boston: Pearson.

Christensen, J. (2017, April 25). *Why reading is good for your health*. Accessed at www.cnn.com/2016/07/21/health /reading-fiction-health-effects/index.html on July 16, 2017.

Christensen, L. (2009). *Teaching for joy and justice: Re-imagining the language arts classroom*. Milwaukee, WI: Rethinking Schools.

Ciarrochi, J., Deane, F. P., Wilson, C. J., & Rickwood, D. (2002). Adolescents who need help the most are the least likely to seek it: The relationship between low emotional competence and low intention to seek help. *British Journal of Guidance and Counselling, 30*(2), 173–188.

Ciarrochi, J., Kashdan, T. B., Leeson, P., Heaven, P., & Jordan, C. (2011). On being aware and accepting: A one-year longitudinal study into adolescent well-being. *Journal of Adolescence, 34*(4), 695–703.

Cisneros, S. (1991). *The house on Mango Street*. New York: Vintage Books.

Durlak, J. A., Weissberg, R. P., Dymnicki, A. B., Taylor, R. D., & Schellinger, K. B. (2011). The impact of enhancing students' social and emotional learning: A meta-analysis of school-based universal interventions. *Child Development, 82*(1), 405–432.

Dweck, C. S. (2015, September 22). Carol Dweck revisits the 'growth mindset'. *Education Week*. Accessed at www.edweek.org/ew/articles/2015/09/23/carol-dweck-revisits-the-growth-mindset.html on April 16, 2019.

eFoodhandlers. (2014, September 2). Basic food safety for Oregon: Chapter 4, "Avoiding cross contamination" (English) [Video file]. Accessed at www.youtube.com/watch?v=_Hx_f_S1rXs on April 19, 2019.

Elbow, P. (1989). Toward a phenomenology of freewriting. *Journal of Basic Writing, 8*(2), 42–71.

Fluckiger, J. (2010). Single point rubric: A tool for responsible student self-assessment. *The Delta Kappa Gamma Bulletin, 76*(4), 18–25.

Foody, M., Barnes-Holmes, Y., Barnes-Holmes, D., Torneke, N., Luciano, C., & McEnteggart, C. (2014). RFT for clinical use: The example of metaphor. *Journal of Contextual Behavioral Science, 3*(4), 305–313.

Friman, P. C., Hayes, S. C., & Wilson, K. G. (1998). Why behavior analysts should study emotion: The example of anxiety. *Journal of Applied Behavior Analysis, 31*(1), 137–156.

Geiger, K. B., Carr, J. E., & LeBlanc, L. A. (2010). Function-based treatments for escape-maintained problem behavior: A treatment-selection model for practicing behavior analysts. *Behavior Analysis in Practice, 3*(1), 22–32.

Gilbert, P. (2009). Introducing compassion-focused therapy. *Advances in Psychiatric Treatment, 15*(3), 199–208.

Gilbert, P. (2010). *The compassionate mind: A new approach to life's challenges*. Oakland, CA: New Harbinger.

Goldson, E. (2010, August 5). *Valedictorian speaks out against schooling* [Video file]. Accessed at www.youtube.com/watch?v=9M4tdMsg3ts on December 26, 2016.

Hacker, T., Stone, P., & MacBeth, A. (2016). Acceptance and commitment therapy—do we know enough? Cumulative and sequential meta-analyses of randomized controlled trials. *Journal of Affective Disorders, 190*, 551–565.

Hansberry, L. (1994). *A raisin in the sun*. New York: Vintage Books. (Original work published in 1959)

Harris, R. (2009). *ACT made simple: An easy-to-read primer on acceptance and commitment therapy*. Oakland, CA: New Harbinger.

Hayes, S. C. (1995). Knowing selves. *The Behavior Therapist, 18*(5), 94–96.

Hayes, S. C. (2005). *Get out of your mind and into your life: The new acceptance and commitment therapy*. Oakland, CA: New Harbinger.

Hayes, S. C., Barnes-Holmes, D., & Roche, B. (Eds.). (2001). *Relational frame theory: A post-Skinnerian account of human language and cognition*. New York: Kluwer Academic/Plenum.

Hayes, S. C., Fox, E., Gifford, E. V., Wilson, K. G., Barnes-Holmes, D., & Healy, O. (2001). Derived relational responding as learned behavior. In S. C. Hayes, D. Barnes-Holmes, & B. Roche (Eds.), *Relational frame theory: A post-Skinnerian account of human language and cognition* (pp. 21–49). New York: Kluwer Academic/Plenum.

Hayes, S. C., Strosahl, K. D., & Wilson, K. G. (1999). *Acceptance and commitment therapy: An experiential approach to behavior change*. New York: Guilford Press.

Hayes, S. C., Strosahl, K. D., & Wilson, K. G. (2012). *Acceptance and commitment therapy: The process and practice of mindful change* (2nd ed.). New York: Guilford Press.

Homer. (2006). *Odyssey* (R. Fagles, Trans.). New York: Penguin. (Original work 675–725 BCE)

hooks, b. (1994). *Teaching to transgress: Education as the practice of freedom*. New York: Routledge.

House, S., & Vaswani, N. (2011). *Same sun here*. Somerville, MA: Candlewick Press.

Howard, V. (2011). The importance of pleasure reading in the lives of young teens: Self-identification, self-construction and self-awareness. *Journal of Librarianship and Information Science, 43*(1), 46–55.

Hughes, L. (1995). Theme for English B. In A. Rampersad (Ed.), *The collected poems of Langston Hughes* (pp. 409–410). New York: Vintage Books.

Hurston, Z. N. (2013). *Their eyes were watching god*. New York: HarperCollins.

Johnston, P. T. (2012). *Opening minds: Using language to change lives*. Portland, ME: Stenhouse Publishers.

Kanter, J. (2016). *Conceptualization of awareness, courage, and love as clinical targets in functional analytic psychotherapy*. Workshop presented at the Association for Contextual Behavioral Science World Conference, Seattle, WA.

Kolts, R. L. (2016). *CFT made simple: A clinician's guide to practicing compassion-focused therapy*. Oakland, CA: New Harbinger.

Krishnamoorthy, R. (2014, July 28). *Promoting the non-obvious candidate*. Accessed at https://hbr.org/2014/07/promoting-the-non-obvious-candidate on December 26, 2018.

Ladson-Billings, G. (1995). Toward a theory of culturally relevant pedagogy. *American Educational Research Journal, 32*(3), 465–491.

Ladson-Billings, G. (2014). Culturally relevant pedagogy 2.0: a.k.a. the remix. *Harvard Educational Review, 84*(1), 74–84.

Lesnick, A. (2009). Odd questions, strange texts, and other people: Collaborative learning, play, and new knowledge. In T. Vilardi & M. Chang (Eds.), *Writing-based teaching: Essential practices and enduring questions* (pp. 71–94). Albany, NY: State University of New York Press.

LeTourneau, N. (2018). The teacher who helped prepare the Parkland students for activism. *Washington Monthly*. Accessed at https://washingtonmonthly.com/2018/03/02/the-teacher-who-helped-prepare-the-parkland-students-for-activism on April 14, 2019.

Linehan, M. M. (2014). *DBT skills training handouts and worksheets* (2nd ed.). New York: Guilford.

Lithwick, D. (2018, February 28). They were trained for this moment. *Slate.* Accessed at https://slate.com/news
-and-politics/2018/02/the-student-activists-of-marjory-stoneman-douglas-high-demonstrate-the-power-of-a
-full-education.html on April 14, 2019.

Lopez, G. (2018, March 26). It's official: March for Our Lives was one of the biggest youth protests since the
Vietnam War. *Vox.* Accessed at www.vox.com/policy-and-politics/2018/3/26/17160646/march-for-our-lives
-crowd-size-count on April 14, 2019.

Luoma, J. B., & Platt, M. G. (2015). Shame, self-criticism, self-stigma, and compassion in acceptance and
commitment therapy. *Current Opinion in Psychology, 2,* 97–101.

Martinez, S. L., & Stager, G. (2013). *Invent to learn: Making, tinkering, and engineering in the classroom.* Torrance,
CA: Constructing Modern Knowledge Press.

McCarty, T., & Lee, T. (2014). Critical culturally sustaining/revitalizing pedagogy and indigenous education
sovereignty. *Harvard Educational Review, 84*(1), 101–124.

McDonough, W., & Braungart, M. (2002). *Cradle to cradle: Remaking the way we make things.* New York: North
Point Press.

McHugh, L., & Stewart, I. (2012). *The self and perspective taking: Contributions and applications from modern
behavioral science.* Oakland, CA: New Harbinger.

McKenna, M. C., Conradi, K., Lawrence, C., Jang, B. G., & Meyer, J. P. (2012). Reading attitudes of middle
school students: Results of a U.S. survey. *Reading Research Quarterly, 47*(3), 283–306.

Miller, W. R., & Rollnick, S. (2013). *Motivational interviewing: Helping people change* (3rd ed.). New York:
Guilford Press.

Moore, C. (2009). Radical revision: Toward demystifying the labor of writing. In T. Vilardi & M. Chang (Eds.),
Writing-based teaching: Essential practices and enduring questions (pp. 119–140). Albany, NY: State University
of New York Press.

National Governors Association Center for Best Practices & Council of Chief State School Officers. (n.d.).
Frequently asked questions. Accessed at www.corestandards.org/resources/frequently-asked-questions on March
23, 2018.

Nellen, T. (n.d.). I heard, I noticed, I wondered. Accessed at www.tnellen.com/cybereng/method.html on July 7,
2017.

Nevin, J. A., & Grace, R. C. (2000). Behavioral momentum and the law of effect. *Behavioral and Brain Sciences,
23*(1), 73–90.

Nitko, A. J., & Brookhart, S. M. (2007). *Educational assessment of students* (5th ed.). Upper Saddle River, NJ:
Pearson Prentice Hall.

Ogle, D. M. (1986). KWL: A teaching model that develops active reading of expository text. *The Reading Teacher,
39*(6), 564–570.

Paris, D. (2012). Culturally sustaining pedagogy: A needed change in stance, terminology, and practice. *Educational
Researcher, 41*(3), 93–97.

Plutchik, R. (2001). The nature of emotions: Human emotions have deep evolutionary roots, a fact that may explain their complexity and provide tools for clinical practice. *American Scientist, 89*(4), 344–350.

Porosoff, L., & Weinstein, J. (2018). *EMPOWER your students: Tools to inspire a meaningful school experience, grades 6–12*. Bloomington, IN: Solution Tree Press.

Powelson, B. F. (n.d.). [Photograph of Harriet Tubman, c1868–69]. Accessed at https://upload.wikimedia.org /wikipedia/commons/f/fc/Harriet_Tubman_c1868-69.jpg on April 18, 2018.

Reilly, K. (2018, March 24). Here's the size of the March For Our Lives crowd in Washington. *Time.* Accessed at http://time.com/5214405/march-for-our-lives-attendance-crowd-size on April 14, 2019.

Roche, B., & Barnes, D. (1997). A transformation of respondently conditioned stimulus function in accordance with arbitrarily applicable relations. *Journal of the Experimental Analysis of Behavior, 67*(3), 275–301.

Rowsell, H. C., Ciarrochi, J., Deane, F. P., & Heaven, P. C. (2016). Emotion identification skill and social support during adolescence: A three-year longitudinal study. *Journal of Research on Adolescence, 26*(1), 115–125.

Sampson, A. (1999). *Mandela: The authorized biography*. New York: Knopf.

Shakespeare, W. (1973a). A midsummer night's dream. In G. B. Evans, H. Levin, H. Baker, A. Barton, F. Kermode, H. Smith, M. Edel, & C. H. Shattuck (Eds.), *The Riverside Shakespeare* (pp. 251–283). Boston: Houghton Mifflin. (Original work published 1600)

Shakespeare, W. (1973b). The tragedy of Romeo and Juliet. In G. B. Evans, H. Levin, H. Baker, A. Barton, F. Kermode, H. Smith, M. Edel, & C. H. Shattuck (Eds.), *The Riverside Shakespeare* (pp. 1101–1145). Boston: Houghton Mifflin. (Original work published 1597)

Sleeter, C. E. (2005). *Un-standardizing curriculum: Multicultural teaching in the standards-based classroom*. New York: Teachers College Press.

Spiegelhalter, D. (2018, April 2). Coffee and cancer: What Starbucks might have argued. *Medium.* Accessed at https://medium.com/wintoncentre/coffee-and-cancer-what-starbucks-might-have-argued-2f20aa4a9fed on April 16, 2018.

Steele, C. M. (2010). *Whistling Vivaldi: How stereotypes affect us and what we can do*. New York: Norton.

Stewart, I., Barnes-Holmes, D., Hayes, S. C., & Lipkens, R. (2001). Relations among relations: Analogies, metaphors, and stories. In S. C. Hayes, D. Barnes-Holmes, & B. Roche (Eds.), *Relational frame theory: A post-Skinnerian account of human language and cognition* (pp. 73–86). New York: Kluwer Academic/Plenum.

Stokes, T. F., & Baer, D. M. (1977). An implicit technology of generalization. *Journal of Applied Behavior Analysis, 10*(2), 349–367.

Sweeney, L. B. (2001). *When a butterfly sneezes: A guide for helping kids explore interconnections in our world through favorite stories*. Waltham, MA: Pegasus Communications.

Taylor, R. D., Oberle, E., Durlak, J. A., & Weissberg, R. P. (2017). Promoting positive youth development through school-based social and emotional learning interventions: A meta-analysis of follow-up effects. *Child Development, 88*(4), 1156–1171.

Than, G. A. (2013, July 16). *Erica Goldson: Graduation speech*. Accessed at http://zenpencils.com/comic/123-erica -goldson-graduation-speech on December 26, 2016.

Torneke, N. (2017). *Metaphor in practice: A professional's guide to using the science of language in psychotherapy.* Oakland, CA: Context Press.

Veehof, M. M., Oskam, M., Schreurs, K. M., & Bohlmeijer, E. T. (2011). Acceptance-based interventions for the treatment of chronic pain: A systematic review and meta-analysis. *Pain, 152*(3), 533–542.

Villatte, M., Villatte, J. L., & Hayes, S. C. (2016). *Mastering the clinical conversation: Language as intervention.* New York: Guilford Press.

Walker, A. (1984). *In search of our mothers' gardens: Womanist prose.* San Diego, CA: Harcourt.

Waltz, T. J., & Follette, W. C. (2009). Molar functional relations and clinical behavior analysis: Implications for assessment and treatment. *The Behavior Analyst, 32*(1), 51–68.

Weinstein, J. H., Wilson, K. G., Drake, C. E., & Kellum, K. K. (2008). A relational frame theory contribution to social categorization. *Behavior and Social Issues, 17*(1), 39–64.

Wiggins, G., & McTighe, J. (2005). *Understanding by design* (2nd ed.). Alexandria, VA: Association for Supervision and Curriculum Development.

Wilson, K. G., & DuFrene, T. (2009). *Mindfulness for two: An acceptance and commitment therapy approach to mindfulness in psychotherapy.* Oakland, CA: New Harbinger.

Wilson, K. G., & Murrell, A. R. (2004). Values work in acceptance and commitment therapy: Setting a course for behavioral treatment. In S. C. Hayes, V. M. Follette, & M. M. Linehan (Eds.), *Mindfulness and acceptance: Expanding the cognitive-behavioral tradition* (pp. 120–151). New York: Guilford Press.

Wilson, K. G., Sandoz, E. K., Kitchens, J., & Roberts, M. (2010). The valued living questionnaire: Defining and measuring valued action within a behavioral framework. *The Psychological Record, 60*(2), 249–272.

Woodson, J. (2014). *Brown girl dreaming.* New York: Penguin.

Zoboi, I. (2017). *American street.* New York: HarperCollins.

Zywica, J., & Gomez, K. (2008). Annotating to support learning in the content areas: Teaching and learning science. *Journal of Adolescent & Adult Literacy, 52*(2), 155–165.

Index

• • • • •

A

academic performance, 5, 7
academic tasks, 9–11. *See also* learning tasks, designing
Acceptance and Commitment Therapy (ACT), 5, 35
achievement, 5–6, 8, 30
actions
    behavioral momentum and, 45
    feedback and suggested actions, 23–26
    hierarchical framing and, 41–43
    values and qualities of, 8
    values-consistent actions, 45–46
adaptive peak, 159
additive approach, 18
analogical framing
    about, 40–41
    protocols and, 44–45, 210
analytic rubrics, 160, 162
annotation, 80, 81, 83. *See also* Focused Annotation protocol
approval-seeking students, 31–32, 33, 169
approximated work products, 134
artistic representation, 63, 117
assessments
    self-assessment after leading a protocol, 49
    self-assessment before leading a protocol, 48
    work products and, 133
avoidance
    responding to common avoidance moves, 32–33
    when students complain, 29–31
    when students do something else, 28–29
    when students seek approval for every decision, 31–32, 33
    when students stay silent, 31
awards. *See* Naming Awards protocol

B

Banks, C., 18
Banks, J., 18
behavioral momentum, 45
behaviors. *See also* avoidance; Intention Icons protocol
    emotional control agendas and, 124
    free choice and, 37
    group commitments flowchart and, 156
    opposite behaviors, 68–69
    positive behaviors, 56
    values and, 7

Booksploration protocol
    about, 106, 122–123
    boosting the impact, 126
    getting ready, 123
    leading the protocol, 123–125
    protocols by framing type and, 44
    using the protocol next time, 126

C

choice, 36–37, 147
Collaborative Conversations protocol
    about, 80, 90
    boosting the impact, 93
    getting ready, 90
    leading the protocol, 91–93
    protocols by framing type and, 44
    teachers and, 27
    using the protocol next time, 94
commitments. *See also* Group Commitments protocol
    group commitments flowchart, 153
    Values in the Field protocol and, 102–103
Compassion-Focused Therapy (CFT), 35
Concentric Self-Portraits protocol
    about, 186–187
    boosting the impact, 189
    getting ready, 187
    leading the protocol, 188–189
    protocols by framing type and, 45
    using the protocol next time, 189–190
connections and outliers, 64
Considerate Editing protocol
    about, 160, 176
    boosting the impact, 179–180
    getting ready, 176–177
    leading the protocol, 178–179
    protocols by framing type and, 44
    using the protocol next time, 180–181
Contextual Behavioral Science (CBS), 3, 35, 36
coverage and uncoverage, 79
criticism, 169, 170
cultural bias, 7
cultural relevance, 18, 19
culture of willingness, creating
    about, 15–17
    delivering lessons and, 19–21
    designing learning tasks and, 17–19
    feedback on student work and, 21–26
    managing your power, 26–28
    onward, 34

responding to student avoidance and, 28–34

D

deictic framing
    about, 38–40
    analogical framing and, 40
    protocols and, 44–45, 210
Dialectical Behavior Therapy (DBT), 35
discomfort, 28
Discovery Writing protocol
    about, 80, 84–86
    boosting the impact, 89
    getting ready, 87
    leading the protocol, 88–89
    protocols by framing type and, 44
    using the protocol next time, 90
discussions
    Collaborative Conversations protocol and, 90
    group discussions, 137
    and one-on-one conversations, 56, 150, 206
    So I Will protocol and, 117
domains of life questionnaire, 58–59
doneness, testing for. *See* Testing for Doneness protocol
drawing, 117, 186. *See also* Concentric Self-Portraits protocol
Dweck, C. S., 30

E

editing. *See also* Considerate Editing protocol
    editing chart, 177
    editing checklist, 179, 180
    editing decisions, 176
    types of, 181
Elbow, P., 142
emotions
    drawing and, 186
    emotional control agendas, 124
    information and, 106–107
    memories and, 2–3
    "Noticing Emotions Chart" reproducible 107, 108
    recognizing, 190
    teaching and, 110
    uncomfortable, 66–68
    values and, 106
Emotions and Values Audit protocol
    about, 105, 106–107

boosting the impact, 110
getting ready, 107–108
leading the protocol, 109–110
protocols by framing type and, 44
using the protocol next time, 110–111
empowerment
about using the science of, 35–36
analogical framing and, 40–41, 44–45
deictic framing and, 38–40, 44–45
free choice and, 36–37
hierarchical framing and, 41–43, 44–45
and language to empower students, 37–38
leading values work and, 48–49
and meaning and vitality at school, 46, 48
and patterns of activity and values, 45–46
endings/last day of school, 210–211
essays. *See also* Considerate Editing protocol;
Strategy Selection protocol
example rubric for Naming Awards essays,
130
So I Will protocol and, 121
work products and, 134, 200
Exemplar Study protocol
about, 135, 146–147
boosting the impact, 150–151
getting ready, 147–148
leading the protocol, 148–150
protocols by framing type and, 44
teachers and, 27
using the protocol next time, 151
extrinsic motivation, 7

F
feedback. *See also* Nonjudgmental Peer Review
protocol; Sentence Expanding protocol
giving feedback on student work, 21–26
judgment and, 169
peer feedback rubric, 174
response to student work and, 25
sentence strips and, 192–194
spoken feedback, 175
field trips, 99–103
flexible context sensitivity, 35–36
Focused Annotation protocol
about, 80–81
boosting the impact, 82–83
getting ready, 81
hierarchical framing and, 43
leading the protocol, 81–82
protocols by framing type and, 44
using the protocol next time, 83
fonts, 176, 178
free annotating, 82
free choice, 36–37
freewriting, 142
fun and meaningful graph, 15
functional coherence, 35
future learning, 187, 191

G
genuine questions prompts, 142, 144
goals
adaptive peak and, 159
attention and, 185
learning goals, 138
reflection activities and, 186

Goldson, E., 6
Gomez, K., 80
grading student work, 21
graphic, Suggested Time, 12
Group Commitments protocol
about, 135, 151–152
boosting the impact, 156–157
getting ready, 152–154
leading the protocol, 154–156
protocols by framing type and, 44
using the protocol next time, 157
group dynamics, 155–156
group work
Group Commitments protocol and, 152
Naming Awards protocol and, 128
Top-Pick Topic protocol and, 140

H
Hayes, S., 15, 29
hierarchical framing
about, 41–43
protocols and, 44–45, 210
high-stakes assignments, 136–137.
See also low-stakes assignments
hooks, b., 28
Howard, V., 122

I
I Heard, I Noticed, I Wondered approach, 170
I-here-now/they-there-then, 38–39
Intention Icons protocol
about, 53–54, 66
boosting the impact, 71–72
getting ready, 67
leading the protocol, 67–71
protocols by framing type and, 44
using the protocol next time, 72
interpretation cards, 170–175
Intervision protocol
about, 54, 72–73
boosting the impact, 76
getting ready, 73
leading the protocol, 73–76
protocols by framing type and, 44
teachers and, 27
using the protocol next time, 77

J
Johnston, P., 31
judgment
feedback and, 169
self-judging thoughts, 190–191
when students stay silent and, 31

K
Kanter, J., 90
knowledge demonstrations, 105, 133–135
Kolts, R., 22
Krishnamoorthy, R., 19
KWL charts, 62

L
last day of school/endings, 210–211
learning goals, 138
learning tasks, designing, 17–19
Lesnick, A., 84
lessons, 19–21

low-stakes assignments, 136
Luoma, J., 17

M
Marjory Stoneman Douglas High School,
Parkland, FL, 18
marking student work, 21
McTighe, J., 79
meaningfulness, 15, 42, 203
memories and emotions, 2–3
memory of school activity, 1–2
metaphors, 40–41
Miller, W., 37
motivation, 7, 159
Motivational Interviewing (MI), 35
mucking about, 142

N
Naming Awards protocol
about, 106, 126–127
boosting the impact, 130–131
getting ready, 127
leading the protocol, 128–129
protocols by framing type and, 44
using the protocol next time, 131
Nellen, T., 170
Nonjudgmental Peer Review protocol
about, 160, 169–170
boosting the impact, 174–175
getting ready, 171–172
leading the protocol, 172–174
protocols by framing type and, 44
using the protocol next time, 175

O
observations
feedback and, 22, 24
Intervision protocol and, 72–77
Nonjudgmental Peer Review protocol
and, 169
observation cards, 170–175
One Time I story prompt, 142, 144
one-on-one conversations, 56, 150, 206
outliers and connections, 64

P
pacing lessons, 20–21
pain, 3
pair-shares, 90
partnerships. *See also* Unit Partner Meet protocol
Collaborative Conversations protocol and,
90–94
conflict and, 61–62
creating, 57–58
peers. *See also* Collaborative Conversations
protocol; Nonjudgmental Peer Review protocol; Represent and Respond protocol;
Support-Push-Inspire protocol; Unit Partner
Meet protocol
Naming Awards protocol and, 129
peer feedback rubric, 174
peer observations, 72–77
peer review direction cards, 170, 171, 172
performances
criteria and, 160
expectations and, 162
work products and, 133–134, 200

personal experience, 23, 24, 27
personal relevance, 17, 19
perspectives
    deictic framing and 38–40
    imagining rubrics and, 161–162,
        163–164, 165
        perspectives on my topic handout, 139
    Testing for Doneness protocol and,
        181–182
plans and reflection activities, 186
Platt, M., 17
Plutchik, R., 107
portfolios, 202. *See also* Values-Based Portfolio
    protocol
portioning tasks, 20
positive behaviors, 56
positive qualities handout, 127
power dynamics, 26–28
practical relevance, 17–18, 19
praise, 31, 169, 170
proficiency, 161
projects, 135–138
"Promoting the Non-Obvious Candidate"
    (Krishnamoorthy), 19
prompts
    Booksploration protocol and, 125
    discovery prompt examples, 85–86
    Genuine Question prompts, 142, 144
    odd-angled prompts, 84
    One Time I story, 142, 144
    sandbox prompts, 144
    So I Will protocol and, 118
    Support-Push-Inspire protocol and,
        196–197
    Testing for Doneness protocol and,
        182–183
    Track and Acknowledge protocol and, 95
    Upcycling protocol prompts, 199–200
    Values-Activating Questions protocol and,
        55–56
protocols
    activities and, 11
    adapting, 209–210
    analogical framing and, 38, 40–41
    deictic framing and, 38–40
    hierarchical framing and, 38, 41–43
    relational framing and, 38
    self-assessment after leading a protocol, 49
    self-assessment before leading a proto-
        col, 48
protocols by framing type, 44–45
protocols to create work product
    about, 133–135
    Exemplar Study protocol, 135, 146–151
    Group Commitments protocol, 135,
        151–157
    Prototype Analysis protocol, 135–138
    Sandbox Mode protocol, 135, 141–146
    Top-Pick Topic protocol, 135, 138–141
protocols to explore new material
    about, 79–80
    Collaborative Conversations protocol, 80,
        90–94
    Discovery Writing protocol, 80, 84–90
    Focused Annotation protocol, 80–83

Track and Acknowledge protocol, 80,
    94–99
Values in the Field protocol, 80, 99–103
protocols to prepare for learning
    about, 53–54
    Intention Icons protocol, 53–54, 66–72
    Intervision protocol, 54
    Represent and Respond protocol, 53,
        62–66
    Unit Partner Meet protocol, 53, 57–62
    Values-Activating Questions protocol, 53,
        54–57
protocols to refine work product
    about, 159–160
    Considerate Editing protocol, 160,
        176–181
    Nonjudgmental Peer Review protocol,
        160, 169–175
    Rubric Response protocol, 160–165
    Strategy Selection protocol, 160, 165–169
    Testing for Doneness protocol, 160,
        181–183
protocols to reflect on the learning
    about, 185–186
    Concentric Self-Portraits protocol,
        186–190
    Sentence Expanding protocol, 186,
        190–194
    Support-Push-Inspire protocol, 186,
        195–198
    Upcycling protocol, 186, 198–202
    Values-Based Portfolio protocol, 186,
        202–207
protocols to review the material
    about, 105–106
    Booksploration protocol, 106, 122–126
    Emotions and Values Audit protocol, 105,
        106–111
    Naming Awards protocol, 106, 126–131
    Review Tournament protocol, 105,
        111–116
    So I Will protocol, 105, 116–122
Prototype Analysis protocol
    about, 135–136
    boosting the impact, 138
    getting ready, 136
    leading the protocol, 137–138
    protocols by framing type and, 44
    using the protocol next time, 138

Q

questions
    do you mean questions, 86
    is it OK if questions, 86
    prompts and, 84
    question cards, 170–175

R

reading. *See also* Booksploration protocol
    independent reading, 122, 123–124
    "Why Reading Is Good for Your Health"
        (Christensen), 123
reflection, 185, 186. *See also* protocols to reflect
    on the learning
Relational Frame Theory, 37

relational framing, 38. *See also* analogical fram-
    ing; deictic framing; hierarchical framing
relationships
    teacher-student relationships, 56
    Top-Pick Topic protocol and, 140
    Unit Partner Meet protocol and, 62
Represent and Respond protocol
    about, 53, 62–63
    boosting the impact, 64–66
    getting ready, 63
    leading the protocol, 63–64
    protocols by framing type and, 44
    using the protocol next time, 66
Review Tournament protocol
    about, 105, 111–112
    boosting the impact, 115–116
    getting ready, 112–113
    leading the protocol, 114–115
    protocols by framing type and, 44
    sample tournament bracket, 112, 113
    using the protocol next time, 116
revision. *See also* protocols to refine work
    product
    considerate editing protocol and, 160
    example revision strategy list, 165–166
rewards, 7
Rollnick, S., 37
Rubric Response protocol
    about, 160–162
    boosting the impact, 164
    getting ready, 162
    leading the protocol, 162–164
    protocols by framing type and, 44
    using the protocol next time, 165
rubrics
    analytic rubrics, 160, 162
    example rubric for Naming Awards essays,
        130
    group membership rubric, 154, 156
    peer feedback rubric, 174
    single-point rubrics, 161, 162
    Testing for Doneness protocol and, 181

S

Sandbox Mode protocol
    about, 135, 141–142
    analogical framing and, 41
    boosting the impact, 145–146
    getting ready, 142–143
    leading the protocol, 143–145
    protocols by framing type and, 44
    using the protocol next time, 146
schoolwork and values, 7
science of empowerment, using. *See*
    empowerment
self-assessment after leading a protocol, 49
self-assessment before leading a protocol, 48
self-evaluations, 22
Sentence Expanding protocol
    about, 186, 190–191
    boosting the impact, 194
    getting ready, 192
    leading the protocol, 192–194
    protocols by framing type and, 45
    using the protocol next time, 194
sentence starters, use of, 75, 88, 120, 169, 192

sentence strips, use of, 192
shame, 17
silence
  students and, 31
  using, 27–28
simulated work products, 134
single-point rubrics, 161, 162
Sleeter, C., 19
small-group discussion, 90
So I Will protocol
  about, 105, 116–117
  boosting the impact, 120–121
  getting ready, 117
  leading the protocol, 117–120
  protocols by framing type and, 44
  using the protocol next time, 122
stereotype threat, 65
Strategy Selection protocol
  about, 160, 165–166
  boosting the impact, 168–169
  getting ready, 166–167
  leading the protocol, 167–168
  protocols by framing type and, 44
  using the protocol next time, 169
strengths, 186
student avoidance. *See* avoidance
student demonstrations, 105
student sharing, 99
students. *See also* peers
  approval-seeking students, 31–32, 33, 169
  struggling to make the material meaningful, 56
  teacher-student relationships and, 56
stylistic choices, 176, 177
suggested time graphic, 12
suggestions and feedback, 169, 170
summarizing lessons, 21
summary strips, using, 119
supervision and intervision, 72
Support-Push-Inspire protocol
  about, 186, 195
  boosting the impact, 197–198
  getting ready, 195
  leading the protocol, 196–197
  protocols by framing type and, 45
  using the protocol next time, 198

T
teachers
  Intervision protocol and, 72–77
  participation and, 27
  self-assessment after leading a protocol, 49
  self-assessment before leading a protocol, 48
  teacher-student relationships, 56
Testing for Doneness protocol
  about, 160, 181–182
  boosting the impact, 183
  getting ready, 182
  leading the protocol, 182–183
  protocols by framing type and, 44
  using the protocol next time, 183
texts, purpose of, 79
Than, G., 6
they-there-then/I-here-now, 39

things, work products, 133–134
thinking
  creative thinking, 95–96
  making thinking visible, 89
  So I Will protocol and, 116–117
thoughts and actions cards, 117, 118
Top-Pick Topic protocol
  about, 135, 138–139
  boosting the impact, 140–141
  getting ready, 139
  leading the protocol, 140
  protocols by framing type and, 44
  using the protocol next time, 141
Track and Acknowledge protocol
  about, 80, 94–95
  boosting the impact, 98
  getting ready, 95
  leading the protocol, 95–97
  protocols by framing type and, 44
  using the protocol next time, 99
transformation approach, 18–19
transformation of function, 37–38
turn-and-talk, 90
two-for-one teaching, about, 3

U
uncomfortable emotions, 66–68
uncoverage and coverage, 79
Understanding by Design (Wiggins and McTighe), 79
un-give up, 88, 89, 146
unit descriptions, 54
Unit Partner Meet protocol
  about, 53, 57–59
  boosting the impact, 61–62
  getting ready, 59
  intervision protocol and, 77
  leading the protocol, 60–61
  protocols by framing type and, 44
  using the protocol next time, 62
unit task organizer, 46, 47
Upcycling protocol
  about, 186, 198–199
  boosting the impact, 201
  getting ready, 199–200
  leading the protocol, 200–201
  protocols by framing type and, 45
  using the protocol next time, 202

V
Valéry, P., 181
values. *See also* Emotions and Values Audit protocol
  communities and, 7–8
  Contextual Behavioral Science (CBS) and, 3, 36
  definitions of, 3–5
  discomfort and, 28
  emotions and, 106, 190
  feedback and, 23, 24
  patterns of activity and, 45–46
  reading and, 122
  Review Tournament protocol and, 111
  schoolwork and, 7
  settings and, 9

  Top-Pick Topic protocol and, 139
  two-for-one teaching and, 3
  values-guided life and, 8
Values in the Field protocol
  about, 80, 99–100
  boosting the impact, 103
  getting ready, 100
  leading the protocol, 100–102
  protocols by framing type and, 44
  using the protocol next time, 103
values work
  about, 3
  academic tasks and, 9–11
  academic units and, 5
  challenges to students and, 16–17
  compliance and, 37
  empowerment and, 46
  leading values work, 48–49
  roots of, 35
  in schools, 5–7, 36
Values-Activating Questions protocol
  about, 53, 54
  boosting the impact, 56–57
  deictic framing and, 39–40
  getting ready, 54–55
  leading the protocol, 55–56
  protocols by framing type and, 44
  using the protocol next time, 57
Values-Based Portfolio protocol
  about, 186, 202
  boosting the impact, 205
  getting ready, 202–204
  leading the protocol, 204–205
  protocols by framing type and, 45
  using the protocol next time, 205–206
Villatte, J., 29, 35
Villatte, M., 29, 35
voice, using, 27–28, 176

W
weaknesses, 186
whole-class sharing, 94–95
"Why Reading Is Good for Your Health" (Christinsen), 123
Wiggins, G., 79
willingness. *See* culture of willingness, creating
work experience, 155
work products. *See also* protocols to create work product; protocols to refine work product
  group commitments flowchart and, 155
  Strategy Selection protocol and, 166–169
  types of, 133–134
writing. *See also* prompts
  freewriting, 142
  Sandbox Mode and, 141–146
  Track and Acknowledge and, 94–99
  ways to keep writing when you are stuck, 87
written representation, 63

Z
Zywica, J., 80

EMPOWER Your Students
Lauren Porosoff and Jonathan Weinstein
Discover how to use the elements of EMPOWER—exploration, motivation, participation, openness, willingness, empathy, and resilience—to make school a positive, meaningful experience in your students' lives. This highly practical resource offers enjoyable, engaging classroom activities, as well as strategies for refining teaching practices, incorporating student values into course content, and deeply connecting with learners.
BKF791

Creating Purpose-Driven Learning Experiences
William M. Ferriter
Motivate and inspire students to learn at high levels. By bringing meaningful work to the classroom, students will develop curiosity, become actively engaged, and have a sense of purpose for their education. Discover strategies and tips for reshaping the traditional classroom environment to give modern students opportunities to exercise choice in their curriculum, master skills, and demonstrate what they've learned.
BKF691

Launching and Consolidating Unstoppable Learning
Alexander McNeece
Adopted by educators worldwide, the Unstoppable Learning model includes seven elements of teaching and learning: (1) planning, (2) launching, (3) consolidating, (4) assessing, (5) adapting, (6) managing, and (7) leading. This book offers strategies for *launching* (introducing content and hooking students) and *consolidating* (facilitating students' comprehension) to help readers cultivate and increase meaningful student engagement.
BKF740

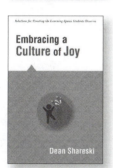

Embracing a Culture of Joy
Dean Shareski
Although fun is sometimes seen as a barrier to real learning, joy is a vital part of effective education. Learn how to have meaningful conversations about where joy gets left out in schools, and discover how to equip students with the skills and qualities they'll need to achieve academic success—as well as to live fulfilling lives—by bringing joy to classrooms each day.
BKF730

You've Got to Reach Them to Teach Them
Mary Kim Schreck
Navigate the hot topic of student engagement with a true expert. The author explores the many factors involved in bringing out the best in students, such as relationships, emotions, environments, and expectations. Become empowered to demand an authentic joy for learning in your classroom. Real-life notes from the field, detailed discussions, practical strategies, and space for reflection complete this essential guide to student engagement.
BKF404

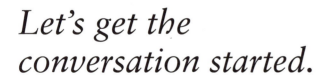